P9-CQS-462

Praise for *Beyond Stewardship*

For several decades now, *stewardship* has been the dominant concept guiding progressive Christian ecological thought and practice. The authors identify various ways in which they and others have come to regard this concept as inadequate and distorting. Then, with vivid stories, up-to-date science, perceptive biblical interpretation, and theological imagination, they propose new ways of thinking. We are *earthlings* responsible for *earthkeeping*. It's a wonderful contribution: fascinating, instructive, inspiring.

–Nicholas Wolterstorff, *Noah Porter professor of philosophical theology emeritus, Yale University; senior fellow at the Institute for Advanced Studies in Culture, University of Virginia*

Ecological theologians have long had an ambiguous relationship with the notion of stewardship. Some have critiqued it for its managerial overtones, while others have embraced it for its biblical resonance. *Beyond Stewardship* does both and neither. What emerges is a rich account of why Christians should view Earth care as integral to the spiritual life, including the types of narratives and actions that are necessary for initiating positive environmental change. Clearly written and inspiring, it should be required reading for Sunday school and college students alike.

–Gretel Van Wieren, *Department of Religious Studies, Michigan State University*

This book is paradigm-shifting and conversation-changing. What would it mean to think about environmental concerns in terms of *reconciliation* rather than merely stewardship or responsibility? Whether you're just beginning to think about environmental discipleship or you've been passionate about creational justice for a long time, this book is a provocative primer.

–James K. A. Smith, *Gary and Henrietta Byker Chair in Applied Reformed Theology and Worldview, Calvin College*

Inspiring … challenging … encouraging … *Beyond Stewardship: New Approaches to Creation Care* will alter paradigms, burst worn-out environmental stewardship models, and shine light on a new way of living in kinship with all God's creation.

–George Heartwell, *former mayor of Grand Rapids, MI*

When I started reading this collection of essays I frankly wondered if I might be bored by a series of ho-hum proposals of alternatives to the old idea of *stewardship*. But the alternative images are interwoven with an exploration of how humans interact with microbes, rusty nails, ecosystems, and the names of trees, as well as with the impact of environmental degradation on racial minorities. The result is an inspiring book that can teach us new ways to think about—and live more fruitfully in—God's good and groaning creation.

–J. Richard Middleton, *Professor of Biblical Worldview and Exegesis at Northeastern Seminary*

Through the process of acknowledging our sinful actions against our Creator through abuse of His creation, our personal responsibility for the harm we have done, and our needed repentance to make things right, the contributors to *Beyond Stewardship* provide the first steps toward a more mature and biblically grounded approach to both environmental ethics and creation care.

–Fred VanDyke, *executive director of Au Sable Institute of Environmental Studies*

These wonderful essays reveal and instruct, but so much more. They delight, refresh, and inspire Christians to greater love of God and of God's good creation. It's a joy to read the book, and spiritually enlarging. I wish I read it twenty years ago before writing the creation chapter of *Engaging God's World*.

–Cornelius Plantinga, Jr., *Senior Research Fellow at the Calvin Institute of Christian Worship*

BEYOND
STEWARDSHIP

BEYOND
STEWARDSHIP

New Approaches to
Creation Care

Edited by David Paul Warners & Matthew Kuperus Heun

Calvin PRESS
COLLEGE
Grand Rapids, MI • calvin.edu/press

Copyright © 2019 David Paul Warners and Matthew Kuperus Heun

All rights reserved. No part of this publication may be reproduced, stored in a retrieval system, or transmitted, in any form or by any means, electronic, mechanical, photocopying, recording, or otherwise without the prior written permission of the publisher.

Published 2019 by the Calvin College Press
3201 Burton St. SE
Grand Rapids, MI 49546

Scripture quotations are from the Holy Bible, New International Version®. NIV®. Copyright © 1973, 1978, 1984, 2011 by Biblica, Inc.™ Used by permission of Zondervan. All rights reserved worldwide. www.zondervan.com. The "NIV" and "New International Version" are trademarks registered in the United States Patent and Trademark Office by Biblica, Inc.™

Publisher's Cataloging-in-Publication Data

Names: Warners, David Paul, author. | Heun, Matthew Kuperus, author.
Title: Beyond stewardship, new approaches to creation care / David Paul Warners;
    Matthew Kuperus Heun.
Description: Grand Rapids, MI: Calvin College Press, 2019.
Identifiers: LCCN 2019937542 | ISBN 9781937555382 (pbk.) | 9781937555399 (ebk.)
Subjects: LCSH Sustainability. | Conservation of natural resources. | Sustainable
    development. | Human ecology--Religious aspects--Christianity. | Nature--Religious
    aspects--Christianity. | Environmental ethics. | Ecology--Moral and ethical aspects. |
    BISAC NATURE / Environmental Conservation & Protection | RELIGION / Christian
    Living / General | BUSINESS & ECONOMICS / Development / Sustainable
    Development | HOUSE & HOME / Sustainable Living | RELIGION / Ethics
Classification: LCC BT695.5 .W37 2019| DDC 241/.691--dc23

Additional resources for *Beyond Stewardship: New Approaches to Creation Care* may be available at www.calvin.edu/press.

The Calvin College Press has no responsibility for the persistence or accuracy of URLs for external or third-party internet websites referred to in this publication and does not guarantee that any content on such websites is, or will remain, accurate or appropriate.

Cover photo: Abby Anaday on Unsplash
Cover design: Robert Alderink
Interior design and typeset: Katherine Lloyd, The DESK

To our parents,
Jane and John Warners
and
Alice and Loren Heun,
who
always supported us,
always encouraged us,
and
always believed in us.

CONTENTS

Part Three
REORIENTING: Hopeful Ways Forward

Additional Resources

Acknowledgments

We extend our thanks and appreciation to the following:

Loren Wilkinson and the authors of *Earthkeeping* for leading the way;

Chapter authors for dedication, persistence, and perseverance;

Observers (Bill Deutsch, Michelle Loyd-Paige, and Randy Van Dragt) for helpful comments and encouragement;

Barbara J. Bjelland, Richard Blackburn, Nate Bradford, Debra Buursma, Tracy Kuperus, Michelle Loyd-Paige, Allysa Metzner, Garth Pauley, Lillie Spackman, Micah Warners, Rachel Warners, Janet Weathers, and John Wertz for helpful comments on chapter drafts;

Rick Hammer for comments and insights on the first manuscript draft; and

Susan Felch and the Calvin Center for Christian Scholarship for extensive guidance and support.

David Paul Warners
Matthew Kuperus Heun

FOREWORD

Bill McKibben

To say this is an important book understates the case. For decades now, Christian environmentalism has operated under the assumption that "stewardship" is the best possible description of how humans should behave in relation to the larger world. But as the authors of this book point out, stewardship is a limited idea, suggesting at best a dutiful sense of earnest commitment. For some reason, the word always gives me the nagging sense that it's time again to mow the lawn. It is not particularly joyful. It misses the gospel call to love. Oh, and beyond that it clearly isn't working: in the most Christian nation on earth, the most Christian people have grown ever more attached to leaders and causes antithetical to the idea of taking care of the earth.

So the time has come to suggest alternatives, ones that simultaneously reduce the overweening importance of people and yet give people a more satisfying role in their engagement with the world around them. As you read these earthy theological reflections, think about your own engagement with the world: What moves you? What calls to your soul? Much of modern life has succeeded in separating us from all that God, on the first page of his Book, offered to us for companionship. Removing that separation will go some way, perhaps, toward restoring our love, and ultimately our accountability, for the world we inhabit.

I say "some way" advisedly. I hope this is not the end of new theological examinations of the problem, because I think there is more distance to travel. The fine reflections on environmental racism—essentially, on powerlessness—toward the end of this volume suggest harder, darker topics to come. There are powers and principalities that actively threaten the natural order, doing so out of a jarring discord with God's plan. We know, for instance, that oil companies, part of the richest industry on planet Earth, systematically lied about climate change for a generation, costing us the time we needed to address this great crisis. I don't know how, as a Christian, to understand that deception, but I know it needs to be understood.

For now, however, this gentle and wise volume marks a real advance in our understanding of how to live in the world around us. I am grateful for it, and I think all who read it will be grateful for it as well. This book leaves one hopeful, which is not a common experience at this moment in history. Let us all use that sense of hope to leverage the action that alone can make change.

PREFACE

Matthew Kuperus Heun and David Paul Warners

W e never know where simple questions might lead.

"How are you doing?" Mark asked when I (editor MKH) returned to South Africa for the first time in three years. His simple question unleashed a flood of memories and reflections.

"I'm still recovering from 2009."

Indeed, there was much to recover from. The year 2009 had been a year of focused teaching and research at two universities in South Africa. A year of learning about renewable energy. A year of understanding the grand challenges facing humankind from a developing country perspective. And a year of learning about the difficulties of living well in God's creation.

Mark was my teacher and friend in both courses and conversations at Stellenbosch University. In addition to many others, he helped me branch out from my engineering-centered point of view to learn about the social and economic aspects of the environmental and sustainability challenges that interested us both.

And he helped me more deeply understand an irony: the year was made possible by airliners that transported my family and me; by cars that ferried me between home and office; by refrigerators that prevented food from spoiling; by an unsustainable food-industrial complex; by computers on which I wrote lectures, reports, and papers; by a home that provided safety and shelter; and by high-rise buildings containing offices and class-rooms. Each was a human-invented machine, system, or structure that consumed energy and materials. During that year, I came to appreciate

1

how modern life requires ever-increasing consumption of resources. Ironically, I was emitting pollution and using up the ecosystems I yearned to preserve even as I was deepening my passion for creation care!

In the decade since 2009, the challenges facing our planet have become worse, not better. None of the things that support modern life (airliners, cars, refrigerators, the food system, computers, homes, buildings) have changed—they still require energy and materials. So, we continue to consume portions of the creation just to live our lives. In the process, we emit pollution and deplete the ecosystems that sustain us. In fact, consumption, pollution, and depletion have been increasing every decade since at least the Industrial Revolution.

Another simple question is "Why?" Why are energy and material consumption continuing to rise worldwide? Why does everyday life demand that we cause pollution to be emitted? Why are most of us living more complex lives instead of simpler lives? Why aren't more of us changing our ways? Why should we deal with the environmental problems we face anyway?

Some people think these questions are too difficult and that environmental problems are too big to be solved, so they give up. Some Christians think that caring for the creation is secondary to our main task, which is to bring others to belief in Christ. To these people, "Why should we deal with the environmental problems?" is a rhetorical question that deserves a dismissive answer: "We shouldn't waste our time."

In contrast, the Christian authors in this book share the conviction that the challenge of caring for God's creation is neither too big nor beside the point. Rather, actively working toward the flourishing of God's creation is a central aspect of bearing God's image in the created world. God loves and protects what God made. As God's image bearers, we are privileged to love and protect it as well. Christians who are committed to doing right by the creation wonder, "Why isn't the broader Christian church leading the way?" And we ask ourselves, "How shall we live?"

Simple questions can be profound, and we never know where they will lead. They can cause us to think deeply and well about fundamental issues and core values. They can cause us to rethink assumptions and reimagine the future. As we pursue answers to "Why isn't the broader Christian church leading the way?" and "How shall we live?" we often ask other profound questions that are central to all aspects of the Christian life: "In what does God delight?" and "What does the Lord require of us?" Answers to these important questions guide the way we live out our lives in the creation.

To that end, we editors gathered twelve Christians with deep passion for a flourishing creation and asked them to draw upon decades of experience in creation care activities to help us all collectively rethink and reimagine the relationship between humans and the nonhuman creation. During two three-day workshops in the summer of 2018, the twelve authors were joined by three observers (Michelle Loyd-Paige and Randy Van Dragt from Calvin College and Bill Deutsch from Auburn University) who provided active listening feedback. The results of our collective efforts are contained in the chapters that follow. The project was made possible by generous financial support from several entities at Calvin College: the Calvin Center for Christian Scholarship, the Provost's Office, the Alumni Association, and the Biology Department. Susan Felch, director of the Calvin Center for Christian Scholarship and editor at the Calvin College Press, provided guidance throughout. Janice Wharton, our intern, chased countless details, contributed first-pass editing, and performed background research for the introduction.

Reformed Christianity is the context within which we authors work and think and share ideas with one another. We Reformed Christians often apply a stewardship strategy to creation care, but we seek to go *Beyond Stewardship* with this volume. Willis Jenkins notes that other Christian traditions use other strategies to frame the topic: ecojustice (Roman Catholicism) and ecological spiritualities (Eastern Orthodoxy), in particular.[1] Although *Beyond Stewardship* emerges from the Reformed tradition, astute readers will notice that some authors draw upon the other strategies highlighted by Jenkins, thereby benefiting from and contributing to a broader ecumenical conversation. Our Reformed perspective supplies one piece of a patchwork whole.

---

1   Willis Jenkins, *Ecologies of Grace: Environmental Ethics and Christian Theology* (New York: Oxford University Press, 2008), 19.

The intended audience for *Beyond Stewardship* is Christians with a passion for and concerns about God's creation. Its purpose is to equip Christians to live better in the creation by helping us all think more intentionally about the relationship between humans and the nonhuman creation in which we are necessarily and thoroughly embedded. In the chapters that follow, each author offers an implicit answer to the questions "Why haven't Christians been more engaged in creation care activities?" and "How can they be motivated to do so?" Each author leads with a story and then makes a "turn"—a rethinking or reimagining of the relationship between humans and the nonhuman creation. Each chapter shows how the turn provides benefits for the creation care work that Christians pursue. Discussion questions and further reading can be found in the appendices.

Naturally, the chapters reflect some of the diversity and tension that always exist at the intersection of belief and action. None of the authors pretend that there are quick fixes to the environmental challenges we face today. Indeed, rethinking and reimagining by themselves are not fixes at all. Rather, they are steps that inform our journey of improving the way we daily encounter and engage the world. None of the authors thinks that answering questions such as "Why?" and "How?" is easy. And this volume certainly won't be the final word on this topic. But we hope that *Beyond Stewardship* will encourage readers to develop their own new and fresh ways of making sense of our existence within the beautiful, diverse, messy, damaged, and intimately interconnected creation.

Finally, we urge readers to envision with us a future in which all Christians, as well as their churches and denominations, actively work toward a more sustainable world. We hope this volume offers important themes and principles to bear in mind as we try to lead faithful lives and as we strive to work out an answer to the simple but profound question "How shall we live?"

We never know where simple questions might lead.

Works Cited

Jenkins, Willis. *Ecologies of Grace: Environmental Ethics and Christian Theology*. New York: Oxford University Press, 2008.

INTRODUCTION

David Paul Warners and Matthew Kuperus Heun

D on't strain your eyes!" a gruff voice yelled from the back of the church parking lot. "And what are you doing down there anyway?"

I (editor DPW) was eyeing a large section of lawn that sloped from the parking lot down to a level area at the edge of the church's property. I explained I was evaluating the site as a member of Plaster Creek Stewards, a local watershed group working to restore the nearby stream. I told the man that the lawn looked like a good location for a large rain garden that could collect storm water runoff and help clean up the stream.

"Aw, that creek is way too messed up. If you think you can actually help that creek with a garden, you're wasting your time."

He was right that the creek is "messed up." Because of runoff and erosion, Plaster Creek is cloudy and brown after every rain, and it carries dangerously high concentrations of *E. coli* bacteria. The creek is known to be the most polluted waterway in West Michigan, and fixing it will take a long time. But ten years of trying have taught us that the contaminated creek isn't actually the problem.

In a stewardship model of creation care, nonhuman creation is the thing a steward cares for. So when we began this watershed group and took on the name Plaster Creek Stewards, we anticipated our work would focus on cleaning up the creek and stabilizing its banks. However, we soon realized that our initial emphasis was wrong. We came to recognize that the deeper reason for the creek's damaged condition was the thoughtless mistreatment, neglect, and apathy of watershed residents. The way people were treating this creek resembled an abusive relationship! Thus, to make lasting improvements to Plaster Creek, our goal changed to repairing the broken relationship between people and their creek. We are trying to reawaken and cultivate an affection for the creek that had been lost over time. We are working to help people relearn how to love the nonhuman creation. We are working toward reconciliation.

It turns out that my gruff visitor was also correct that a single garden at one location would not make a big difference to water quality in the creek. Indeed, one garden by itself won't improve any creek enough to justify the investment of time and money. What our visitor didn't appreciate, though, is that a garden at this church would be about more than cleaning up the creek. The wildflowers and native plants in the garden and the birds and insects they would attract could provide a positive example of creek-friendly landscaping for the neighborhood. A garden could serve to educate local residents, raise awareness, and testify to how people can live more carefully in this watershed with the creek in mind. A garden could help begin to heal the relationship between watershed residents and their creek. A garden could start to reconcile the relationship between people and creation.

After a recent talk I gave on these themes, a student asked why we don't call ourselves "Plaster Creek Reconcilers." She had an excellent point. We have come to understand that contaminated water (or any human-caused environmental problem for that matter) is merely a symptom of a deeper problem. And when we focus on improving the nonhuman creation, a stewardship approach can prevent us from seeing the deeper problems. If we don't address the deeper problems, we won't develop lasting solutions. A cleaned-up creek this year will be dirty next year if behaviors and attitudes don't change. Plaster Creek doesn't need a cleaning; it needs reconciliation.

The student's question shows that new words can emerge from careful thinking about our creation care work. New thinking and new words can lead to a redirection of our efforts. (See Groenendyk, chapter 2 and Rienstra, chapter 8.) At least for now, the word *stewards* is retained in our name and serves as a reminder of our beginnings and of the importance of staying open to new and better ways of thinking about our presence in the creation.

Plaster Creek Stewards' evolving understanding of the relationship between people and the nonhuman creation illustrates one limitation of the stewardship model of creation care. "Stewardship" focuses on the thing to be stewarded, possibly blinding us to root causes of environmental degradation. But before doing some more careful thinking about other limitations of stewardship, it is helpful to review the history of the term and how it has become associated with care for the nonhuman creation.

Stewardship

The term *stewardship* has been used in the North American church since the 1700s, but its meaning has shifted significantly over time. One outcome of the American Revolution was a separation of church and state, and American churches had to generate nongovernmental sources of income. The tithe was the answer, and churches referred to faithful tithing as stewardship.[1] In the early 1800s, missionary outreach work emerged that was also supported through tithing, extending the reach and purpose of stewardship. Tithing fell periodically during economic low points such as the Civil War, World War I, and the Great Depression but always recovered afterward. This financial understanding of stewardship endured well into the 1900s.[2]

However, the finance-centered understanding of stewardship in the church did not indicate a lack of regard for environmental concerns in greater society beyond the church. In a 1911 book on the Country Life movement in the United States, Liberty Hyde Bailey conveyed that the beauty of the land held spiritual value. He claimed that small farmers could better protect the land than large agricultural corporations.[3] In the concluding essay to his 1949 book, *A Sand County Almanac*, Aldo Leopold coined the phrase "land ethic," claiming that all humans have a moral responsibility to care for and conserve land, even if doing so is

---

1   George A. E. Salstrand, *The Story of Stewardship in the United States of America* (Grand Rapids, MI: Baker, 1956), 41–46.
2   Gene Wunderlich, "Evolution of the Stewardship Idea in American Country Life," *Journal of Agricultural and Environmental Ethics* 17 (2004): 81.
3   Liberty Hyde Bailey, *The Country-Life Movement in the United States* (New York: Macmillan, 1911).

not economically beneficial. Leopold conceded that such an ethic would require Americans to reorient their beliefs significantly.[4]

During post–World War II economic prosperity, stewardship saw a revival in the church. No longer a solely financial concept, stewardship was expanded to include time, talent, and treasure.[5] But more than any other decade, the 1960s saw big changes in the use of the term *steward-ship*. Christians began to ask why stewardship was so focused on church needs (as opposed to all parts of life), and the term soon fell out of favor in Christian circles. At the same time, secular environmentalists picked up stewardship to describe the human responsibility to preserve the environment and help the disadvantaged.[6] Then in 1967, historian Lynn White Jr. wrote his landmark article, "The Historical Roots of Our Ecologic Crisis."[7] He blamed the Judeo-Christian tradition for using the Genesis 1:28 dominion mandate as a license to abuse the creation. Anthropocentrism, he believed, enabled technological advancement, which led to destruction of nature.[8] White's article, which was quickly accepted by the secular environmentalist community, caused Christians to reexamine Genesis.[9] In this era, theologians developed a new paradigm: Christian Environmental Stewardship (CES). CES was a significant and important move away from dominion of nature toward a less-destructive care for the creation.[10]

But CES was still mostly just a theory in theological circles until the Calvin Center for Christian Scholarship (CCCS) convened its first project, "Christian Stewardship and Natural Resources." This initiative produced the book *Earthkeeping*, the goal of which was "to discuss, in a general yet scholarly way, the broad issues surrounding Christian stewardship of

---

4   Aldo Leopold, "Substitutes for a Land Ethic," in *A Sand County Almanac and Sketches Here and There* (New York: Oxford University Press, 1949), 210–26.

5   Wunderlich, "Evolution of the Stewardship Idea in American Country Life," 82.

6   Wunderlich, "Evolution of the Stewardship Idea in American Country Life," 82.

7   Lynn White Jr., "The Historical Roots of Our Ecologic Crisis," *Science* 155, no. 3767 (March 10, 1967): 1203–7.

8   White, "The Historical Roots of Our Ecologic Crisis," 1204–5.

9   Ian G. Barbour, ed., *Western Man and Environmental Ethics: Attitudes Toward Nature and Technology* (Reading, MA: Addison-Wesley, 1973), 6.

10 Willis Jenkins, "The Strategy of Christian Stewardship," in *Ecologies of Grace: Environmental Ethics and Christian Theology* (New York: Oxford University Press, 2008), 77–92.

natural resources, and to do so at a level appropriate for the intelligent lay-person."[11] The CCCS project also informed and inspired the emergence of Au Sable Institute,[12] which did much to promote evangelical scholarship on the theology and practical implications of CES.[13]

The authors of *Earthkeeping* urged Christians to consider themselves caretakers (stewards) who are in charge of resources (the creation) that belong to someone else (God). The concept of CES as described in *Earthkeeping* is more biblical and creation affirming than the previous notion of dominion. Yet the lament in *Earthkeeping* that "Christians have not shown much concern for the world's health"[14] seems as appropriate today as it was forty years ago.

Unfortunately, the concept of CES has not inspired broad swaths of North American Christianity (or other groups for that matter) to take creation care seriously, which leads us to reconsider the concept of stewardship today. With the benefit of hindsight, we can see that stewardship has a number of drawbacks in addition to its benefits. And the authors in this volume provide fresh ideas for what comes beyond stewardship. But before outlining those fresh ideas, it is important to summarize some weaknesses of the CES paradigm.

Biblical Support for Stewarding Creation Is Limited

The introduction to *Earthkeeping* says, "In this book we consider the enormously difficult and important problem of . . . how to care for the creation in which [God] has placed us as stewards."[15] Interestingly, there are no biblical references commanding human beings to *steward* the creation. While various terms in Hebrew are translated as "steward" in English, none of those terms are used in Genesis 1–2. The Hebrew expression

---

11 Loren Wilkinson, ed., *Earthkeeping: Christian Stewardship of Natural Resources* (Grand Rapids, MI: Eerdmans, 1980), viii.

12 Jenkins, "The Strategy of Christian Stewardship," 78–79.

13 "Evangelical Christianity and the Environment: Summarizing Committee Report of the World Evangelical Fellowship Theological Commission and Au Sable Institute Forum," *Evangelical Review of Theology* 17, no. 2 (April 1993): 122–33.

14 Wilkinson, *Earthkeeping*, 3.

15 Wilkinson, *Earthkeeping*, viii.

translated "steward" later in Genesis (43:16; 43:19; 44:1, 4) literally means "the man who is over" (*ish asher al*)[16] or "the man who is over the house." (Here the word *man* means male, not female.) In Greek, the most common term used is *oikonomos* (Luke 12:42; 1 Corinthians 4:1; 1 Peter 4:10), which means "someone who controls the affairs of a large household" (e.g., oversees service at the master's table, directs servants, and controls household expenses; in short, a household manager). None of these references to stewarding involve the natural world specifically. However, there are several scriptural directives for how we are to *engage* the nonhuman creation. A complete reading of the Scriptures shows that we are to both serve and protect the nonhuman creation. Servants and protectors of the creation are likely to act quite differently than stewards of the creation. (See Bouma-Prediger, chapter 6.)

Words have power, and they can expand or limit our understanding. (See Groenendyk, chapter 2; and Rienstra, chapter 8.) In this case, the extrabiblical language and understanding of stewardship may be hindering our ability to think about and care for the creation well. If we understand that humans are simply stewards, the richness of our "job description" is lost, and we become merely managers of the creation. We narrow the scope of our responsibility and absolve ourselves of many other tasks with regard to the creation.[17]

CES Causes Separations

The CES paradigm separates both humans and God from the creation. By definition, CES overemphasizes human distinctness from the nonhuman creation and underemphasizes our creatureliness within it. (See Meyaard-Schaap, chapter 3; Joldersma, chapter 4; and Al-Attas Bradford, chapter 5.) Stewardship is something we humans do *to* the creation. So stewardship connotes an I-it relationship, promoting the notion that we humans are somehow situated apart from the nonhuman creation.

---

16 For the sake of readability, we have chosen to spell Hebrew words with their closest English rendition, and are not including the more theologically proper diacritical marks.

17 H. Paul Santmire, *Before Nature: A Christian Spirituality* (Minneapolis, MN: Fortress Press, 2014).

Words that construct humans as separate from creation and emphasize direct action upon the creation can also relieve us from responsibility for our subtle (or not so subtle) daily behaviors that contribute to creation's degradation. For example, a good steward could clean up a polluted stream without addressing the human behaviors that caused the stream to be polluted in the first place (even, possibly, by the steward himself or herself as illustrated by the Plaster Creek story above). To a greater extent than we usually understand or accept, humans are a part of, are embedded within, and have a reciprocal relationship with the rest of creation. We completely and utterly depend on the nonhuman creation for our existence. While we certainly affirm that human beings are the only species created in God's image, this unique status does not make us any less dependent on the broader creation than other species. A more balanced anthropology is needed. Unhelpfully, CES tends to promote a dissociated sense that humans are somehow separate from the rest of creation.

But that is not the only separation that CES entails. A steward oversees a resource *while the owner is away*. Thus, stewardship can be understood as taking care of resources God has left for us. In this way, stewardship may be separating God from the creation, contradicting Christian teachings of God's immanence. Paradoxically, stewardship can make using creation as we please more acceptable, with occasional reminders to undo any damage before the owner (God) returns.[18] Unfortunately, this strand of thought also enables those who urge consuming the earth's resources to quicken the day of Christ's return.[19]

CES Leads to an Instrumental View of the Nonhuman Creation

When we envision ourselves as stewards who are separate from the rest of creation, a necessary question arises: "How should we relate to the

---

18 J. Richard Middleton, *A New Heaven and a New Earth: Reclaiming Biblical Eschatology* (Grand Rapids: Baker Academic, 2014), 72, 82ff.

19 Barbara R. Rossing, "'Hastening the Day' When the Earth Will Burn? Global Warming, Revelation and 2 Peter 3 (Advent 2, Year B)," *Free Library*, October 1, 2008. https://www.thefreelibrary.com/%22Hastening+the+day%22+when+the+earth+will+burn%3f+Global+warming%2c...-a0186594230.

nonhuman creation?" Stewardship answers this question in two ways that contribute to an instrumental view of nonhuman creation.

The first is evident in the introduction to *Earthkeeping*, which says, "Thus, in this book we consider the enormously difficult and import-ant problem of how human beings should *use* the world."[20] The subtitle of the first edition of *Earthkeeping*, namely, *Christian Stewardship of Natural Resources*, reinforced this framing of the nonhuman creation. Clearly, we humans rely on the nonhuman creation to provide resources to sustain us: food, shelter, and water. But viewing the cosmos merely as a collection of resources for us to use constructs an instrumental relationship between humans and the nonhuman creation. Within an instrumental view of creation, the challenge is simply to figure out how to take things from the creation in better ways. But surely the creation is worth more than its value to humans, and its value should not be so narrowly defined.

The second way that stewardship can lead to an instrumental view of the nonhuman creation arises from the notion that God values everything God has made. If we view God as owner, that means we humans should steward everything on God's behalf. But given our finitude and ignorance, we simply cannot do this. So, in practice we end up mostly stewarding only that which *we* understand to be valuable to *us*. Through this own-er-possession reasoning, an instrumental relationship between humans and the nonhuman creation is advanced. (See Joldersma, chapter 4.)

Asking the question "How shall we use natural resources?" might not be the right question to ask. Rather, the most appropriate approach at times may be to exercise restraint and *not use* the creation at all. Choos-ing to live with less (the virtue of frugality) can allow other elements of the creation to be fruitful and multiply as they have been commanded to do (Genesis 1:22). (See Warners, chapter 14.) And indeed, apart from the question of using the creation or not, human beings can choose to engage in behaviors that improve or enhance the creation too.

---

20 Wilkinson, *Earthkeeping*, viii (emphasis added).

Problems Arise from Financial Connotations of Stewardship

Several problems emerge from stewardship's financial meanings. The first difficulty is that focusing on financial aspects of stewardship downplays creation's inherent value. A steward watches over *valuable* resources that belong to others. A good steward takes more care with the most valuable things. In today's world, value is usually quantified monetarily. But if one resource is valuable, other resources are less valuable. Thus, elements of the creation that lack monetary value can be easily overlooked. In contrast, Scripture encourages us to see beyond financial concerns, instead valuing the creation precisely because it was brought into being and is deeply loved by the Creator.

Fundamentally, stewardship presumes *ownership* of resources. To speak of ownership conveys that something is a possession. CES rightly disabuses humans of the idea that we possess the creation. But it transfers ownership of the creation to another (God). However, God's ownership of creation is a problematic concept as it relates to creation care. A proprietary ownership relationship between God and creation is much too simplistic to encompass God's deep love for creation, God's immanence in creation, and the freedom God has infused into creation. When stewardship frames the creation as an object that is possessed, God's relationship to the creation is diminished.

Furthermore, the concepts of ownership and stewardship are encumbered by their connections with our dominant economic system: capitalism. The foundation of capitalism is private ownership of the means of production, including land and resources. In capitalism, ownership conveys a right to use resources as we human owners see fit. Although capitalism has improved the quality of life for many people over the last few centuries, it has also led to unsustainable rates of natural resource consumption and widespread environmental damage. Capitalism can rightly be criticized for its role in environmental degradation. But what can provide that critique? Not stewardship! The stewardship model is too intertwined with capitalism and notions of ownership and rights to provide a compelling critique. In the end, both capitalism and stewardship too readily sanction humans (as owners or stewards) to use natural resources as they see fit.

CES Has Blind Spots

CES has several blind spots. The first arises from the common understanding that a steward is an individual, not a group, who cares for a resource. Collective, international action is necessary to address the global nature of many of today's creation care challenges (e.g., plastic pollution, climate change, and species loss). Stewardship of the nonhuman creation by individuals, even if each person is dutifully engaged in their own stewardly actions, is insufficient given the global nature of the challenges we face.

To be sure, there are isolated examples of representatives coming together to engage in creation care on the global scale, such as the Montreal Protocol's ban on chlorofluorocarbons to protect the ozone layer. But collective responses to many other global-scale creation care challenges have been inadequate. The orientation of stewardship toward individualistic, small-scale action is a weakness. The CES paradigm is ill-suited to address global-scale creation care issues.

Furthermore, the individualistic connotations of CES imply that each person has responsibility for a piece of the creation. But at most, individuals have agency over a small and limited area: the land they call their own. (And land ownership is not a given!) Implicitly, CES assumes further that each individual can exercise that responsibility. But too often those assumptions are false. And CES ignores the question "Who can be a steward?" When CES ignores this important question, it underemphasizes the importance of the social interactions and power dynamics that mediate the relationship between humans and the nonhuman creation. CES too often incorrectly assumes that individuals have agency to actually be stewards. (See Bouma, chapter 12.)

In addition, nearly all thinking and writing about CES incorrectly assumes that all people share a common experience of the nonhuman creation. But in reality, those experiences are mediated by the social construct of race. Another blind spot of CES is that it ignores racial dimensions of our experiences with the nonhuman creation. When race is ignored, the road is paved for environmental racism. (See Heffner, chapter 11.)

Finally, when stewardship of natural resources is the focus of CES, or when stewardship is referred to as "environmental" stewardship, the implication is that "unnatural" (e.g., urban, agricultural, commercial, industrial) areas are lesser parts of the creation that do not need stewarding or care. In reality, solutions to environmental problems are desperately needed in these beloved portions of God's creation too. The concept of stewardship, as typically understood, makes recognizing the expansive nature of creation care more difficult. (See Bjelland, chapter 13.)

Overview

The spiritual home of this book is the Reformed branch of historic Christianity. A motto from the second Dutch Reformation states, "The church is Reformed and always being reformed according to the Word of God." Times change, knowledge changes, issues change. The way we make sense of the world from a faith perspective should change too. In fact, the book *Earthkeeping* itself provides a good example of the openness to change implied by "always being reformed": its subtitle changed from *Christian Stewardship of Natural Resources*[21] in the first edition to *Stewardship of Creation* in the second edition,[22] a positive move that updated the relationship between humans and the nonhuman creation. The nonhuman creation is more than natural resources.

Even today, we understand more and think about things differently than we did when the *Earthkeeping* editions were published. We now see that the model of creation care embodied by the phrase "Christian Environmental Stewardship" has weaknesses. But the problems in creation run so deep that we need to do more than coin a new phrase. We need a richer and deeper understanding of our relationship with the nonhuman creation. We need to reimagine no less than the place and the role of humans in this world.

As we pursued this reimagining, we started with the questions "What if God didn't place humans on earth to be *stewards* of creation but something else?" And "If not stewards, then what?" This volume is the result of much thought and conversation around these questions by a diverse group of scholars. Some authors reimagine the relationship between humans

---

21 Wilkinson, *Earthkeeping*.

22 *Earthkeeping in the Nineties: Stewardship of Creation*, rev. ed. (Grand Rapids, MI: Eerdmans, 1991).

and the nonhuman creation by expanding on the traditional notion of stewardship. Others dismiss the stewardship model altogether and offer alternative ways of understanding our presence within the broader creation. Throughout this project, we have found synergy emerging from the heterogeneity of author voices. Collectively, these essays continue the process of reimagining how we should live out our lives in the places we inhabit as individuals, communities, and institutions.

The book is organized into three sections as follows. The first section, "Rethinking: Expanding Awareness," invites readers to reassess their actions and rhetoric. Engineer Matthew Kuperus Heun identifies the importance of recognizing the damage that has been done to the creation, which should lead to lamenting our human complicity. One hopeful outcome of lament is a determination to act differently. Communication professor and rhetorician Kathi Groenendyk begins by noting that the word *stewardship* works well for some groups but not for others. She provides a cogent reminder that those involved in Christian environmental thought and action must understand their audience and make sure they choose the right words for each audience.

The second section, "Reimagining: How Things Could Be," offers new directions for developing relationships within the created world. Biblical scholar and activist Kyle Meyaard-Schaap proposes that instead of understanding ourselves as *stewards of* the creation, we should consider ourselves to be *in kinship with* the creation. He argues that kinship inspires a more appropriate and effective response to problems of species loss and climate change. Professor of educational philosophy Clarence W. Joldersma urges readers to see themselves less as stewards and more as earthlings. Along with this reoriented understanding of self, he calls for a new way of seeing the rest of creation too—by recognizing that the nonhuman creation has independent moral standing regardless of its utility to humans. The intimacy and mutual dependency of our relationship with the creation is brought into sharper focus by theologian Aminah Al-Attas Bradford. She leans on microbes (of all things!) to rein in our anthropocentric inclinations and to explain why matter matters even for redemption, the end result being that creation care must be understood as mutual and symbiotic. Religion professor Steven Bouma-Prediger criticizes CES as limited in scope and too easily confused with other meanings of stewardship. He argues that the broader and biblically based notion of earthkeeping is a decided improvement. Concluding the second section, environmental historian James R. Skillen claims that human actions to improve the creation are challenged by two limitations: sin and finitude. We sin by choosing to serve ourselves and not the creation. And even when our intentions are right, human finitude means that we can't know how best to steward the creation. We need a new way of envisioning human responsibility toward the nonhuman creation; we need to reimagine stewardship as humbly seeking first the Kingdom of God.

The third section, "Reorienting: Hopeful Ways Forward," highlights some active ways in which Christians can relate to the creation. To begin, English professor Debra Rienstra shows that to care well for anything (including the creation), we need a fundamental level of knowledge and understanding. Thus, effective creation care can begin with learning the names and basic ecologies of the creatures we are to care for. Philosophers Matthew C. Halteman and Megan Halteman Zwart offer a concrete and specific way to reimagine the relationship between humans and the nonhuman creation by understanding animals differently (especially animals used for farming), as co-creatures. Economist Becky Roselius Haney explains how human-made ecological disasters such as the Dust Bowl are the result of a faulty worldview and the pride, ignorance, and impatience that accompany it. With humility, wisdom, and patience, Christians in the technologically sophisticated twenty-first century can and must relearn both individually and collectively their interdependence with the nonhuman creation. Urban studies scholar Gail Gunst Heffner points out that degradation of urban spaces and subsequent negative consequences for human health have disproportionately affected lower-income communities of color. Indeed, the limited and selective application of stewardship principles has contributed to environmental injustice and demands attention. International development professor Dietrich Bouma notes that injustice and inequality create barriers for some people to live out the universal call to care for the creation. He contends that a critical part of caring for the creation well is making sure that all human voices are empowered and heard. If Heffner and Bouma expand who is involved with creation care, urban geographer Mark D. Bjelland expands our imagination for what counts as the creation. He calls Christians to recognize that the creation is not only snow-capped peaks and lush rainforests but also the "streets, fields, neighborhoods, watersheds, towns, and cities" in which most of us spend our daily lives. These parts of the creation need to be brought under the umbrella of creation care too. In the final chapter, ecologist David Paul Warners provides a concluding reflection on the "How?" question posed in the preface. He urges us to recognize that we move daily through a world filled with gifts. Gifts given by a loving Giver are to be highly prized, deeply cherished, and carefully tended. The generosity conveyed through gifts also encourages reciprocity, inspiring grateful lives that give back, both in response for the gift and in praise of the Giver.

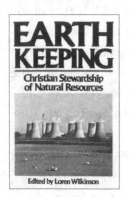

The cover design of *Beyond Stewardship* is meant to both evoke and pay homage to *Earthkeeping* (1980), as we stand on the shoulders of its authors to again wrestle with the important challenge of restoring a right relationship between humans and the nonhuman creation. Both cover photos contain expansive sky and landscape to draw readers into their respective books. On the *Earthkeeping* cover, a fossil-fuel power plant separates farmland from sky. Its design illustrates demand for energy resources, the resulting pollution, and human impacts on the nonhuman creation in general.

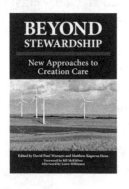

In the *Beyond Stewardship* cover photo, wind turbines replace the cooling towers of the power plant, signifying new ways of thinking about our relationship with the nonhuman creation. The perspective of the turbines, together with blue sky, clouds, and green landscape, suggests there are hopeful ways to move forward. The multiple-use land patterning, including a forested strip, offers a reminder that we must better fit our existence into God's creation so that all creation flourishes together.

As the *Earthkeeping* book included a work of art ("A Steward's Hymn"), this book also offers an artistic contribution entitled "No More Room." We were delighted to work with the energetic and passionate student artists who willingly modified their original children's story to fit into this book as a compelling Postlude. In addition, we were blessed by the willingness of the editor and surviving members of the original *Earthkeeping* book (Loren Wilkinson, Eugene Dykema, and Calvin B. DeWitt) to offer their thoughtful reflection in an Afterword; both the cover and the closing of this book honor their groundbreaking work.

Finally, a note about terminology. We use the terms "cosmos" or "universe" to refer to everything God has created. The terms "creation" and "the creation" typically refer to the earth, or that part of the cosmos in which we live and with which most of us typically interact (people included). When we reference elements of earth excluding human beings, we apply the term "nonhuman creation." Readability considerations dictate when the article "the" is used to accompany these terms. In addition, we have chosen to spell Hebrew words with their closest English rendition and do not include the more theologically proper diacritical marks. Additional resources for this book can be found at https://www.calvin.edu/press.

Works Cited

Bailey, Liberty Hyde. *The Country-Life Movement in the United States*. New York: Macmillan, 1911.

Barbour, Ian G., ed. *Western Man and Environmental Ethics: Attitudes Toward Nature and Technology*. Reading, MA: Addison-Wesley, 1973.

"Evangelical Christianity and the Environment: Summarizing Committee Report of the World Evangelical Fellowship Theological Commission and Au Sable Institute Forum." *Evangelical Review of Theology* 17, no. 2 (April 1993): 122–33.

Jenkins, Willis. "The Strategy of Christian Stewardship." In *Ecologies of Grace: Environmental Ethics and Christian Theology*, 77–92. New York: Oxford University Press, 2008.

Leopold, Aldo. "Substitutes for a Land Ethic." In *A Sand County Almanac and Sketches Here and There*, 210–26. New York: Oxford University Press, 1949.

Middleton, J. Richard. *A New Heaven and a New Earth: Reclaiming Biblical Eschatology*. Grand Rapids, MI: Baker Academic, 2014.

Rossing, Barbara R. "'Hastening the Day' When the Earth Will Burn? Global Warming, Revelation and 2 Peter 3 (Advent 2, Year B)." *Free Library*, October 1, 2008. https://www.thefreelibrary.com/%22Hastening+the+day%22+when+the+earth +will+burn%3f+Global+warming%2c...-a0186594230.

Salstrand, George A. E. *The Story of Stewardship in the United States of America.* Grand Rapids, MI: Baker, 1956.

Santmire, H. Paul. *Before Nature: A Christian Spirituality.* Minneapolis: Fortress Press, 2014.

White, Lynn, Jr. "The Historical Roots of Our Ecologic Crisis." *Science* 155, no. 3767 (March 10, 1967): 1203–7.

Wilkinson, Loren, ed. *Earthkeeping: Christian Stewardship of Natural Resources.* Grand Rapids, NI: Eerdmans, 1980.

Wilkinson, Loren, Peter De Vos, Calvin DeWitt, Eugene Dykema, and Vernon Ehlers. *Earthkeeping in the Nineties: Stewardship of Creation.* Rev. ed. Grand Rapids, MI: Eerdmans, 1991.

Wunderlich, Gene. "Evolution of the Stewardship Idea in American Country Life." *Journal of Agricultural and Environmental Ethics* 17 (2004): 77–91.

Part One

RETHINKING: Expanding Awareness

1

SMASHING PROTOTYPES

Matthew Kuperus Heun

Each May, teams of senior engineering students at Calvin College exhibit prototypes from their yearlong capstone design course. This public showcase is followed by a large banquet attended by family and friends. The entire day celebrates the students' hard work and commissions them for a life of service as professionals. An engineering department professor usually gives a short after-dinner speech filled with parting wisdom for the graduates. If I were asked to speak, my reflections would begin as follows.

Good evening, ladies and gentlemen. I own a sledgehammer. It's small: a five-pound sledge. I brought it with me tonight, as you can see. I also own a circular saw. As you know, these tools can be extremely useful. For example, I removed an ugly interior brick wall in my previous home with this sledgehammer. And the saw can be used to construct a house.

But tonight, let's consider a different use for my tools. What if, last night I went completely berserk and used these tools to demolish your prototypes? For some electrical projects, I could obliterate your circuit boards with a single swift strike of the hammer or slice of the spinning blade. For larger prototypes, I might need to work harder. But in just a few minutes, I could destroy all your prototypes with these two simple tools.

Let's consider your reaction to the resulting piles of wires and parts. I bet that most, if not all, of you would be devastated by my actions. You might say, "I worked so long and hard on my prototype, and now it's ruined!" You might ask, "Now what's left to show my family and friends who traveled hundreds of miles to see the results of tens of thousands of tuition dollars?" You might wail, "How could you *do* this to the work of my hands?" You have a very appropriate pride in all you accomplished in your senior year, not to mention the previous three. And because you are so pleased with the results of your efforts, you would grieve the heap of parts that my hammer and saw produced.

We professors give you an assignment in September. But as the spring banquet looms, you are inwardly driven to complete your prototype well. You exhaust yourself on your project, working long days and longer nights. You want to do well, not simply for the grade you will receive but because your prototype says something about you to the world. And there is a sense in which a part of yourself remains in the prototype that you and your teammates create. In fact, nobody else would design it exactly the same way you did, and the prototype emerges as an expression of yourself. Once you commit to this process, you *spend* yourself on it, and you would be devastated if your prototype was needlessly destroyed.

In his book *Engaging God's World*, Cornelius Plantinga describes God's creative acts in this way: "Creation was a way for God to *spend* himself."[1] You worked very hard on your prototype. But Plantinga notes that God "made room in the universe for other kinds of beings, . . . generating ten to one hundred billion galaxies, . . . salamanders and sandhill cranes and fringed gentians, . . . more than 750,000

---

1   Cornelius Plantinga Jr., *Engaging God's World: A Reformed Vision of Faith, Learning, and Living* (Grand Rapids, MI: Eerdmans, 2002), 22 (emphasis added).

species of insects[2] and 250,000 species of plants, . . . grasshoppers that look like leaves, and beetles that hitchhike on the backs of bees."[3]

Do you see the parallels? God *spent* God's self on the creation. You *spent* yourself on your prototype. The creation is an expression of the Creator as your prototype is an expression of you. The parallels are not perfect, of course. God creates *ex nihilo*, while we humans create from what we find around us. God's original creation was perfect and good in every way, and our creations are, of course, imperfect and finite. We are not little gods, but we do create. So, it is right and fitting that we celebrate your accomplishments this evening. When all of God's creating was done, God declared that "it was very good" and rested (Genesis 1:31; 2:2). And in your own small way, you can sit back now and rest a bit; you too can celebrate and say, "It is good."

Why can you celebrate? Note that on the sixth day of creation, "God said, 'Let us make [hu]mankind in our image'" (Genesis 1:26). I submit that both the pride you feel about your prototype and the celebration we are having tonight are rooted in your image-bearing nature. In fact, because you are fashioned in God's image, you *will* create, and you will be justifiably satisfied with your designs, just as God's creation was "good" and God celebrated it. Your creative work on your prototype and in all your future engineering endeavors will be one way (not the only way, to be sure) that you reflect God's image in your lifetime. And because you spent yourself on your design and know it is good, you wouldn't be just a little upset if you walked in today to find your prototype in pieces. You would be devastated. You would be outraged. And I suspect that after the outrage subsided, you would feel a deep sadness, and you would *lament* what has been lost.

I would continue the speech to my students by discussing further how engineers reflect God's image and the responsibilities that image bearing

---

2 Plantinga's estimate of 750,000 species of insects is from the early 2000s; a more recent estimate indicates that earth is home to around 5.5 million species of insects.

3 Plantinga, *Engaging God's World*, 23.

entails. But here I want to focus on lament, defined as "a passionate expression of grief or sorrow."[4]

There are three actors in my story, and each has cause to lament. My students will lament their destroyed prototypes. I will lament my actions after I understand the harm I have done. And the prototypes, if they were sentient, would lament their inability to perform their tasks and fulfill their purposes.

As we explore lament, we can consider the story in my speech to be an allegory and draw upon the following parallels. The prototypes, being created things, correspond to the creation. I, as destroyer, play the role of humans who spoil the creation. The students, as makers of prototypes, are analogous to God, the Creator of the creation. By exploring each lament in the context of the allegory, we will discover that lament prompts us to rethink and restore our relationship to the nonhuman creation. Let's begin with the students and proceed in reverse order.

The Makers' Lament

Because humans reflect God's image, we can discern something about the Creator by exploring the students' reaction to their destroyed prototypes. My students will be devastated that their hard work has been destroyed. How much more devastated must God be at the state of God's creation? Mountaintop removal coal mining and hydraulic fracturing scar ancient landscapes, eliminate jobs, and poison nearby residents. (See Meyaard-Schaap, chapter 3.) The Western microbiome profile is disappearing, and our chemical, antimicrobial, and toxic ways of manipulating the creation are causing the next wave of mass microbial extinction.[5] (See Al-Attas Bradford, chapter 5.) We raise and slaughter almost ten billion land animals annually in the United States, and feeding this many animals requires unsustainable consumption of oil, land, and water. (See Halteman and Zwart, chapter 9.) Makers lament when their good work is

---

4 *New Oxford American Dictionary*, 3rd ed., s.v. "lament," accessed 20 November 2018, http://www.oxfordreference.com/view/10.1093/acref/9780195392883.001.0001/m_en _us1262018?rskey=gLi8qC&result=46641.

5 Bruce Goldman, "Gut Bust: Intestinal Microbes in Peril," Stanford Medicine, last modified Spring 2016, https://stanmed.stanford.edu/2016spring/gut-bust.html.

destroyed, and the students' lament can help us imagine and understand God's expressions of lament for what has become of God's good creation.

But lament can be more than an endpoint of sorrow. It can also be an important step in an active and difficult process that moves us from recognition to empathy and ultimately to forgiveness, improved relationships, and recommitment. (See Heffner, chapter 11.) To understand this second type of lament, we need to shift attention from my students to me, from maker to destroyer.

The Destroyers' Lament

If I am callous and insensitive, I will be unconcerned about my students' reactions to their piles of wires and parts. But what if I enter into thoughtful conversation with them? What if I invest the time to learn the intricacies of my students' now-destroyed prototypes, the care my students put into them, and the usefulness they provided? I would begin to recognize why my sledge and saw caused such deep pain and sorrow. I would come to empathize with my students' grief. Becoming aware of what I had done would lead *me* to a deep sadness, also to a place of lament. And here we find that the lament of a destroyer is different from the lament of a maker.

My lament will motivate me to begin a process of putting things right, and my first thought will be to try to rebuild or re-create the prototypes that I destroyed. Upon further reflection, I will come to understand that the process of putting things right will be long and difficult. It might even be impossible! Indeed, if I try to make amends by re-creating my students' prototypes, I will not be able to remake their machines in the same way they did, because their prototypes were expressions of them, not me. I will come to the point where I lament not only my destructive actions but also the fact that I don't know how to make amends or put things right. I will be paralyzed by the knowledge that my sledge and saw have done irreparable damage with no apparent way for me to fix it. I will sit in despair between the world as it is (piles of wires and parts) and the way I wish it would be (repaired and functioning prototypes). I might express my lament passionately as I give voice to my grief and sorrow. ("Oh, this is terrible!" "Oh, what have I done?" "I cannot believe I caused such deep pain!" "How can I ever put this right?" "Oh, what can I do?") My lament is deep and reaches to my core as I empathize with the pain of my students. Although my sorrow is nearly debilitating, I want to do something. I want to somehow make things right again between my students and me. But "Oh, what can I do?" And words alone cannot put things right.

When we assess the state of the creation, we recognize that we humans are the ones who are smashing prototypes. In my fictional story, I smashed my students' prototypes with a sledge and a saw. But we are smashing God's good creation with ever more powerful machines and excessive consumption, often in pursuit of economic growth. Indeed, human activity is contaminating the water, polluting the air, eroding the soil, decimating species, and changing the climate. Admitting our complicity unsettles and disturbs us destroyers. But when we come face-to-face with what we have done to the creation, we lament. We sit between the way the creation is (damaged) and the way the creation ought to be (flourishing), and we don't know what to do. We search for solutions. But the challenges are so extensive that we don't know where to begin. We find that our words alone cannot put things right. And we are scared that we alone can't fix them. The problems are, in a word, daunting. The situation is enough to make us cynical, to make us give up. The destroyers' lament is hard work indeed.

But as we work at our lament, lament works on us. In my deep lament over my destructive actions and in the process of trying to find a way forward, I will focus on understanding the motivations and objectives of the prototypes' creators, my students. I will learn the finest details of their designs. I will ask forgiveness for destroying their work. As I emerge from lament and with their blessing, I will start the process of remaking their machines. This will be halting and imperfect work, maybe starting from preliminary sketches that aren't *exactly* as-built drawings. If they extend some forgiveness and grace, perhaps we will, together, re-create their prototypes to be more-or-less similar to the originals. I will work alongside my students, learning about them as I learn about the work of their hands.

Just as I want so deeply to make things right between my students and me, we Christians want so deeply to make things right between God and us. In the midst of our lament, our thoughts focus on the God of the universe and the Christ of Colossians: "He is before all things, and in him all things hold together" (Colossians 1:17). Although we want to make things right ourselves, focusing on the God of the universe and the Christ of Colossians changes us. We are compelled to humbly ask for and receive forgiveness from the God whose creation we destroy. A faint understanding grows and becomes clearer through time. It is true that we alone can't make things right, but that is beside the point. We come to accept that we are in God's hands. The creation is in God's hands. Even the damage we have done to the creation is in God's hands. We begin to understand that we are not necessarily called to be successful; our job is to be faithful.

Even as we wallow in lament, we are kinetic, trying our best to figure out how to move forward, how to be better. We collectively engage in deep self-reflection, which leads to a realistic assessment of our twin limitations: sinfulness and finitude. (See Skillen, chapter 7.) We critically and realistically evaluate roadblocks and barriers to effective action. With thankful but still heavy hearts, we praise God for being God, the Creator, the Redeemer, and the Ruler over all. We understand, more deeply than before, that everything—everything—is in God's sovereign hands.

Freed from the self-imposed responsibility to put things right ourselves, we are surprisingly compelled to action. We orient ourselves away from despair and dead-end cynicism. Guided by the humility born of deep reflection and the desire to be faithful, we recommit to pointing in the right direction to heal the wounded creation, fully aware that we alone can't provide the fix. Our humility leads us to continually ask what God would have us do to restore creation. We move ahead, even if our actions are small and we aren't sure of the best way forward. We experience setbacks, yet we also gratefully celebrate successes when they occur. And we learn more about the Creator as we work to heal the creation.

The Creation's Lament

But can the third actor in the allegory (the prototypes) also participate in lament? The students created the prototypes to provide some benefit to someone or something somewhere. But the piles of wires and parts are unable to perform their intended tasks or fulfill their intended purposes. If they were capable, the demolished prototypes would surely lament their inability to fulfill their intended purposes or their calling. They would lament their destruction.

So, too, the creation laments. Famously, Romans 8:22 describes a creation that longs to fulfill its potential, its calling: "The whole creation has been groaning as in the pains of childbirth right up to the present time." And we must pay attention to its lament.

When we listen to the creation's lament, we hear a call to understand the creation on its own terms, despite our finitude and sinfulness. The creation's lament prompts us to rethink and reimagine our relationship to it. When we do, we come to understand that we are intimately tied to the nonhuman creation. Indeed, we are symbiotic with it. (See Al-Attas Bradford, chapter 5.) We are kin with it. (See Meyaard-Schaap, chapter 3.) We understand that we have a responsibility toward it that is deeper than stewardship. (See Joldersma, chapter 4.) We learn that we are called to serve and to "keep" it. (See Bouma-Prediger, chapter 6.)

Beyond Stewardship is a book for Christians who are distraught by the lament of the Maker and compelled by the lament of the creation. It is for those who recognize their role as destroyer and find themselves on a path through lament to forgiveness, improved relationships, and recommitment to repair the damage they have done in the past and to do less harm in the future. If successful, this book will equip us for that journey.

Works Cited

Goldman, Bruce. "Gut Bust: Intestinal Microbes in Peril." Stanford Medicine. Last modified Spring 2016. https://stanmed.stanford.edu/2016spring/gut-bust.html.

Plantinga, Cornelius, Jr. *Engaging God's World: A Reformed Vision of Faith, Learning, and Living.* Grand Rapids, MI: Eerdmans, 2002.

2

WORDS MATTER, BUT AUDIENCE MATTERS MORE

Kathi Groenendyk

Recently, my husband was asked to preach at a small rural church. The church has been without a minister, and he served as their temporary pastor the previous summer. While he served the church, he got to know the families well. Many in the congregation either are farmers or have jobs tied to farming. He visited their farms, ate at the local diner, and attended the Independence Day celebration. He learned about the joys and economic struggles of farming. After building connections, he is now often asked to return as a guest preacher.

While my husband was considering the sermon topic for this particular Sunday, he read a *New York Times* story about the plight of the cedars of Lebanon. Many of these trees are hundreds of years old. In ancient times, the cedars of Lebanon were threatened by greedy kings who ordered that the trees be cut. These kings wanted to profit from the trees and did not care if they destroyed the forest in the process. But the cedars today are experiencing a threat greater than the greed of ancient kings: climate change. As temperatures rise, the cedars are declining and are expected to survive only in the northernmost part of the country, an area where they are facing a growing number of insect infestations. These insect problems are also a result of warmer temperatures. My husband felt called to preach on verses from Ezekiel and Isaiah (Ezekiel 27:2–5, 33–34; Isaiah 37:22–25) in which prophets condemn the kings for careless, wasteful destruction. By selecting these verses and describing the current threat to the cedars, he could explore God's call for us to extend care and protection toward the creation by taking action on climate change.

But given today's political climate, few rural church members would want to hear about climate change. So how best to raise a sensitive topic in a sermon? My husband decided to apply lessons learned from interactions with other friends and acquaintances who don't believe that climate change is happening. We have learned that when we discuss environmental issues, we first need to find common ground and ways to talk about the subject so that no one shuts down the conversation. When we talk to people who disagree with us, we realize the importance of starting small and building trust with them in dialogue. For the sermon, my husband identified common ground: farmers spend their lives in God's great creation and know the importance of caring for it. The farmers in the church see themselves as stewards of the land. Despite the differences in location (we are city dwellers) and careers (farmers versus pastor), he and the congregation both believe that God's creation is a gift and that we can see God's greatness in it. (See Warners, chapter 14.)

Much of the sermon's language focused on caring for the land and our responsibilities to the land. My husband hardly mentioned the phrase "climate change" but referred to "stewardship" more. Choosing to talk about stewardship with this particular group led to more engagement with the idea of creation care, expanding the congregation's understanding of what stewardship should be. After the church service, many members thanked him for the message. One congregant said she appreciated that he was thoughtful and sensitive in talking about these issues. In her opinion, many people were engaged with the message because they trusted him and because he didn't offend their political sensibilities. The number of positive responses was encouraging.

My husband has an honest, trusting relationship with the parishioners, many of whom hold cultural and political views different from his. But by remembering, acknowledging, and referencing their shared values, he was able to explore potentially divisive issues—climate change, materialism, and environmental responsibilities—in a way that encouraged engagement with the topics. Using the word and concept of stewardship in this situation was a positive way to broaden the congregation's understanding of creation care.

Rhetorical scholar Kenneth Burke theorizes that when we talk with others, we should be constantly looking to bridge the divisions between us.[1] We should understand our audience so well that we become one with them: we should walk a mile in their shoes. Then we must use rhetoric to build identification with our audience. Identification—becoming one with our audience—can lead to persuasion. We invite our audience to share our view of the world, but we do not force that view upon them. As we work to build identification and to persuade, we should use language that builds on common ground rather than heightening our differences or angering our listeners. Because words have multiple meanings and connotations, we must choose our words wisely.

Stewardship is an example of a term that must be used carefully. The concept of stewardship may be flawed (see the introduction; Meyaard-Schaap, chapter 3; Bouma-Prediger, chapter 6; and Bouma, chapter 12), but that does not mean that all audiences know the flaws or even agree that there are problems. Therefore, for some groups, the concept of stewardship works well as a starting point to introduce them to a broader understanding of creation care. My husband's sermon is just one example.

Yet stewardship does not resonate with every group. Attempts to promote creation care must always begin with efforts to understand one's audience (as we rhetoricians like to emphasize), followed by careful selection of language that will engage that particular audience. If we carefully think about our listeners and wisely choose our words to communicate well with them, we can find unexpected common ground with people we

---

1   Kenneth Burke, *A Rhetoric of Motives* (Berkeley: University of California Press, 1969), 55.

thought were adversaries. By doing so, more people will be engaged in creation care.

In this chapter, I first establish that there are multiple audiences on environmental topics. Then I expand on the idea that for some groups (like my husband's parishioners), *stewardship* is a beneficial term to use to build identification before moving beyond stewardship to creation care (or other concepts). Finally, I illustrate why stewardship cannot be used for every group by discussing a significant flaw with the concept.

Knowing Your Audience

Around the holidays, many environmental groups such as the Sierra Club publish online guides on how to talk to your family about climate change. These guides acknowledge that climate change is a political issue and that families fight about political issues. These fights are painful. Everyone becomes angry, but no one changes their mind. So how do we begin to have productive, positive conversations? Communicating well with others starts with the knowledge that people have different reasons for acting. If we want to influence attitudes or encourage action, we need to understand what our listeners value and believe.

We should learn all we can about our listeners. What are their values? What are their experiences? What do they know? What words and expressions do they use when they talk about the creation? As we consider how *they* express themselves and what words *we* wish to use, we need to examine if our words about creation care resonate with our listeners. Do our words match theirs? Misunderstandings (at the very least) occur when we ignore the fact that words have multiple meanings and connotations.

To show the wide range of public reaction to environmental topics, the Yale Program on Climate Change Communication researched Americans' beliefs regarding the politically contentious subject of climate change.[2]

---

2   C. Roser-Renouf, E. Maibach, A. Leiserowitz, G. Feinberg, and S. Rosenthal, *Faith, Morality and the Environment: Portraits of Global Warming's Six Americas*, Yale Program on Climate Change Communication (New Haven: Yale University and George Mason University, 2016), http://climatecommunication.yale.edu/wp-content/uploads/2016/01/Faith-Morality-Six-Americas.pdf.

Researchers identified six distinct American audiences. Twenty-one percent of the American public is alarmed about climate change; 30 percent is concerned; 21 percent is cautious; 7 percent is disengaged; 12 percent is doubtful; and 9 percent is dismissive. Each group has different motivations, different amounts of knowledge and commitment, and different political awareness regarding environmental action. The "alarmed" and "concerned" groups are more likely to believe that humans are responsible for protecting the nonhuman creation. The "dismissive" group is more likely to emphasize the use of resources for human and economic benefit. (See Haney, chapter 10.) Clearly, such large disparities mean that messaging about climate change and other environmental issues needs to be tailored appropriately for each audience.

The Yale researchers found that appealing to moral values is one of the more effective ways to persuade an audience about environmental issues. Thus, a way to tailor messages concerning climate change is to connect with the shared values and principles of an audience. The Yale research points to the impact of Pope Francis on the environmental awareness of American Catholics. Researchers found that American Catholics are now more likely to view climate change as a moral and social justice issue because of the pope's teachings. After publication of the encyclical *Laudato Si'*,[3] 42 percent of US Catholics say that global warming is a moral issue compared to 34 percent before publication.

Pope Francis is an effective communicator, in part because he knows his audience well. He starts with shared beliefs. He extends what his listeners know and believe and reshapes their understanding of environmental stewardship. Finally, he challenges them to take environmental action. In *Laudato Si'*, Pope Francis evokes the revered St. Francis of Assisi by praising God for the gift of the creation that sustains us. But, Pope Francis writes, we have harmed our home, because we have been irresponsible and abused the earth. The pope reminds us of the shared knowledge that we are dust of the earth and depend on air and water for life. He leans on

---

3 Pope Francis, *Encyclical Letter Laudato Si' of the Holy Father Francis on Care for Our Common Home* (Rome: Libreria Editrice Vaticana, 2015), http://w2.vatican.va/content/francesco/en/encyclicals/documents/papa-francesco_20150524_enciclica-laudato-si.html.

the long and shared tradition of Catholic social thought when he urges Christians to care for the earth and to care for the least of these in our communities who suffer when the earth suffers. Pope Francis stands on the common ground of the sanctity of the family and builds on the metaphor of the earth as sister and mother. We have a familial, reciprocal connection to the creation, and because the creation cares for us, we should care for the creation. He reshapes our understanding of the human role in the creation when he mentions that stewardship is a helpful correction to the earlier concept of dominion and that we should not think of ourselves as masters of the world. The pope ends with a moving call to dialogue and action on international, national, local, and personal levels.

Deciding if the Stewardship Concept is a Good Starting Point

As we talk with others about environmental issues, we must understand their underlying beliefs about the creation and how they think about the relationship between humans and the nonhuman creation. Are we stewards of nature? Are we kin with the earth, as Pope Francis suggests? (See Meyaard-Schaap, chapter 3; and Haney, chapter 10.) If they use the language of stewardship, does their definition match ours? When we look closer at the meanings of the words we use, we may be surprised with whom we connect and what work we can do together.

Twenty-five years ago, when I was a graduate student at Texas A&M University, I was part of a research team that studied how local community groups could more effectively solve land use conflicts. Our team went to local communities and discussed ethical and practical frameworks that community members could use in these conflicts. One team member who specialized in environmental ethics used Aldo Leopold's *A Sand County Almanac*[4] in his discussions with the town's ranchers, business owners, and environmentalists, encouraging them to think about how Leopold's insights could help solve land use disputes. Leopold worked in forestry and wildlife ecology, and he wrote often for scientific journals and

---

4   Aldo Leopold, *A Sand County Almanac and Sketches Here and There* (New York: Oxford University Press, 1968).

conservation magazines. *A Sand County Almanac* is a collection of Leopold's essays about the natural world, how it works, and why we should ensure a healthy land. The book is a classic of environmental literature.

Our team was surprised to learn that two very different community groups—environmentalists and ranchers—both enjoyed reading *A Sand County Almanac*. These two groups often seemed at odds with each other, but they loved the same book. Environmentalists were drawn to Leopold's thoughtful call to ecological action. Ranchers connected with the concept of stewardship because they self-identify as stewards of their land. If you farm the land, you should care for it so that you can continue to farm it. Leopold's brilliance was merging a human-focused interpretation of stewardship with active ecological care for the sake of nonhuman creation. His new meaning for the word *stewardship* bridged the usual gap between environmentalists and ranchers. With this reshaped view of stewardship, the two groups found common ground and identified with each other.

Farmers and ranchers are not the only groups to view stewardship positively. The example of my husband's sermon shows that some Christians might also respond positively to the word *stewardship* because they believe that God's creation has been entrusted to us and we must handle it respectfully. For farmers, ranchers, and some other Christians, the word *stewardship* evokes the biblical metaphor of the steward: someone who cares for a vineyard that belongs to another. The word directs their attention to responsible care for creation.

We can easily see that North Americans are divided on environmental issues. It sometimes seems as if our experiences and political views are so different that we cannot find a way to discuss environmental topics. Yet with a closer look, we may find common ground and overlapping perspectives. For some audiences, the responsible care aspect of stewardship can become common ground on which to build environmental awareness and to encourage creation care.

Why Stewardship Does Not Work for Every Group

Stewardship does not have a single meaning: its meaning, connotations, and associated actions depend on both the speaker and the audience. Not everyone shares the same understanding of stewardship. Thus, not all see it as a helpful framework for environmental action. (Indeed, much of this book is a response to the limitations of stewardship.)

As noted in the introduction, one problem is that stewardship has meaning in both financial and environmental contexts. One can exercise stewardship over both money and the creation. Often, individuals and organizations set economic stewardship in opposition to environmental stewardship. Then they privilege economic stewardship over environmental stewardship in the name of economic growth and development. (See Haney, chapter 10.)

One recent example of exploiting the multiple meanings of stewardship comes from President Trump's first term. Scott Pruitt was Trump's first administrator of the Environmental Protection Agency (EPA). As head of the EPA, Pruitt sought to roll back environmental legislation so that industries would have more freedom in their operations. The EPA was created by President Nixon (a Republican) in 1970 to ensure a healthy environment for all citizens. And historically, the EPA has prioritized environmental stewardship over economic considerations. But Pruitt took full advantage of the ambiguities in the word *stewardship* as he moved the EPA in a different direction. In June 2018, he tweeted two pictures of meetings with industry leaders. He wrote, "Discussed the importance of the regulatory reform taking place @EPA with a great group of job creators at the WH [White House]. We are ensuring we approach decisions with stewardship in mind, rather than prohibition" (@EPAScottPruitt, June 19, 2018). Pruitt tied the word *stewardship* to job creation, not creation care. He viewed environmental concerns to be in opposition to economic considerations and privileged the economy over the nonhuman creation. And his tweet provides a crystal-clear example of the blurring of the economic and environmental meanings of the word *stewardship*. We can debate how best to relate jobs and environmental protection but using the word *stewardship* to refer to both job creation and creation care confuses the issues.

To audiences who favor environmental stewardship, Pruitt's words and actions are no different from the old concept of dominion over the creation. The result can be evisceration of environmental meaning from the word *stewardship* and the blurring of any distinction between the concepts of stewardship and dominion. To these audiences, stewardship is an unhelpful framework for environmental action. And stewardship becomes an obstructive, even harmful, way to think about the relationship between humans and the nonhuman creation.

Selecting the Right Words for an Audience

One implication of going beyond stewardship is being nimble in how we talk with others about creation care. When addressing audiences for whom stewardship is a helpful environmental framework, we need to build identification with them first. For certain groups, like the farmers and ranchers mentioned earlier, the concept of stewardship can provide common ground for productive conversations. Once common ground has been established, we can work to introduce other environmental perspectives and terms and collectively move our environmental discussions and actions forward.

We also should recognize that different groups may need to hear different words first. Because of the negative connotations associated with the word *stewardship* and because, for some, stewardship does not suggest a right strategy for environmental action, stewardship may not provide common ground. Therefore, we need to understand our audience and choose language that reflects a shared environmental perspective. Other terms emphasize different aspects of the relationship between humans and the nonhuman creation. "Creation care" highlights the responsible care aspects of stewardship while minimizing its financial or human-focused connotations. "Christian environmental thought and action" calls attention to links between how we think and act regarding the creation. "Earthkeeping" focuses on tending the earth. (See Bouma-Prediger, chapter 6.) "Kinship" emphasizes connectedness between the human and nonhuman elements of creation. (See Meyaard-Schaap, chapter 3.)

Adapting a message to identify with and ultimately persuade an audience does not distort one's principles: we can stay true to our environmental convictions while we work to understand and relate to others who may not share them. We need to shift our lens beyond stewardship, but first we must understand urgent environmental issues from others' perspectives, find common ground with them, and move forward in talking and working together. Words are important, but knowing our audience is paramount.

Works Cited

Burke, Kenneth. *A Rhetoric of Motives*. Berkeley: University of California Press, 1969.

Leopold, Aldo. *A Sand County Almanac and Sketches Here and There*. New York: Oxford University Press, 1968.

Pope Francis. *Encyclical Letter Laudato Si' of the Holy Father Francis on Care for Our Common Home*. Rome: Libreria Editrice Vaticana, 2015. http://w2.vatican.va /content/francesco/en/encyclicals/documents/papa-francesco_20150524 _enciclica-laudato-si.html.

Roser-Renouf, C., E. Maibach, A. Leiserowitz, G. Feinberg, and S. Rosenthal. *Faith, Morality and the Environment: Portraits of Global Warming's Six Americas*. Yale Program on Climate Change Communication. New Haven: Yale University and George Mason University, 2016. http://climatecommunication.yale.edu /wp-content/uploads/2016/01/Faith-Morality-Six-Americas.pdf.

Part Two

———

REIMAGINING:
How Things
Could Be

3

FROM FOREIGN TO FAMILY:

Kinship as Pathway toward
Radical Care for the Earth

Kyle Meyaard-Schaap

t midmorning, our group of students met Larry Gibson at a West
Virginia gas station off Route 3. We were there to observe the
impacts of mountaintop removal coal mining on local communities, and Larry was to provide a front-row seat. He owned property at
the top of Kayford Mountain, a small piece of land that had been in his
family since the 1700s. Kayford and the mountains surrounding it are rich
in coal, but most of their unharvested seams are too shallow for coal companies to safely dig down and mine as is typically done. Instead, it is much
cheaper to blow the tops off the mountains to expose the coal seams and
then scrape the surface. Larry's neighbors had sold their mineral rights,
one by one, and moved off the mountain. Larry was the lone holdout, and
the coal company had undertaken ever more extreme measures of intimidation to force him to sell.

Fog swirled in the headlights and gravel crunched under our tires
as we made our ascent up the mountain. When we reached Kayford's

summit, we finished the last bit of the journey on foot. The coal is so close to the surface that it studs the path like black tree roots. Larry led the way, his flat-brimmed hat barely visible above the rising and falling heads in front of me. Suddenly, he stopped and extended his arms like a school crossing guard. We had reached the end of the ridge to which he was leading us, but we couldn't see it because of the dense fog. We fanned out along the ridge crest and stared into the misted void, unable to see through the foggy veil before us but knowing nonetheless what we were looking at.

Topless mountains. Thousands of acres of scarred earth and miles of buried river. An expanse of neatly terraced brown and tan that once was wild, vivid green.

We knew what we were looking at because we had studied images of the mining operation across the holler. We also knew because of what we heard as we stood on the ridge. Or rather, what we didn't hear. We didn't hear the cacophony of birds singing to one another from the branches of Appalachia's old-growth pines. We didn't hear the abundance of life that should have been pulsing to us like an electric current across the expanse. Instead, we heard the vast emptiness left by the thousands of feet of ancient elevation now leveled forever. We heard nothing out of the void. Nothing at all. Who knew silence could be so deafening?

After several minutes of silent vigil, we made our way back down the short path that wound toward Larry's cabin. As his home came into view, several in our group noticed a sinister addition to Larry's landscaping: a rope hanging in the oak tree beside his cabin. The noose hadn't been there twenty minutes earlier.

A few days after our time at Kayford Mountain, we visited a small country church nestled in a nearby holler. As we recounted our experience, the pastor—a former coal miner—listened attentively. When we finished, he told us that all the residents of the holler either are currently employed or have family members who have been employed by the very coal company terrorizing Larry. Coal mining is their heritage, their livelihood, their identity. Then he said, with all sincerity and earnestness, words that echo in my ears to this day: "After all, God gave us the coal to bless us. He wants us to use it!"

In his own way, the pastor was articulating a theology of stewardship. To him, what was happening around Kayford Mountain and to Larry was regrettable, but how else could we harvest God's good gifts? It was simply the necessary cost of exercising stewardship, of managing the resources God has given for our use. The creation has inherent value, but if creation's well-being conflicts with human advancement, the winner is obvious: humans. (See Haney, chapter 10.)

The pastor was sincere. But his point of view shows that the Christian Environmental Stewardship paradigm, combined with powerful economic and political forces, can limit our understanding of the interdependent relationship between humans and the nonhuman creation. In the remainder of this chapter, I hope to provide a larger, scriptural, and more expansive picture of that relationship. Namely, I claim that Scripture does not ultimately call us to use and manage the creation. Rather, it calls us to be in intimate kinship with it.

Kinship in Genesis

Kinship is a strong word. It conjures images of family and notions of deep-seated commitment and love. It indicates commonality and honors both difference and diversity. Consider the relationship between a mother and her newborn child. The mother and child are woven together with deep and mysterious ties of love and affection and by the biological needs of the baby to be fed and nurtured. Mother and child are physically and emotionally connected. They share the same nose and DNA. And places of meaning bind them together—the nursery in the quiet hours between waking and sleeping, the walking route through their neighborhood. And as human beings, they share the common task of being responsible image bearers of the Creator in the creation. Yet mother and child are not the same. They are unique, distinct individuals. Kinship requires two poles to be fully expressed: commonality and difference. Mother and child are bound together in a relationship of commonality that honors—and indeed requires—their differences.

Similarly, Scripture holds that commonality in difference is the essence of our relationship to the nonhuman creation. Already in Genesis 1, we see this relationship on display. Humans are created on the sixth day alongside the rest of the land creatures, sharing the stage with badgers, beavers, and billy goats. In Genesis 2, the Hebrew text employs a pun that is often lost in translation to explain the intimate kinship of humans to the earth. Humans, says Genesis 2, are *adam* ("human") from the *adamah* ("earth," "soil"). (See Bouma-Prediger, chapter 6.) We are, quite literally, soil-creatures, formed from the dust of the earth and vivified by the very breath of the Creator God. We share a common origin with the nonhuman creation.

In Genesis, we also find a common vocation shared between human and nonhuman alike, namely, to worship and glorify God by participating in the ongoing work of creating. The Genesis creation narrative makes clear God's desire to delegate his divine power to the rest of creation that it might participate in the work of ongoing creation and re-creation. God commands the earth to "produce vegetation" (Genesis 1:11) and "living creatures according to their kinds" (Genesis 1:24), and it obeys (Genesis 1:12, 24). God commands human beings to "be fruitful and increase in number" (Genesis 1:28), and the progeny that fill the pages of scripture thereafter make clear that they too obey. A careful reading of the creation narrative reveals that both God and the Earth are subjects of the creative verbs, and that humans are also invited to create alongside the Creator. God desires his creation (humans and nonhumans alike) to be more than passive recipients of his creative will. The creation is to actively and freely participate in the creative process. (See Heun, chapter 1.) By blessing them (Genesis 1:22, 28), God filled both human and nonhuman creatures with divine power to participate with God in the ongoing work of creation. God established a common vocation for humans and nonhuman creatures alike.

Despite both our common origins and our common vocation with nonhuman creatures, God did not create identical creatures. The dizzying diversity jam-packed into the first chapter of Genesis removes any notion that God's ultimate plan for the creation is sameness. God values difference and diversity, and he hardwires it into his good creative design. Indeed, basic reproductive processes ensure diversity among and across species. The Genesis narrative highlights differences between human and nonhuman creatures when it notes that humans alone have been made in the image of their Creator. Yet this distinction is not a summons to human-centered privilege. It is a call to humble service. (See Bouma-Prediger, chapter 6.) Our uniqueness relative to nonhuman creatures is a crucial distinction, and we should resist any temptation to erase it. Instead, we can both celebrate the distinction as part of God's good design and recognize it as a critical piece of the kinship formula: commonality *in difference*.

Kinship in the Incarnation and the Sacraments

We see this relationship of kinship—of commonality in difference—not only in Genesis but also splashed throughout the pages of Scripture. We see it in the writings of the prophets (Hosea 4 and Joel 1) when they remind God's people to do right by both human and nonhuman creatures, recognizing their common vocation and noting that oppression of one means suffering for both. We see it in Job 38–41 and in many Psalms (19; 24; 65; 104), which attest to God's delight in both the human and the nonhuman creation for their own sake. It is made plain in the Gospels when Jesus communicates the character and nearness of the Kingdom of God using soil, plants, seeds, and birds. But the most striking examples of similarity in difference are found in the incarnation and in the institution of the sacraments.

With the incarnation, we see the enduring union of God and God's creation. And this union is located in a human body. It is no accident of salvation history that God became flesh to bring the world back to God's self. God's choice provides a tremendous affirmation of the goodness of God's creation in general and the goodness of humanity in particular. God's choice is also perfectly consistent with humanity's vocation to participate with God in the ongoing work of creation.

John 1 draws this connection between Genesis and the incarnation most clearly by choosing a loaded Greek word to describe Jesus: *logos*, translated as "the Word." In Greco-Roman cosmology, the *logos* was understood to be the animating force that infuses the world with being and life. *Logos* created the world in the beginning and sustained it from one moment to the next. And according to Hebrew cosmology, words were the building blocks of reality.

According to both the Greek and Hebrew worldviews of John's original audience, words are the operative force in the ongoing work of creation. The author of John is clearly drawing a straight line from the creation story in Genesis (when God creates with words) to the incarnation, because the incarnation—the joining together of God and humanity forever—is the culmination of humanity's role in the creative vocation set out in Genesis 1 and 2. Christ, the *logos*, is the firstfruits of the new creation, and everywhere he goes in the Gospel accounts, new creation (re-creation) follows: sight from blindness, healing from disease, order from chaos, life from death. In the person of Jesus Christ, redeemed creation flows through human fingertips. In him, humanity is finally faithful to its vocational calling. But in Christ, the creative vocation is extended and advanced too. The original call to create alongside God becomes a calling to re-create in the footsteps of Christ.

If the incarnation affirms and advances humanity's role in a shared vocation, then the sacraments do the same for the nonhuman creation. The sacraments of baptism and communion are many things. (See Al-Attas Bradford, chapter 5.) But for the purposes of this chapter, let us simply recognize that, like the incarnation, the sacraments require a partnership between God and the physical world (bread, wine, and water) to communicate the redeeming work of God. Without the elements of communion or the water of baptism, both would be devoid of meaning and power. The nonhuman creation (represented by bread, wine, and water) is a necessary participant in fashioning the new creation that is brought about by celebrating the sacraments. Just like the incarnation, the sacraments affirm the role of the nonhuman creation in the common task given to human and nonhuman alike in Genesis, and the sacraments extend the nonhuman creation's calling to include the task of redemption.

In both the incarnation and the sacraments, we see clearly the bonds of kinship between humans and the nonhuman creation, oriented around the redeeming work of Christ. By taking on a physical human body in the incarnation and instituting the sacraments as physical signs of his redeeming work, God underscores the intimacy of the human and the nonhuman in our shared physicality. By including both human and nonhuman in the act of communicating God's grace and redemption, the incarnation and the sacraments reach back to our common creative vocation in Genesis while at the same time reorienting it toward the new creation for which we hope. In all this, the incarnation and the sacraments maintain and honor the creational difference between human and nonhuman. The incarnation and the sacraments serve different functions in God's economy of salvation, and humans and nonhumans each have different but equally important roles to play. In the incarnation and the sacraments, we see clearly the equation of kinship: commonality in difference.

The Cultivation of Kinship: Worship

Scripture, the incarnation, and the sacraments attest to a kinship relationship between the human and the nonhuman creation, implying the closeness of family. Yet the paradigm of Christian Environmental Stewardship draws disproportionate attention to a separation between human stewards and the nonhuman creation. (See the introduction.) How is our commonality with the nonhuman creation to be rediscovered? In worship, of course. After all, it is in worship that we are taught the liturgies of life, where we are offered the imagination for what is possible and what is not. It is in worship that we are taught who we are and are invited into the story that shapes our lives.

For centuries, the church has enacted liturgies rich in the formula of kinship. "Canticle of the Sun," composed by St. Francis of Assisi, thanks God for his kin "Brother Sun," "Sister Moon," "Brother Wind," and "Sister Water." *The Exsultet*, an ancient Easter vigil liturgy, recognizes the work of the bees who made the wax for the candle that is lit as "a solemn offering . . . an evening sacrifice of praise."[1] These ancient liturgies understand the intimate relationship of human and nonhuman instituted in Genesis and

---

1   "The Exsultet: The Proclamation of Easter," United States Conference of Catholic Bishops, 2019, http://www.usccb.org/prayer-and-worship/liturgical-year/easter/easter-proclamation -exsultet.cfm.

heightened in the incarnation and the sacraments, and they are eager to include our nonhuman kin in the task of worshiping the Creator.

Though many of these liturgical practices have been lost over time, particularly in American Protestant contexts, there are contemporary efforts to reintroduce the kinship relationship into our worshiping practices. The Season of Creation movement, begun in Australia in 2000, is an effort to establish a new liturgical season, like Advent and Lent, in the church calendar. The Season of Creation is dedicated to the participation of nonhuman creation in worship. Running for five Sundays from September to early October, the liturgical Season of Creation has been endorsed by several denominations and ecumenical bodies, including the World Council of Churches.[2] Like the ancient *Exsultet*, liturgies for the Season of Creation "invite the cosmos to worship with us."[3] Everything from "glittering galaxies high in the sky" to "the turtle, the toad and the elephant, the earthworm, the ant and the dragonfly" are summoned to "dance with cosmic energy,"[4] the cosmic energy that flows from the risen Christ, whose "presence fills the cosmos."[5]

In addition to discovering liturgies of kinship, both ancient and new, we must cultivate worship practices that connect us to the nonhuman creation. For millennia before the Western Enlightenment, human cultures understood that the specific places in which we live and move matter. (See Bjelland, chapter 13.) We are formed and nurtured and blessed by the particular nonhuman creation around us, and our worship must reflect this reality. (See Warners, chapter 14.) Given how the celebration of the sacraments already unites us with the nonhuman creation in our common creative vocation, why not name names in our worship? (See Rienstra, chapter 8.)

We can name and give thanks for the local water source during baptisms. We can identify fields, bakeries, vineyards, and wineries during

---

2   "Season of Creation," World Council of Churches, 2019, https://www.oikoumene.org/en/what-we-do/climate-change/time-for-creation.

3   "The Season of Creation," Series C, Cosmos Sunday, Call to Worship, Uniting Church in Australia, Synod of Victoria and Tasmania, 2019, https://seasonofcreation.com/wp-content/uploads/2010/04/liturgy-cosmos-sunday-1.pdf.

4   "The Season of Creation," Series C, Cosmos Sunday, Call to Worship.

5   "The Season of Creation," Series C, Cosmos Sunday, Gathering.

Holy Communion. We can give thanks to the sources themselves for their participation in the holy moment. We can give thanks to our place for its participation in worship. We can gather soil from the church's property and place it at the front of the sanctuary throughout Advent to remind ourselves that in the incarnation God forever joined the stuff of earth to his divine self. We can take a prayer walk around the property, praying for specific parts of creation that are found there. We can take special note of any sort of pollution or degradation on the church's property and offer lament. We can invite a local expert (i.e., historian, botanist, or energy efficiency consultant) to offer information about the church's specific history, ecology, or mechanical systems during a worship service. We can research which local birds from the community migrate south for the winter and pray in anticipation of their return in the spring as the community prays for the return of Christ, thanking God for the beauty and mystery of the creation. We can identify and implement renewable energy options for the sanctuary and for parishioners' homes as an act of worship.

When we rediscover the church's liturgies of kinship, both ancient and modern, celebrate those elements of creation that already inform our worship, and invite more of the nonhuman creation into active worship with us, the possibilities are myriad! As we begin to practice these liturgies, our closeness to and commonality with the nonhuman creation begin to form us into a new kind of people. Our assumptions about human exceptionalism are challenged. Our imaginations expand beyond the limitations of mere stewardship toward right relationships with nonhuman creation marked by commonality in difference. We become kinship people.

The Fruit of Kinship: Love and Protection

If Scripture—from Genesis to the incarnation to the sacraments and beyond—makes the case that our proper orientation toward the nonhuman creation is not management but kinship, and if our worship practices form and deepen our kinship bonds with the rest of creation, what outcomes could this have for our lives, for the church, and for the world?

One fruit will be the cultivation of genuine affection and love. Remember our mother and newborn child. There is something chemical that spurs the love of a mother toward her child. But love also needs time, proximity, and common purpose to grow. Attention toward and awareness of one's beloved lead to affection, which in turn fosters deep and abiding love.[6] Careful attention to a newborn's differentiated cries, hunger cues, unique facial expressions, and early mannerisms contributes to an awareness of the precious little one. As awareness of the child grows, affection wells up with every coo, smile, and cry. In this rich soil of attention, awareness, and affection, love takes root and blooms.

The same is true with our relationship to the nonhuman world. As we embrace our commonality with the nonhuman creation, our attention is piqued. As we participate with the nonhuman creation through worship in the common task of communicating God's redeeming work to the cosmos, we become aware of the uniqueness of the nonhuman world in new ways. We become aware of the baptismal power of a local stream and the spiritual nourishment offered by local grains and grapes. Our awareness generates affection for the many ways that the nonhuman creation sustains us physically and spiritually. We fall in love.

This love for the nonhuman world, then, is the fount from which flows the church's unique answer to the powerful economic, cultural, and political forces at work in Larry's story and many others. When fully realized, our love for the nonhuman creation, anchored by our kinship bonds, will lead the church toward radical acts of protection and preservation of both human and nonhuman alike. This radical protection and preservation is in fact part of our human calling, as evidenced in God's command to the *adam* in Genesis 2:15 to "serve and protect" the garden. (See Bouma-Prediger, chapter 6.)

We will reject the idea that the nonhuman creation is merely inert raw material to fire our industrial machines and a passive recipient of our actions upon it. Our kinship love will not allow us to stand idly by while creation is exploited and abused for short-term profit. We will have an answer for those who seek to weaken protections for the nonhuman

---

6   Calvin B. DeWitt, *Earthwise: A Guide to Hopeful Creation Care*, 3rd ed. (Grand Rapids, MI: Faith Alive Christian Resources, 2011), 121-122.

creation in the name of scoring ideological points. Our fierce sense of protection will draw us to the streets and into the halls of power. We will confront the prevailing economic, political, and social domination of creation. We will treat the nonhuman creation as family and a coparticipant in the work of creation and re-creation. We will view the nonhuman creation not as resources but as kin.

In all but the most extreme cases, and as far as it is within her power, a mother will do everything she can to serve and protect her newborn child. The love she has for her kin will not allow her to do anything else. To do anything else would be unthinkable. When the church comes to understand fully its intimate kinship relationship with the physical world, refusal to take radical action to serve and protect the nonhuman creation will be just as unthinkable.

The Promise of Kinship: Creation Renewed

Larry Gibson died of a heart attack in 2012, mere months after our visit. He died before anything could come of his advocacy. He died with bullet holes in his cabin and nooses swinging in the trees outside his door. He died with Kayford Mountain still in desperate danger.

I can't help but wonder how a broadly held vision of kinship might have changed Larry's story. What if the small congregation in Larry's holler had been formed into kinship people? What if the theology of the pastor we met hadn't been shaped by the prevailing economic and political forces benefiting from the abuse of the land around him but rather by a vision of kinship love and protection for the nonhuman creation? What if Christians in America were increasingly being formed, week after week, into kinship people by worship practices that facilitated closeness to and recognized our commonality with the physical world, while celebrating our differences?

Perhaps the local church would have protected Larry from the harassment he suffered. Maybe they would have protected the mountains surrounding Kayford. Maybe the pastor could have recognized as kin the birds, the mountains, the streams, Larry, and all the people negatively affected by the company's practices and could have acted out of love and protection rather than rationalizing the problem away. Perhaps Christians across the country would have known Larry's story and would have marched in the streets and knocked down the doors of Congress demanding a stop to the abuse. It is possible that today Christians would be exerting persistent pressure on corporations to find alternative means of energy production that treat humans like Larry and the nonhuman creation alike as kin. Maybe they would be leading the charge to transform all of humanity's relationship to the created world by protecting endangered species, eliminating dangerous pollutants, and stopping climate change in its tracks.

If the American church had been formed by this vision, Larry could have died peacefully. He could have been surrounded by neighbors long-since driven out. He could have had the sound of hymns in his ears sung by members of the local church standing guard at his door. He could have known that his kinship with Kayford Mountain was not an isolated relationship but was shared by Christians the world over who had been shaped by worship to enact a vision of love and protection for human and nonhuman creatures alike.

Works Cited

DeWitt, Calvin B. *Earthwise: A Guide to Hopeful Creation Care*. 3rd ed. Grand Rapids, MI: Faith Alive Christian Resources, 2011.

"The Exsultet: The Proclamation of Easter." United States Conference of Catholic Bishops, 2019. http://www.usccb.org/prayer-and-worship/liturgical-year/easter/easter-proclamation-exsultet.cfm.

"The Season of Creation." Uniting Church in Australia, Synod of Victoria and Tasmania, 2019. https://seasonofcreation.com/worship-resources/liturgies/.

4

The Responsibility of Earthlings for the Earth:

Graciousness, Lament, and the Call of Justice

Clarence W. Joldersma

It is the clay of our own body, dust that shall return to dust,
that knows the earth and knows itself as terrestrial.
—Alphonso Lingis, *The Imperative*

When I was a young boy, my grandparents lived with our family on a small, poor farm. They, along with my parents, were recent postwar immigrants to Canada, hoping to create a better life. As a young kid, seven to eight years old, I adored my grandfather. He was resourceful and creative, building and repairing things around the farm, using the materials at hand. I would constantly shadow him, no doubt getting in the way but trying to help. Rather than shoo me away, he would draw me in, giving me tasks that were part of the project.

One of my strongest memories is that he taught me how to straighten old, bent nails that had been pulled from previous projects. Straightening a nail required patience and care. Rolling a nail with an index finger while tapping the bends in the nail with a hammer was tricky. The nail needed to be tapped in just the right spot and with just the right force to nudge it straighter, then rolled slightly to locate another bend and tapped again. The process required keen eye-hand coordination and feeling the nail's roll under the touch of the finger and the hammer's weight as it landed in just the right spot.

After a while, bent nails seemed to call out, "Straighten me!" And it was like I could almost feel the straightness in a crooked nail as I began to work on it. This felt like a goodness calling—that I should reuse this scarce resource and practice frugality. It was part of developing an eye for positive possibilities of used material, beyond its current use. Straightening nails turned out to be part of a nest of social practices that I later recognized as something Christians call stewardship.

In looking beyond the bend of a nail, I was acquiring the stewardly values of "don't waste" and "be frugal." But more, my understanding of things and of myself was also changing. The stewardship practice of straightening nails taught me that bent nails were not trash but something with continuing value. I learned through this practice that a nail itself was more valuable than my time. Despite our poverty, we could have afforded a pound of new nails for a new project. But I came to know that a nail itself had intrinsic value. Although a thing, a nail deserved straightening. It had a goodness that called me to invest time and energy. An inanimate thing had a right to dictate the use of my time.

Stewardship Is Not Enough

Stewardship involves using resources in a way that goes beyond our selfish greed, teaching us that we don't have an absolute right to do what we want with our resources. It makes relative our own claims to absolute ownership. In my religious tradition, we often say, "This world belongs to God." God is the absolute owner rather than humans. German philosopher Immanuel Kant, by contrast, thought that because the earth was a globe and we could locate ourselves in a specific place on it, this meant that we humans had an original right to own and possess it. His idea was that the earth's surface was a common property for human beings and that each human thus had a primary right to own a part of it. On this account, the earth was originally human property.

Stewardship modifies but does not overturn Kant's idea. In stewardship, we are called to be responsible with the resources that we proximally own, on behalf of God, who is the ultimate owner. Nevertheless, in stewardship, the creation is still reduced to being a resource for humans, open to continued domination and exploitation. The earth has suffered under this relationship, even when stewardship is done responsibly. The earth's suffering cannot be resolved by more efficient and responsible resource use.

Clearly, the nails I straightened in my childhood were owned by our family. What is more, nails get their meaning from their use as handy fasteners that help assemble parts into useful artifacts such as furniture, houses, sheds, and decks. Nails are means to achieve certain ends. Further, when the iron out of which they are made is mined, it becomes a resource ready to be fashioned into useful products. When formed into nails and stocked in a hardware store, iron becomes a reserve, a stock ready to be used for human projects at a moment's notice. Stewardship of nails and other stock reserves involves hearing a call to responsible, frugal use of resources that we own on behalf of God.

In stewardship, the moral significance of nails comes through their usefulness. Their moral status rides on our feeling called to recognize them as valuable stock ready for use by humans in responsible ways. Nails have moral standing because they are part of stewardly actions, by humans, that have moral significance. However, stewardship is not enough. In stewardship, our relationship with the nonhuman creation remains instrumental, even when situated in a feeling of responsibility and enacted through careful and frugal use.

To go beyond stewardship's limitations, we need an expanded understanding of our human creatureliness and a deeper understanding of the nonhuman creation. (See Al-Attas Bradford, chapter 5.) These understandings echo Willis Jenkins, who argues that for Christians to have a successful environmental ethic, we need to pay careful attention to three things: the moral significance of the nonhuman creation, the way we interact with that creation, and the way we think about ourselves in that interaction. Stewardship, he says, is that middle thing, the human practice that shapes the nonhuman creation.[1] Jenkins challenges the stewardship tradition to address the other two aspects as well, the moral standing of the nonhuman creation and an expanded self-understanding of being human.

In the next two sections of this chapter, I will develop Jenkins's first and last dimensions in reverse order. My claim is that we need an expanded self-understanding of humans beyond our role as stewards of resources for human projects and interests. I will use the term *earthlings* to designate this expanded understanding of ourselves. And we need to view the nonhuman creation as having an independent moral standing beyond its use for humans. I will use the metaphor "earthly depth" to name this.

We Are Earthlings

As humans, we live on the earth. There is an earthiness to our existence. We are not separate from the earth. The ancient story of creation recounted in Genesis echoes that fact, suggesting that we were created to live on the earth and that we are suited for an earthly existence. We are *earthlings*.

Recognizing that we are earthlings expands what it means to be a person. For example, we might believe our ability to think and act separates us from the nonhuman creation. But conscious thoughts and actions, which help us make our way in the world, are based in our sensorimotor structures. We share this sensorimotor embodiment with nonhuman living creatures. As cognitive beings, we already have an inkling of a depth to our human experience, that we are earthlings.

But the enduring presence of our emotions also reveals that we are earthlings. Our experience of the world always has a positive or a negative feeling, and emotions always color our actions and thoughts. Our emotions are not mere add-ons to our rational agency. Rather, the thoughtful freedom in which we do things is always embedded in an emotional mattering that conditions and supports it. In other words, emotions are

---

1   Willis J. Jenkins, "The Strategy of Christian Stewardship," in *Ecologies of Grace: Environmental Ethics and Christian Theology* (New York: Oxford University Press, 2008), 77-92.

affective experiences of how things matter. In this, emotions connect us to other living creatures. Nonhuman primates, mammals more generally, and even reptiles and birds are all motivated by primal emotions. They too experience things in how they matter to them. Our emotions show that part of the essence of being human is older than humanity itself. As earthlings, we share with many other creatures our experiencing the world as mattering.

Our experiences of mattering include primary emotions such as caring for others, playing together, being angry at siblings, desiring romantic connections, seeking novel experiences, and fearing dangers. When we experience these emotions, what is welling up inside us is something ancient, shared with nonhuman living creatures. For example, grief might overcome us when we learn that our beloved grandfather has died. He mattered to us. Grief is the mournful feeling of sudden loss of someone with whom we had an intimate bond, someone who mattered. Neuroscientists suggest that such grief is likely a maturation of the panic emotion that occurs when a newborn is suddenly separated from a parent, something that happens in primates, mammals, and even birds. Humans grieve, but so do chimpanzees, elephants, and geese. The very human emotion of grief is an ancient experience, an earthiness that has been incorporated into our embodied nature. Sharing this emotion with nonhuman creatures shows our relatedness and earthly kinship with the teeming array of living creatures on the earth. (See Meyaard-Schaap, chapter 3.)

But what matters is also more basic than what our primary emotions indicate. We can think back to the ancient creation stories in the first chapters of Genesis. In the second story the author relates that God fashioned humans out of dirt, with the first humans emerging out of the earth's elements. What is more, this fashioning might be a special case of God's general creational invitation in the first creation story: "Let the earth bring forth living creatures". These creation stories echo what we now know about human life: the most ancient emergence of biotic life from the elements is present in every human being, in the very elements that constitute us as living creatures. We are all composed of elements such as oxygen, hydrogen, carbon, and nitrogen. What matters shows in our dynamic metabolism, in our need to breathe in oxygen and breathe out carbon dioxide. (See Al-Attas Bradford, chapter 5.) Already our elemental makeup and our need to breathe show that we are earthlings. This earthiness reveals our relatedness to other living creatures and our earthly kinship with what matters for the teeming creatures on earth.

Our elemental mattering as earthlings shows that as living creatures, we are dynamic systems. This means that what matters to us as creatures are certain conditions outside of us. To remain alive, we are dependent on the continual dynamic interchanges across our bodies' boundaries. This is obvious not only in exchanges such as breathing in and out or eating and eliminating but also in our adjustments to weather, including to temperature and moisture. The dynamics of the earth matter to us. At its most comprehensive, the earth is a dynamic system constituted by various subsystems: atmosphere (air), biosphere (living creatures), cryosphere (ice), hydrosphere (water), and lithosphere (earth's crust). These specific systems compose a comprehensive earth system and jointly form the livable conditions that matter and on which we depend.

For the last ten thousand years, the earth system has been very supportive of human and other creaturely life. This elemental support also shows us to be precarious as living creatures. We are vulnerable to the elements and ultimately to the supportive stability of the earth system. Because we require constant elemental interaction with our surroundings, the stability of human life is dependent on the generosity of the elements within which we constantly bathe. As living creatures, we are constantly exposed to the elements and dependent on their gracious support for our independent living. This fragility, this exposure to the earth system as a milieu in which we live and on which we depend, reveals us as earthlings.

Kant's idea of original property is called into question when we realize that more ancient than the right to ownership is that we are bathed in the elemental environment constituting the earth's surface. Original property is called into question when we understand that the earth is a dynamic system, sustaining us as living creatures. The earth is fundamentally a medium in which we live, making it originally nonpossessable. Human ownership is situated within this nonpossessable milieu, a planetary earth system that supports us. This suggests that belonging to the earth is original, not the right of ownership.

My aim is to uncover an expansive responsibility of humans toward the nonhuman creation, one that goes beyond the practical agency we associate with stewardship. That expansive responsibility, which I address in the last section of this chapter, is an ethical call that is felt as part of our ancient earthiness. Stewardship is important, but our self-understanding as earthlings suggests a responsibility that goes beyond stewarding. A more complete understanding of our responsibility for the creation requires understanding that we are earthlings.

Looking back, I was awakened to my earthiness under my grandfather's guidance. He helped me to become aware of an expansiveness to my being human. As a child, I didn't understand that, of course. But the expansiveness of what it means to be human is increasingly evident to me, as I recognize more and more that being human means that I am an earthling.

The Nonhuman Creation Has Independent Moral Standing

I learned from my grandfather something about the moral status of nails. His practices gave me the space to ask broader questions: Do nails have some significance beyond their status as useful things? Do nails have a moral standing independent of being a useful resource? If so, how might we experience such moral standing? And more generally, how might we experience the nonhuman creation's moral standing independent of its status as stock reserve? Experiencing the goodness in a nail was my clue.

The Christian tradition often appeals to the creation stories to say that the creation itself has a kind of sacredness. Its sacredness suggests that the nonhuman creation is an end and not merely a means. The goodness that was declared in the first ancient creation narrative of Genesis names creation as an end, with its own moral standing. The sweep of goodness in that narrative was comprehensive, including plants and animals, water and land, day and night. The goodness was declared for the elements within which we bathe, ultimately for the planet as earth system. The sacredness of earth itself is something beyond utility, involving an intrinsic worth. The declared goodness in the creation narrative indicates that the Creator loves not only humans but also nonhumans and the earth itself. My term *earthly depth* is meant to indicate a sacredness so deep that degradation of the creation offends the Creator's love. (See Heun, chapter 1.) Experiencing earthly depth reveals the creation's independent moral standing.

To uncover how we might experience the moral standing of nails and other useful things means we need to uncover this earthly depth. A nail is useful as a fastener. But hidden in this usefulness is its perhaps unnoticed reliability. A nail is an effective fastener because it remains faithfully at work over decades keeping together pieces of wood. A nail is trustworthy in our reliance on it. This faithful support is a nail's earthly depth. Earthly goodness shows up in experiencing the trustworthiness of useful things: the sturdiness of a road, the reliability of a car, the supportiveness of a chair. This ancient creational goodness also shows up when our bodies are reliable and stable grounds for our work and play. It appears in the supportive dependability of the nutrition in the food that nourishes us, in the supportive way that houses shelter us, the sun warms us, water refreshes us, and the wind cools us. Most comprehensively, it is revealed in experiencing the earth as a supportive dynamic system for living. Over the last ten thousand years, that planet-wide system has been a proper fit for human and nonhuman life. This ancient condition is a faithfulness that makes possible our practical activities and daily lives.

When we are attentive to this faithful goodness, we begin to experience how radically we depend on the earth's generous support. With regard to the elements in which we bathe, the earth shows itself generously trustworthy. The sustaining ground of earthly depth is a deep graciousness, a reliability we experience as a generous gift, freely given even before we have had a chance to ask for it. (See Warners, chapter 14.) When realized, this generosity elicits an appropriate feeling of gratefulness. It is a debt that can never be repaid, for which we at least owe thanks. For example, the last ten thousand years of favorable climate have been a continuous gift, supporting wide-ranging human projects. Living on the earth, as earthlings, we experience this depth as an ancient owing. The earth's goodness manifests itself as a generous gift for which we owe thanks. Its generosity matters to us.

But earth's supportiveness is not automatic or guaranteed. Feeling the contingency of earth's generosity also means experiencing the vulnerability of earth's support. Nails can rust and break, losing their trustworthy grip as fasteners. Ocean currents can weaken and change course, allowing severe weather to emerge on land. Seen in this light, climate change is not merely change but an undermining of the generosity of the earth as a supportive dynamic system. Disruptions of the global earth system threaten to undermine the well-being of the many living creatures that constitute the intricate web of life. There is a fragility and a vulnerability to the conditions supporting biotic life, including our own. And life has become more precarious because the trustworthy planetary conditions have been disrupted recently by human activities. We have damaged what matters to us, harmed that to which we owe thanks.

Earlier I suggested that part of our being earthlings is the emotion of grief. Grief is also an appropriate response to the experienced disruption of our earth as dynamic system. We can rightly mourn the damage we have inflicted on the generous gift of support that is our earth system. (See Heffner, chapter 11.) Grief is mourning the loss of something that has a moral status, something that matters. The earth's freely given gift of trustworthy support has a moral status that goes beyond its utility. Mourning disruption of the earth's trustworthy support signals its independent moral status.

But grief is not uniquely human, for nonhuman creatures also can mourn. Extending this metaphorically to the earth system as a whole, the damage to the earth's generous support can also be thought of as the earth's own lament, a grieving in its own voice. (See Heun, chapter 1.) The New Testament narrates that the earth itself has been groaning. This groaning signals the earth's lament for its diminished ability to provide reliable conditions for the flourishing of living creatures. The earth's lament in its own voice can be heard as a refusal to willingly go along with the destructive changes brought on by human activities. The earth's lament is felt in its resistance to our projects, through its disruptive effects in response to human-induced perturbations.

Earth's lament uncovers an ancient call to responsibility, deeper and more expansive than the one associated with stewardship. The lament is an ancient summons to let nonhuman earthlings be themselves, as creatures with independent moral standing. We humans are called to leave them be, including the earth system as a whole. Slight changes in any direction of our long-term planetary conditions would make earth uninhabitable for most types of living creatures. Earth's lament is a call to responsibility *by* the earth *for* the earth to let the earth *be*. Earth's lament is a call by the generous goodness of the earth for us to be responsible for maintaining, as best we can, the conditions that make on-going life on the earth possible. Earth's lament demands a liberation from our human quest for domination and exploitation of the earth. It invites us to understand ourselves as located in the interconnectivity of all earthly beings. Earth's lament calls us to see ourselves as earthlings, acknowledging our own earthiness in solidarity with the earth.

Our felt debt of gratitude to the earth gives rise to an ethical stance. We feel it as an earthly depth that undermines our false notion of the absolute nature of our ownership, agency, and freedom. This debt unsettles our practical self-interests, revealing that we radically depend on something with independent moral status to which we owe something. This debt of gratitude reveals an ethical claim on us for restraint and simplicity. This debt shows that earth's generous support can be withdrawn, because our productive control can have violent consequences for the earth's trustworthiness (see Haney, chapter 10). The earth's lament is an ethical appeal to an expansive, deep responsibility. We ought to say yes to the earth.

Responsibility Deeper than Stewardship

To understand a nail is to sense how we might hold it in one hand while approaching it with a hammer in the other. To know a nail is to be familiar with it through the dexterity of our hands. Hammering a nail is a responsive exploration in which a hammer and a nail together draw our bodily posture into the task at hand. As they order our bodies' dynamics, the nail shows up as an imperative, to use Alphonso Lingis's term, an invitation to which our earthy bodies respond.[2] We know a crooked nail through its call

---

2   Alphonso Lingis, *The Imperative* (Bloomington: Indiana University Press, 1998).

to be straightened, to which we respond with exploratory manipulations of hammering as we roll the nail in one hand and tap it with the other. Our sensorimotor activities are, in their earthiness, bodily responses to the things we interact with.

Kant was famous for suggesting that our moral subjectivity is connected to a moral imperative, and he called our response to this invitation respect. He restricted the moral imperative to relationships with other humans. But what if our sensorimotor responses to things as imperatives also involve respect? Then useful resources, in their earthly depth, are not merely instrumental means but also moral ends. Because things show up as imperatives, they call from an earthiness deeper than usefulness. In their earthly depth, things as imperatives call for ethical respect, as things with independent moral standing. These imperatives are an earthly summons, a demand for a kind of ethical responsibility toward the creation that is deeper than stewardship, the mere management of resources.

A nail, then, isn't something merely useful but also earthy. Even when I see a nail as ready to use in projects, my experience of it as an imperative means that its earthiness intrudes into its usefulness. I experience its earthiness as an intrinsic moral standing that intrudes into my practical experience. Earthiness interrupts my strategic viewing of the nail purely as a resource, uncovering a deeper responsibility to something with independent moral standing.

The responsibility that emerges through this earthly depth means feeling that, as earthlings, we are to bear witness to the earth's independent moral standing. This means bearing witness not only to nails as having independent moral standing, but also, more comprehensively, to the dynamic planetary earth system. The earth system summons our respect. It matters. Earthy responsibility is experiencing the goodness of the creation, that it matters intrinsically, beyond our interests. And the earth, through its lament in its own voice, reveals its vulnerability as the earth system. The creation's goodness does not protect it against human interests and projects. So it calls for respect, a summons for the protection of its vulnerability as something that matters, as something worthy of respect.

This call for respect is a call of justice. The Old Testament prophets proclaimed that a call of justice was coming from the vulnerable humans in society—the widow, the orphan, the alien, the poor. Although they had independent moral standing, these persons existed on society's margins, oppressed and exploited. Their vulnerability and harm called out for justice, because they mattered. Justice showed up as a claim, an imperative arising because they also had independent moral standing. Justice summoned the people to ensure that the marginalized persons were not harmed and to look after their welfare. That claim was based in experiencing the claimant's moral standing as a being of worth, an end worthy of respect. The goodness of the creation shows up in this same way. We experience the goodness of the creation as a felt claim, as an imperative that the nonhuman creation matters. The imperative becomes, then, a summons to protect the vulnerable earth from harm. Earth matters. The experience of creation's disruption, the harm of the earth itself, is a call of justice.

We are touched by the earth in this call of justice. We are touched by the earth's gracious and contingent support. Our response to earth's call of justice should be a deep, expansive environmental responsibility. We are touched by grace, grace given corporeally, by the gift of grace experienced as the earth. This independent moral standing of earth should spur a response. It should awaken our fundamental responsibility to the creation as something to respect and care for intrinsically. This reorientation is a call for restraint and a call to care for creation for its own sake.

Works Cited

Jenkins, Willis J. *Ecologies of Grace: Environmental Ethics and Christian Theology.* New York: Oxford University Press, 2008.

Lingis, Alphonso. *The Imperative.* Bloomington: Indiana University Press, 1998

SYMBIOTIC STEWARDSHIP

Aminah Al-Attas Bradford

Over four hundred applicants and not one of them mentioned the creation. These were Calvin College student leaders applying to be faith facilitators in their residence halls. At the end of their interviews, I asked for a one-hundred-word explanation of the gospel. Without fail the students mentioned God, God's Son Jesus, humans, and sin. Some mentioned the devil, hell, and heaven. A few mentioned incarnation and resurrection. But no one mentioned the creation. To be fair, when you are given only a hundred words to summarize the gospel, why mention muskrats or glaciers or microbes? After all, in the end, what does the creation really have to do with salvation?

I also asked students about their service experiences, and some were advocates for environmental causes. Their reasons for serving far surpassed anything I could have offered when I was a college student. Some mentioned that Christ is Lord of all things (Colossians 1:15–20), others that every square inch of creation is the Lord's.[1] Some students celebrated

---

1 Abraham Kuyper, *Abraham Kuyper: A Centennial Reader*, ed. James D. Bratt (Grand Rapids: Eerdmans, 1998), 461.

that creation is the theater of God's glory,[2] others that humans are to be stewards of creation (Genesis 1:26–28). But in these students' minds, and I imagine in the minds of many ecologically sensitive Christians, when giving a bare-bones gospel account, the creation doesn't merit mention. Creation is a matter of ethics, or obedience, but not salvation.

I press on this phenomenon of separating the creation from salvation because this book is framed by a shared lament aptly put by my colleague James R. Skillen. Given all the theological and biblical justifications mentioned above, he asked in a discussion, "Why isn't ecological stewardship the bread and butter of the church?" Scholars are beginning to think that part of the problem is the logic of stewardship itself. Stewardship is a problematic concept.

A key critique of stewardship is that it depends on the twin prides of thinking too highly and centrally of humanity (anthropocentrism) and thinking too lowly of everything else (objectification). Stewardship emphasizes humanity's exceptional capacity and responsibility while minimizing the creation's inherent value. After all, how can we steward if we are not separate from and somewhat superior to the rest of the creation? This distorted way of thinking about the human and the nonhuman creation may not seem problematic because modern theology itself functions with this segregated and marginalizing view of the nonhuman creation, what I call matter or flesh. Modern Christianity often operates with this same puffed-up picture of humans. We are taught that the gospel revolves around us. As God's image bearers, we imagine humans are set apart, the only characters in a drama about divine rescue. We think of ourselves as distinct from and more important than the rest of creation—more rational than animal and more "spiritual" than creaturely. This view of humanity corresponds to an anemic picture of the rest of the creation. We think of the creation as special scenery, a backdrop to our lives. Acknowledging these twin prides offers a critique of stewardship and raises questions about *who* we are and *where* we are.

This critique is bolstered by new biological insights. Learning that trillions of microbes living in and on our bodies (known as the human

---

2   John Calvin, *Calvin: Institutes of Christian Religion*, 4th ed., vol. 1, trans. Ford Lewis Battles, ed. John T. McNeill (Philadelphia: Westminster Press, 1967), 61, 179, 341.

microbiome) contribute to our digestion, cognition, sleep, immunity, and more erodes the biological notion that we are an independent, superior species. These discoveries of humanity's intimate entanglement with microbial life also complicate the theological idea that we are separate from and superior to the rest of creation. How superior to animals can we be if we depend on them to be ourselves?

These critiques alone, that stewardship operates with an exaggerated, prideful, and now biologically untenable idea of the human being, are reason enough to reconsider the language of stewardship. But anthropocentrism and objectification are not the cause of stewardship's failure to make ecological concerns the bread and butter of the church. In fact, they are symptoms of a deeper problem. Anthropocentrism and objectification are endemic to a Christian culture that cannot account for why the non-human creation matters. Christians may be waking to *ecological* reasons why all people should care for the creation, but few Christians seem to have a *theological* imagination for why the creation matters to the central drama of salvation. The student interviewees who championed ecological stewardship didn't know how to connect the creation to the gospel. They didn't know why the creation matters.

Stewardship is a problematic term, but not in the way we usually think. The real problem is that Christians do not know why matter matters for redemption. When we understand why the creation matters for redemption, stewardship becomes symbiotic and its tendencies toward anthropocentrism and objectification fall away.

At one level, creation matters because, without it, humans would cease to exist. Coming to grips with humanity's biologically symbiotic relationship with the creation is a good start. That is why I focus on our dependence on microbial life. Biological dependence wakes people from their false sense of independence, superiority, and centrality. But our dependence on the creation goes beyond biology. The creation matters for salvation. Cultivating a new imagination for biological *and* spiritual dependency primes us to finally acknowledge that stewardship is a mutual task between humans and the nonhuman creation. Stewardship becomes symbiotic when our dependence on creatures moves beyond matters of biology to matters of redemption.

We should not be naïve. Accepting humanity's entanglement or kinship with other creatures (especially spiritual dependence) is a hard pill to swallow for many Christians. That is why, before we can turn toward symbiotic stewardship, we must first explore the roots of our resistance to dependence on nonhuman matter. I suspect that whether we call it stewardship, earthkeeping, creation care, or kinship, until Christians understand why they place themselves above the nonhuman creation and until they have an imagination for how the nonhuman creation is related to salvation, environmental stewardship will never be the bread and butter of the church. Stewardship won't matter until matter matters.

Our Microbial Symbionts

I am a theologian, not a microbiologist. But I like microbes because they expose unexamined assumptions about what it means to be human. Sometimes we don't realize the deep beliefs we hold about ourselves and the world until something, like the microbiome, challenges them. Looking at microbes is an opportunity to turn the microscope back on ourselves. As we do this, it is important to pay attention to and learn from the questions that arise. (See Halteman and Zwart, chapter 9.) Microbes will reveal and Scripture will reform our understanding of ourselves and our relationships to creatures. Microbes are like tiny prophets. They prepare the way for a deepened imagination for how matter might matter for salvation.

Humans depend on nonhuman matter, the flesh of the world, for food and shelter. This is not news. The discovery that humans themselves are food and shelter for trillions of microscopic creatures is news, and it is making headlines: "We Are Our Bacteria,"[3] "Microbes Maketh Man,"[4] "The Human Microbiome: Me, Myself, Us."[5] When we count up the cells

---

3   Jane E. Brody, "We Are Our Bacteria," *New York Times*, July 14, 2014, https://well.blogs
    .nytimes.com/2014/07/14/we-are-our-bacteria/.
4   "Microbes Maketh Man," *Economist*, August 18, 2012, https://www.economist.com
    /leaders/2012/08/18/microbes-maketh-man.
5   "The Human Microbiome: Me, Myself, Us," *Economist*, August 18, 2012, https://www
    .economist.com/science-and-technology/2012/08/18/me-myself-us.

that comprise a human body, we find there are at least as many nonhuman cells as there are human cells. Microbes inhabit our skin and line our digestive pathway. Collectively, they are sometimes referred to as a person's microbial organ. Even inside our human cells there are mitochondria, the organelles that power each cell. The microbial DNA contained in mitochondria indicates that mitochondria were formerly free-living microbes themselves. The multiple layers of human-microbe intimacy make it difficult to conceive of human life as we know it without these invisible partners.

For example, what you eat becomes a meal for your gut microbes, who feast as they aid your own digestion. Their waste supplies neurochemicals that contribute to feelings of being full, happy, sleepy and help you crave your next meal. But your intimate entanglement with microbes goes even deeper. You were inoculated with your first microbial inhabitants as you passed through your mother's birth canal. The composition of your mother's breast milk was tailored to suit your new microbiome. Her breast milk contained nutrients that could not nourish you directly but fed your microbes, who then aided you in early stages of digestion, immune system development, and even brain function.

In light of such discoveries, scientists are reconsidering the very nature of humanity. They no longer treat the idea of a biological individual as tenable. They can't easily determine where you end and your microbes begin.[6] Biologically, humans are an amalgam of us and them, us plus our symbionts. Scholars are straining for new language to describe this reality. Instead of calling ourselves human, they suggest ecosystem, waystation, or my personal favorite, holobiont—from the Greek meaning "a whole set of lives." If symbiosis was previously studied as plants and pollinators, today humans, or shall we say holobionts, are the new textbook example of mutual dependence.

---

6 "These findings lead us into directions that transcend the self/non-self, subject/object dichotomies that have characterized Western thought. . . . Animals cannot be considered individuals by anatomical or physiological criteria because a diversity of symbionts are both present and functional." Scott F. Gilbert, Jan Sapp, and Alfred I. Tauber, "A Symbiotic View of Life: We Have Never Been Individuals," *Quarterly Review of Biology* 87, no. 4 (December 2012): 325–26.

Self-Analysis

How does the idea of the microbiome settle in your mind? What questions rise to the surface? Where do you get stuck? News of humanity's thoroughgoing microbial dependencies can be unnerving for Christians raised on the values of independence and personal responsibility. You might be asking, "If I am not in charge of my own behaviors, thoughts, and feelings, who am I? What about Genesis and being made in God's image? And how does individual salvation work if I am more of an amalgam of creatures than an independent agent? Don't my reason and free will distinguish me as human? Aren't all these distinctions the tools I need to get beyond my animal instincts and lean into Christlike behaviors . . . like stewardship, for example?"

News that humans are holobionts may seem so incompatible with Protestant ideas of individual salvation and discipleship that some might be tempted to ignore or deny the science of the microbiome altogether. Another danger is that young Christians, especially young Christian biologists, might feel their only choice is to abandon not the science but their Christian faith, finding it too inflexible to accommodate new biological discoveries. But the questions and hesitations that arise are important. They reveal that the impulse to distinguish and elevate ourselves above the rest of creation isn't accidental. It is theological. The questions and hesitations are driven by how we are taught to think about ourselves and the world in which we live, the way we interpret the Bible, and especially the way we read the account of the Fall in Genesis.

In the following rereading of Adam and Eve's Fall, we will discover that the temptation to draw a dividing line between humans and the rest of creation, elevating the human race above other creatures, is a temptation as old as the human race itself. This ancient, primal temptation explains why environmentalist critiques of stewardship's anthropocentrism and objectification don't motivate the typical modern western Christian. In fact, if these assumptions are understood to be central to Christian theology, criticisms of these assumptions may fuel churchgoers' suspicions of environmentalists. When Christianity itself is built on the divide between the human and the nonhuman creation, critiquing anthropocentrism and objectification will not motivate Christians toward environmental care. Indeed, the critiques become an attack on Christianity itself, and thus the critiques are ignored. Christians are set up to reject environmentalism. If biological dependence and kinship with the creation are to become motivations for creation care, we must first understand why Christians cling so tightly to the distinction between humans and the nonhuman creation in the first place.

The Fall as Creaturely Denial

How would you describe the root cause of Adam and Eve's Fall? One classic interpretation is that they failed to resist temptation. They did not use their God-given gifts of reason, freedom, and willpower to rise above their lower animal instincts and natural cravings. They succumbed to lust and appetite. In so doing, Adam and Eve debased themselves, behaving more like the other creatures than like humans meant to rise above their animality. They moved down toward creatures instead of up toward God. Some suggest that when humans fell, they lost or tarnished the image of God in them, the very dignity meant to distinguish humans from animals.

By this account, the more animal a human is, the more lowly and sinful they are. To heal from the Fall is to get beyond creaturely temptations and to move toward the distinctly human or even divine qualities of our nature. The less animal we are, the more holy we are. (Gender and race also map onto this hierarchy: the darker and more feminine a person is, the more animal and less holy they are imagined to be.) No wonder some Christians resist ecologists' well-meaning attempts to humble humanity by emphasizing our dependence on animals!

But what if there is a different way to read the Fall? Theologians like to emphasize that all of reality is divided by one solid line. That line does not fall between the human and the nonhuman creation but between God the Creator and everything else. While the Creator is independent and needs nothing, everything on the other side of the line is dependent and creaturely, because creatures get their being and life from God. By definition, to be creaturely is to be dependent.

When the snake tempted Eve to eat from the tree of knowledge, he suggested a way to sidestep her dependence on God. In essence, he suggested that humans don't need God for knowledge and wisdom. Rather, they can be independent from God and thus become like God. Adam and Eve weren't dragged down by their creatureliness; they were dragged down because they tried to rise above it. Adam and Eve's sin was not their failure to rise above or transcend their creatureliness. Their sin was rejecting their creatureliness and denying their dependence on God. They did not want to be creatures like other animals. In their attempt to gain independence from God and get beyond their creatureliness, they fell.[7] The Fall was a case of creaturely denial.

In this rereading, we learn that turning a blind eye to our creaturely dependencies and elevating ourselves above the rest of the creation are fallen instincts. Believing that humans exist in their own category of being, that they do not share the same dependencies and fate as the rest of the creation, is a condition of the Fall. In fact, in this understanding of the Fall, both anthropocentrism and objectification are two sides of the same coin—two examples of rejecting our creatureliness. Anthropocentrism and objectification are conditions of the Fall.

Thus, when ecological folk lament stewardship's anthropocentric and objectifying tendencies, they are like prophets crying out against the delusion that we are higher than the rest of the creation. Microbes are prophets too, although tiny ones. They bring us face-to-face with our biological dependency. They are like a flag God waves to get our attention. Humanity's symbiotic existence with microbes is not an affront to human sanctification; it is a reminder of our creatureliness and of God's providence. The microbiome tells us the truth that by God's grace we are embedded, enmeshed in the creation that mutually and symbiotically supports our being.

Hopefully, microbial witness of our enmeshed dependence makes the old attitudes of human exceptionality and centrality seem strange. Hopefully, this interpretation of the Fall gives Christians permission to reconsider such attitudes. But when the language of stewardship separates and elevates humanity over and against the rest of the creation, the

---

7   Sebastian Moore, *Jesus the Liberator of Desire* (New York: Crossroad, 1989). I am indebted to Gene Rogers for showing me this interpretation.

stewardship paradigm reinforces the very attitudes that rereading the Fall might help us shed. However, if we can separate stewardship from anthropocentrism and exceptionalism by embracing our mutual dependence with the nonhuman creation, stewardship becomes symbiotic. When the ailing planet ceases to be an object out there and becomes a world embedded in our very being, the objectionable aspects of stewardship shift. As we learn to pay attention to and care for the microbial life that supports our own, it becomes a matter of repentance that we acknowledge biological stewardship goes both ways. In light of our intimate symbioticism, any attempts to care for and restore the creation that cares for and restores us can only be conceived as symbiotic stewardship.

Beyond Biological Symbioticism

Coming to grips with the biological mutuality of stewardship begins to rehabilitate the language of stewardship. The image of microbes dining on the breast milk my daughter suckled but couldn't digest until her symbionts broke it down becomes iconoclastic. It exposes the idolatry of one-sided biological stewardship and anthropocentrism. It destroys our objectification of the nonhuman creation. But it is not enough for matter to matter biologically. Acknowledgment that our symbioticism is a biological gift of God's providence is the beginning, but it is not the end. It is the yeast (another microbe) that expands our imaginations as we explore the deeper ways that nonhuman flesh matters in humanity's redemption and recovery from the Fall.

How do we grow wonder for nonhuman matter's contribution to humanity's restoration to God? We look at Jesus. We look at the biblical story of incarnation and baptism. My hope is that our new sense of biological dependencies and a reformed reading of the Fall give us eyes to see the contributions of the flesh that have been present in the Scriptures all along. (See Meyaard-Schaap, chapter 3.)

The Word Became Flesh and Was Made Holobiont

When many Western Christians think about the incarnation, they think about God becoming human—that is to say, Christians tend to emphasize

God becoming a *Homo sapiens* rather than the more general miracle of God becoming matter, flesh, the tissue of the world. But incarnation literally means "in the flesh," "in the body"—as in God became matter. One way to tune our attention toward nonhuman contributions to human redemption is to prioritize Jesus becoming flesh before emphasizing the particularities of his becoming human, male, Middle Eastern flesh.[8] This is not to say that Jesus came as all flesh. Jesus was not a river or a monarch butterfly, and it does matter that Jesus became human. Rather, it is to say that we must not rush past the significance that God united God's self to flesh, to biological matter. In the incarnation, God becomes related, becomes kin, to the flesh of the world as a fleshed human, or holobiont.

Because Jesus is a real human and because he was born of Mary, Jesus is just as much a holobiont as you and I. Jesus was inoculated with his mother's microbial symbionts. The DNA he carries is mostly bacterial. If we squirm at these implications of Jesus taking on real flesh, it is because we harbor vestiges of the fallen desire for saviors to be more than creaturely. We are not alone. The desire to protect Christ from tainted, lowly realities of embodiment has fueled gnostic heresies, which pit matter against spirit, from the earliest days of the church. But Jesus was a human, not a ghost or an angel. Which means he is hydrogen, oxygen, carbon, nitrogen. His bones are made of energy from the sun that was stored in the grains of wheat that became the bread that Jesus digested, but not without the help of his symbionts. Matter matters biologically for Jesus as much as it does for us. When Christ crosses the Creator-creature divide, he doesn't just dip his toe into the world of flesh; he submerges himself in it.

Most importantly, Jesus' connection with flesh does not begin with the incarnation. The incarnation makes *visible* the connection that the Second Person of the Trinity has always had with the creation. From Irenaeus and Athanasius to Calvin, the church affirms that the Word has from all time

---

8   Duncan Reid, "Enfleshing the Human: An Earth-Revealing, Earth-Healing Christology," in *Earth Revealing; Earth Healing: Ecology and Christian Theology*, ed. Denis Edwards (Collegeville, MN: Liturgical Press, 2001), 69–83. Using the two phrases from the Nicene creed, "became flesh" and "was made human," Reid proposes that ecological Christologies must prioritize Jesus' flesh as foundational and Jesus' humanity as an amplification rather than a negation of Jesus' enfleshment.

been present and active with creation as the one through whom all things were made. From this we know that matter matters to Christ, not only because Christ is matter but because Christ has always been the Lord of matter, the one in whom all things hold together (Colossians 1:16–17). Christ's Lordship reflects an intimate, creative relationship with matter. And Christ's relationship to flesh is not just because it's the scenery or the sideshow to our human drama. In fact, Christ's central relationship with matter becomes increasingly clear as we reread the story of Jesus' baptism, where, if anything, *we* become the sideshow, the awe-filled observers of an encounter between Jesus and a river. In Jesus' baptism, we can explore further how matter might matter for redemption. Such exploration further erodes those patterns of anthropocentrism and objectification that falsely suggest that stewardship is a one-way street.

Jesus and the Jordan

Why did Jesus get baptized? Jesus was the only pure and holy human to walk the earth. He was the last human in need of baptism. Early Christian theologians puzzled over this and offered a surprising explanation. Jesus got into the Jordan River not to purify himself but to purify the water.

Theologians spanning a millennium explain: "Christ was baptized in order that by the experience he might *purify* the water."[9] Jesus "is cleansed for the purification for the waters, for he indeed did not need purification, who takes away the sin of the world."[10] Thomas Aquinas quotes Ambrose: "I answer that, 'Our Lord was baptized because He wished, not to be cleansed, but to cleanse the waters.'"[11]

By these ancient accounts, Jesus' entry into the Jordan was less about a holy God getting wet and more about water getting holy. Here water, nonhuman matter, or flesh, is center stage and not because humans need

---

9   Ignatius of Antioch, "Letter to the Ephesians 18.2," in *The Holy Spirit in the Syrian Baptismal Tradition*, by Sebastian Brock (Piscataway, NJ: Gorgias Press, 2008), 92 (emphasis added).

10 Gregory of Nazianzus, "Oration 38.16," in *Festal Orations: St. Gregory of Nazianzus*, trans. Nonna Verna Harrison (Crestwood, NY: St. Vladimir's Seminary Press, 2008), 74.

11 Thomas Aquinas, *Summa Theologiae: Volume 53, The Life of Christ (3a. 38–45)*, trans. Samuel Parsons and Albert Pinheiro (Westminster: Blackfriars, 1971), 23.

water to survive. This scene is not about us. As Lord of all things, Christ has always had a relationship with nonhuman creation, and he gives his own purity and righteousness to the water. And the water and all creation are grateful! As an ancient liturgy says, "Christ sanctified it when he went down and was baptized in it. At the moment he went up from the water, heaven and earth accorded him honour, the sun inclined its rays, the stars worshipped him who had sanctified all rivers and springs."[12] Not just the Jordan River but all rivers and streams were sanctified. This logic, that when one creature undergoes transformation all of its relatives get changed too, may seem surprising, but it is central to how theologians make sense of the gospel. For example, when Adam falls, all humans fall. When the Word becomes flesh, all flesh becomes Christ's kin. When Jesus purifies the Jordan, all water gets healed.

When we train our imagination to view the creation as more than scenery in the Scriptures, what we see at Jesus's baptism is his direct interaction with the tissue of the world. With our imagination materially retuned, the creation is no longer a backdrop. Matter becomes a main character, and humans are the bystanders. Here the geography is a main character, and humans are the scenery.

Creation Stewards Humanity

This is not to say that humans are excluded from the larger story of baptism. On the contrary, Christ purified the rivers for their own sake so that they could become part of the mystery of human baptism. Rivers, water, flesh, *and* humans all participate in baptism. When we get into the water that Christ baptized, our own purification is sealed and signaled. Although humans participate, water leads the way. Water gets baptized and then shares its baptism with us. By the power of the Spirit, water stewards the grace of baptism. Just as microbes (flesh) facilitate our biological life, water (creation) facilitates our sacramental life. (See Meyaard-Schaap, chapter 3.) Christ refuses to let us sidestep the creation. And thank goodness, for our baptism becomes yet another opportunity to repent of the

---

12 Severus of Antioch, "Fenquitho III," in *The Holy Spirit in the Syrian Baptismal Tradition*, 95.

lie of independence from the nonhuman creation. Matter contributes to our reorientation to God as we recover from denying our creaturely dependence.

And we have not even mentioned the bread and wine, our spiritual food. Grain and grapes do not grow without microbes, which prepare the soil. Grain and grapes are converted and preserved as bread and wine by microbial yeast. And we would struggle to digest this holy meal without our own microbial symbionts. Our Lord doesn't want us to think about phantasmic, immaterial things. He wants us to touch and taste, to embrace our entanglement and dependence on flesh. As it tends generations of humans, flesh becomes a steward of humanity. Nonhuman flesh assists in human repentance and restoration. As we heal from the sin of denying our creatureliness, Christ employs the water of baptism and the bread and wine to steward our material journey of redemption. Flesh becomes the bread and butter of the church.

When we can imagine how matter contributes to our biology *and* to our redemption, the falsehoods fade away. And as anthropocentrism and objectification fade away, so do the problems of stewardship. When we understand that matter matters for redemption, caring for the creation becomes a mutual stewardship wherein we acknowledge that the flesh that supports our biological and spiritual renewal needs us to return the favor. We move beyond mere stewardship to symbiotic stewardship as we embrace our creaturely dependence.

I do not mean to minimize the problems of the Christian Environmental Stewardship paradigm. Rather, I suggest that the problems run deeper than stewardship itself. The root of stewardship's problem is us, specifically a version of Christianity that overemphasizes humanity and underemphasizes everything else. Until we address the root of stewardship's failure, no amount of tinkering with names and paradigms will move the needle in a moment of great ecological urgency.

My hope is that rereading Scripture in these creaturely, materially attentive ways clears theological weeds for those chapters that rightfully suggest that our relationship to creatures is one of embedded kinship. I hope it stretches Christian imaginations so that we read the Scriptures for a gospel account that shows our need to repent of creaturely denial and celebrates Christ's and our own entanglement with flesh. This clearing makes way for symbiotic stewardship. My hope is that we all learn to narrate the gospel to show that the nonhuman creation matters for salvation—even if we are given only one hundred words. *For God so loved the world, that while we were yet denying our creaturely kinship with all flesh, Christ chose to depend on such flesh for our rescue.*

Works Cited

Aquinas, Thomas. *Summa Theologiae: Volume 53, The Life of Christ (3a. 38–45)*. Translated by Samuel Parsons and Albert Pinheiro. Westminster, UK: Blackfriars, 1971.

Brock, Sebastian. *The Holy Spirit in the Syrian Baptismal Tradition*. Piscataway, NJ: Gorgias Press, 2008.

Brody, Jane E. "We Are Our Bacteria." *New York Times*, July 14, 2014. https://well.blogs.nytimes.com/2014/07/14/we-are-our-bacteria/.

Calvin, John. *Calvin: Institutes of Christian Religion*. 4th ed. Vol. 1. Translated by Ford Lewis Battles. Edited by John T. McNeill. Philadelphia: Westminster Press, 1967.

Gilbert, Scott F., Jan Sapp, and Alfred I. Tauber. "A Symbiotic View of Life: We Have Never Been Individuals." *Quarterly Review of Biology* 87, no. 4 (December 2012): 325–41.

Gregory of Nazianzus. "Oration 38.16." In *Festal Orations: St. Gregory of Nazianzus*. Translated by Nonna Verna Harrison. Crestwood, NY: St. Vladimir's Seminary Press, 2008.

"The Human Microbiome: Me, Myself, Us." *Economist*, August 18, 2012. https://www.economist.com/science-and-technology/2012/08/18/me-myself-us.

Kuyper, Abraham. *Abraham Kuyper: A Centennial Reader*. Edited by James D. Bratt. Grand Rapids, MI: Eerdmans, 1998.

"Microbes Maketh Man." *Economist*, August 18, 2012. https://www.economist.com/leaders/2012/08/18/microbes-maketh-man.

Moore, Sebastian. *Jesus the Liberator of Desire*. New York: Crossroad, 1989.

Reid, Duncan. "Enfleshing the Human: An Earth-Revealing, Earth-Healing Christology." In *Earth Revealing; Earth Healing: Ecology and Christian Theology*, edited by Denis Edwards, 69–83. Collegeville, MN: Liturgical Press, 2001.

From Stewardship to Earthkeeping:

Why We Should Move beyond Stewardship

Steven Bouma-Prediger

Mitch and May Term

In the spring of 2018, after finishing his third year at Hope College, Mitch had the opportunity to take a May term course in upstate New York. He and ten other students enrolled in "Ecological Theology and Ethics," an upper-level religion course that I teach each year. The course includes a nine-day wilderness expedition in the Adirondack Mountains. Using Camp Fowler, a Christian camp in the south-central part of the park as our base of operations, we go whitewater rafting, spend four days canoeing (and portaging), have a solo day, and backpack for four days on a forty-three-mile stretch of the famous Northville–Lake Placid Trail. Students learn wilderness skills, enhance their leadership ability, and put into practice ideas about ecology, ethics, and theology discussed in the traditional classroom setting. In short, the course combines, as Mitch put it,

"Christian theology and ecology with hands-on, full-body learning." I will let Mitch tell his story in his own words.[1]

> On the van ride to Camp Fowler, I had a conversation with Prof. Bouma-Prediger about the importance of this class and where caring for the earth fits into the Christian life. Although I grew up in the church, I had never considered, let alone heard of earthkeeping as a responsibility for Christians. It was simply not talked about. I had heard the term stewardship, but was desperately trying to figure out what the role "steward of creation" meant in the Bible, church, worship, prayer, etc.
>
> As we began our nine-day expedition, I started to discover answers to my questions in more ways than one. While practicing canoe strokes during the day and developing fire-building and bear-line throwing skills at night, I gradually learned more about creation, the Creator, and my place on the earth. Throughout the trip we read the *Spiritual Field Guide* by Bernard Brady and Mark Neuzil.[2] Not only did that book help me articulate the spiritual and intellectual growth I was experiencing, but it was also an essential catalyst for our group discussions at night around the campfire. One of the most important things Brady and Neuzil stress is how frequently earthkeeping is brought up in the Bible. Countless passages—from Genesis to Job, Isaiah to Luke, Psalms to Revelation—clearly showed me, for the first time, how caring for the earth is biblical and important. These passages from the Bible demonstrated the legitimacy of humans as earthkeepers. As I continued to make sense of the questions I brought up with my professor, it turned out that earthkeeping is in fact a much more important part of what it means to be a Christian than I had thought.

---

1 The text that follows (and at the end of this chapter) is taken with Mitch's permission from his final paper for the course.
2 Bernard Brady and Mark Neuzil, *A Spiritual Field Guide: Meditations for the Outdoors* (Grand Rapids, MI: Brazos Press, 2005).

Mitch's story is quite common. Many people grow up in the church but hear virtually nothing about caring for the earth. And what they do hear—the term *stewardship*, for example—is unclear and unhelpful. The Christian life, as they hear it described and see it lived out, does not include caring for the earth as part of what it means to be a faithful Christian.

My thesis is simple: care for creation is integral to the Christian faith and is well described by the term *earthkeeping*. In other words, although *stewardship* has been a useful term for the past few decades, *earthkeeping* is a better word to capture the biblical vision of our relationship to the creation and our calling to care for the world of which we are a part. The benefits of using the term *earthkeeping* are that it provides a more accurate understanding of the biblical vision of who we are and offers a richer image for explaining why we act the way we do in caring for our home planet. Indeed, the idea of earthkeeping helped Mitch better understand the biblical story and more effectively explain to his family and friends his desire to care for creation. But before exploring the Bible, first some background on the term *stewardship*.

Stewardship: Some Limitations

The tradition of describing Christian responsibility to care for creation in terms of stewardship has both supporters and critics. One of the most articulate advocates is Robin Attfield, who convincingly shows how stewardship, as a way of stressing human responsibility for the nonhuman creation, is rooted in the Christian tradition. He argues that "whatever the causes of the [ecological] problems may be, our traditions offer resources which may, in refurbished form, allow us to cope with these problems."[3] One of those resources is the stewardship tradition, with roots going back to prominent church theologians such as Chrysostom, Augustine, and Calvin. This tradition affirms that humans are "the stewards of the earth" and thus "responsible for its conservation, for its lasting improvement, and also for the care of our fellow-creatures, its nonhuman inhabitants."[4]

---

3 Robin Attfield, *The Ethics of Environmental Concern*, 2nd ed. (Athens: University of Georgia Press, 1991), 34.
4 Attfield, *The Ethics of Environmental Concern*, 45.

Among the critics, the most ardent is Paul Santmire. Santmire cogently argues that it is best "to retire" the word *stewardship*. He gives four reasons. First, the term *stewardship* carries "too much baggage from the anthropocentric [human-centered] and indeed androcentric [male-centered] theology of the past."[5] Second, the term is "too fraught with the heavy images of management, control, and exploitation of persons and resources."[6] Third, the term *stewardship* has such a broad meaning that it is too easily co-opted to mean nothing more than "wise use." [7] And fourth, stewardship is most often understood in terms of fund-raising for the church. Santmire asks, ". . . what if the Scriptures in fact teach us something richer and more complex?"[8] To summarize, in understanding our calling to care for the earth, we can do better than stewardship.

While Attfield and others insist that *stewardship* is a valuable term worthy of continued use today, Santmire's critique is compelling. Neither Santmire nor I disagree with Attfield's main claim, namely, that the Christian tradition has rich resources for addressing the ecological crisis before us. Our quarrel has to do with the usefulness of the term *stewardship* in today's discussions and debates. For most people, the term primarily refers to giving money to the church. For those who see it having to do with the natural world, stewardship connotes exploitation or (at best) wise use. The Bible, by contrast, teaches us something much more compelling.

In sum, if we wish to talk about the importance of caring for the earth and all its inhabitants, then we should use another term. While the term *stewardship* has been a fruitful way of thinking about our responsibility as Christians to care for our home planet and a positive move beyond earlier notions (and misunderstandings) of dominion, the limitations of the term

---

5   H. Paul Santmire, *Nature Reborn: The Ecological and Cosmic Promise of Christian Theology* (Minneapolis, MN: Fortress Press, 2000), 120.

6   Santmire, *Nature Reborn*, 120.

7   H. Paul Santmire, "Partnership with Nature According to the Scriptures: Beyond the Theology of Stewardship," *Christian Scholar's Review* 32, no. 4 (Summer 2003): 383. This edition of CSR focused on "The Fate of the Earth" and included essays by Cal DeWitt, Joe Sheldon and Dave Foster, Loren Wilkinson, and Kenneth Peterson, along with this essay by Santmire.

8   Santmire, "Partnership with Nature According to the Scriptures: Beyond the Theology of Stewardship," 382.

have grown such that at least in some circumstances it should be replaced by something better.

While I agree with the limitations of the term *stewardship* expressed by Santmire, I articulate them in a somewhat different way. (See the introduction for a more expanded treatment.) First, in the minds of many Christians, stewardship connotes giving money to the church, or more broadly, as the common phrase puts it, stewardship means giving your "time, talent, and treasure" to the Christian community. In common usage, stewardship does not mean caring for God's good earth. Second, the term *stewardship* has ambiguous biblical backing. There are better biblical images with more robust passages in the Bible that support the idea of earthkeeping. (See below for details.) Third, the term *stewardship* underwrites a dualism of culture over nature—that is, the notion of stewardship assumes a split between human and nonhuman, with an undue priority of value given to humans and human culture. (See Al-Attas Bradford, chapter 5.) Fourth, this dualism sanctions only a managerial role for humans. While we clearly are called to rule in a certain way, the role of manager is not our only or most important role. (See Meyaard-Schaap, chapter 3.) Fifth and finally, the stewardship paradigm leads to the assumption that nature has only instrumental value and not also intrinsic value. (See Joldersma, chapter 4.) In other words, the natural world is seen as being valuable only by virtue of its usefulness to humans rather than being of value in and for itself as a creation of God.

I agree with Santmire that we should "retire" *stewardship*. My proposed alternative is *earthkeeping*.

An Alternative: Christians as Earthkeepers

In his essay "Christianity and the Survival of Creation," Kentucky farmer, novelist, essayist, and poet Wendell Berry resolutely affirms, "We have no entitlement from the Bible to exterminate or permanently destroy or hold in contempt anything on the earth or in the heavens above it or in the waters beneath it. We have the right to use the gifts of nature but not to ruin or waste them."[9] Berry rightly argues, "The Bible leaves no doubt at

---

9   Wendell Berry, *Sex, Economy, Freedom, Community* (New York: Pantheon, 1993), 98.

all about the sanctity of the act of world-making, or of the world that was made, or of creaturely or bodily life in this world. We are holy creatures living among other holy creatures in a world that is holy."[10]

To Berry's claims I offer a loud amen. The Bible begins (Genesis 1–2) and ends (Revelation 21–22) with rivers and trees. The Bible speaks of humans as earth-creatures who are earthkeepers: creatures made from the stuff of the earth who have the God-given responsibility of caring for the earth and its plethora of creatures. The Bible portrays God's good future as earthly and earthy. Although there is much more that could be said,[11] what follows is a brief presentation of the biblical case for earthkeeping.

First, Genesis 1–2 speaks about both who humans are and what humans are to do. These chapters speak both of our being and of our doing. With respect to who we are, Genesis 1:26 clearly distinguishes between human creatures and nonhuman creatures by speaking only of the former as created *imago Dei*—in the image (*selem*) and likeness (*demut*) of God. We humans are distinct in some important sense—unique among all the creatures to come from God's hand. The story of the naming of the animals in Genesis 2:19–20 likewise points to human uniqueness. The human creature has the responsibility of giving names to the other creatures—no small task given the significance of names in the Bible, for names signify identity. (See Rienstra, chapter 8.) Abram becomes Abraham, ancestor of a multitude. Jacob becomes Israel, one who wrestles with God. To name something or someone properly implies personal knowledge. To get the name right one must intimately know the creature being named. But naming also indicates a kind of authority. To name is to have power. Clearly, therefore, humans, being namers, are unique in important ways. While animals are similar to humans in certain ways—being sentient and showing elements of language and puzzle solving—humans as a package are unique. To use a technical term, only humans are *persons*. We are response-able and responsible persons. That is an inescapable part of who we are.

---

10 Berry, *Sex, Economy, Freedom, Community*, 98–99.
11 For a more in-depth discussion, see the revised second edition of my book *For the Beauty of the Earth: A Christian Vision for Creation Care* (Grand Rapids: Baker Academic, 2010).

But what is often ignored or intentionally overlooked is that humans are not only distinct from but also similar to nonhuman creatures. (See Meyaard-Schaap, chapter 3; and Al-Attas Bradford, chapter 5.) We are, human and nonhuman alike, embedded in the creation. For example, in Genesis 1, the creation of humans occurs on the same day as the creation of other animals. There is no separate day for humans. On the sixth day, as Genesis 1:24–31 tells it, all kinds of living creatures come forth: domestic animals, wild animals, and creeping things. Humans and other animals of the earth, the text implies, have something in common. (See Halteman and Zwart, chapter 9.) And as Genesis 2:7 indicates, the human earth-creature (*adam*) is made from the earth (*adamah*). Humans are made of dirt and soil. To carry the Hebrew wordplay into Latin, we are humans because we are from the humus. We are earthy and earthly creatures. (See Joldersma, chapter 4.) Other creatures, to take seriously the language of Joseph Sittler and St. Francis, are our sisters and brothers.[12] In sum, these texts indicate that we humans are not only different from but also similar to our non-human neighbors. We humans are both responsible persons and earthy creatures.

With respect to what we are called to do, the Hebrew verbs in Genesis 1:26–28 indicate that one dimension of the human calling is dominion. The human earth-creature is called to subdue (*kabash*) and to rule or have dominion over (*radah*) other creatures. But what does this mean? Do subdue and rule, as is often assumed, necessarily mean domination? A larger canonical perspective sheds light on this important question. For example, Psalm 72 speaks clearly of the ideal king: one who rules and exercises dominion properly. The psalm unequivocally states that such a ruler executes justice for the oppressed, delivers the needy, helps the poor, and embodies righteousness in all things. In short, the proper exercise of dominion yields shalom: the flourishing of all the creation. This is a far cry from dominion as domination. And Jesus, in the Gospel accounts, defines dominion in terms clearly contrary to the way it is often understood. For

---

12 See, for example, Joseph Sittler, "Ecological Commitment as Theological Responsibility," *Zygon: Journal of Religion & Science* 5, no. 2 (June 1970): 172–81.

Jesus, the ideal king, to rule is not to subdue but to serve. To exercise dominion is to suffer, if necessary, for the good of the other. Domination, exploitation, or misuse is unacceptable. We humans are called to rule, but ruling must be understood rightly.

The calling to dominion is only part of the picture in Genesis 1–2. Yes, we are called to exercise dominion, but we are also called to service. Genesis 2:5 speaks of humans serving the earth (*adam* is to *abad* the *adamah*). From the verb *abad* comes the most commonly used Hebrew word for servant (*ebed*). And Genesis 2:15 defines the human calling in terms of service: we are to serve (*abad*) and protect (*shamar*). We are to serve and protect the garden that is creation, for its own good as well as for our benefit. Taking seriously both callings implies that dominion must be defined in terms of service. We are called to dominion as service. It is faulty exegesis and a selective and tendentious reading of Genesis 1–2 to focus only on dominion texts and to interpret them as entailing domination.

The word *shamar*, often translated "protect," can also be interpreted as "keep," not in terms of possession but as "providing for the sustenance of (someone)."[13] For example, in the famous blessing by Aaron, found in Numbers 6 ("The LORD bless you and keep you" [v. 24]), the word translated "keep" is *shamar*. To keep is to care for. To keep is to preserve and protect. We "keep" the garden when we serve and protect it. Thus, my shorthand for the right relationship between humans and the nonhuman world is "earthkeeping."[14] The term is biblically rooted. It focuses on our home planet rather than, like the term *creation care*, all of the universe. It captures our human identity as earthy and earthly creatures. It reminds us that we are not owners but conservers of a world we hold in trust from God. It acknowledges that we humans have an important calling to serve the earth and its creatures so that all will flourish. According to Scripture, we are earthkeepers called to serve and protect the world that God made, loves, and sustains.

---

13 *New Oxford American Dictionary*, 3rd ed. (2010), s.v. "keep."

14 This term I borrow from Loren Wilkinson, ed., *Earthkeeping in the Nineties: Stewardship of Creation* (Grand Rapids, MI: Eerdmans, 1991), an updated and revised version of the earlier 1980 volume, *Earthkeeping: Christian Stewardship of Natural Resources*.

This earthkeeping teaching is found not only in Scripture. It is also in our creeds, prayers, and songs. In the Apostles' Creed, we begin with a confession of God as Maker of heaven and earth. God is our Creator, and we are creatures. In the Lord's Prayer, we pray that God's will be done "on earth as it is in heaven." This prayer is not about going to heaven but about heaven being realized on earth. In the Doxology, we declare that "all creatures here below" praise God. That is our calling: to serve and protect the earth in such a way that all creatures—dolphins and daffodils, hawks and hemlocks, penguins and people—are able to praise God. In sum, earthkeeping is woven into the fabric of our faith, if only we have the eyes to see. (See Halteman and Zwart, chapter 9.) In contrast to the term *stewardship*, the term *earthkeeping* more fully captures the biblical vision of who we are and what we are called to do.

Mitch and May Term Again

During the May term course, Mitch continued to reflect on his faith. He thought long and hard about why caring for the earth was part of his identity as a Christian and how he might be a better earthkeeper once the course was over and he returned to "normal life." Again, here are Mitch's own words.

> Like most Christians, I grew up with the belief that human beings are separate from and elevated above the rest of creation. My lack of serious regard for my ecological impact largely came from my lack of care, which I can now see ultimately came from my lack of understanding of my role within creation. A careful reading of Genesis indicates that human beings should properly assume a status right alongside the trees and birds. Humans are created on the sixth day and God makes them in conjunction with the wild animals. Humans do not have their own day, and though God assigns them the task of dominion, they are, like the rabbits, rocks, and rivers, small parts of God's creation.
>
> Elsewhere in the Bible we find evidence that everything in creation needs God. For example, in Psalm 104 waters flee, mountains

rise, and all wild animals look to God for food. Humans are scarcely mentioned among the entirety of an actively responding creation. This passage very clearly teaches us that all creation is made for God. All creation is alive with the activity of God, from human to hyrax, hippo to hibiscus. All creatures are made to serve God and are invited, daily, to respond to God.

The Bible clearly shows humans as part of something much bigger than themselves. And when Christians enter into the body of Christ, they are stepping into something much bigger than a local collection of fellow religious folk. Little do they know that they are joining not just a body of people but a living creation—becoming one with a living, breathing planet that glorifies its creator every second. As Paul tells us plainly in Colossians 1:15–17: "[Christ] is the image of the invisible God, the firstborn over all creation. For in him all things were created: things in heaven and on earth, visible and invisible, whether thrones or powers or rulers or authorities; all things have been created through him and for him. He is before all things, and in him all things hold together."

More than an "exclusive savior" for the select few who follow him, Christ himself is the one who unites all things together. So Christ is not only important for his followers. Christ is central to all created things in heaven and on earth. This means, as Dr. Bouma-Prediger puts it, "Jesus comes to save not just us but the whole world."[15] Christ is the firstborn in and for whom all things are created and held together and reconciled.

Ecological literacy and good earthkeeping tend to be forgotten, even neglected, by most professing Christians. To say the least, this is incredibly dangerous. Not only is bad earthkeeping inconsistent with what the Bible teaches, it is also direct disobedience for followers of Christ. It is, as Wendell Berry puts it, "the most horrid blasphemy" against God himself.[16] True Christians profess not themselves, but Christ. And since in Christ all created things in heaven and on earth

---

15 Bouma-Prediger, *For the Beauty of the Earth*, 116.
16 Berry, *Sex, Economy, Freedom, and Community*, 98.

are held together in unity, our responsibility is to be good caretakers of the earth.

By the end of my trip, I saw myself walking through the woods with a genuine desire to preserve and protect it. I had totally surrendered my desires, and my selfishness and materialism were replaced by a genuine desire to preserve and protect the world around me. "Earthkeeping Christian" seemed to be the only true way to live, and in those moments I felt more in touch with myself and with life than I ever have when caught up in my own agenda and plugged into the busy way of living back home.

Works Cited

Attfield, Robin. *The Ethics of Environmental Concern*. 2nd ed. Athens: University of Georgia Press, 1991.

Berry, Wendell. *Sex, Economy, Freedom, Community*. New York: Pantheon, 1993.

Bouma-Prediger, Steven. *For the Beauty of the Earth: A Christian Vision for Creation Care*. Grand Rapids, MI: Baker Academic, 2010.

Brady, Bernard, and Mark Neuzil. *A Spiritual Field Guide: Meditations for the Outdoors*. Grand Rapids, MI: Brazos Press, 2005.

Santmire, H. Paul. *Nature Reborn: The Ecological and Cosmic Promise of Christian Theology*. Minneapolis: Fortress Press, 2000.

———. "Partnership with Nature According to the Scriptures: Beyond the Theology of Stewardship." *Christian Scholar's Review* 32, no. 4 (Summer 2003): 381–412.

Sittler, Joseph. "Ecological Commitment as Theological Responsibility." *Zygon: Journal of Religion & Science* 5, no. 2 (June 1970): 172–81.Wilkinson, Loren, ed. *Earthkeeping in the Nineties: Stewardship of Creation*. Grand Rapids, MI: Eerdmans, 1991.

7

Stewardship and the Kingdom of God

James R. Skillen

Then environmental writer Wendell Berry and his friend Wes Jackson were talking one day about American farmland.[1] Erosion has removed more than half of the rich topsoil in Iowa. Irrigation is draining the Ogallala Aquifer under the Great Plains states. Heavy fertilizer use is polluting the Gulf of Mexico. Pesticides may be killing honeybees across the country. Why, they wondered, does agriculture cause so much destruction?

They blamed our market economy, in which corn and soybeans have monetary value but native prairie plants do not. Farmers earn money for the crops they produce but not for protecting fragile ecosystems. Essentially, our market economy is selective rather than comprehensive in what it values. Market economies value certain parts of God's nonhuman creation for their direct utility to humans. They do not value elements of the creation that have no monetary usefulness to humans or the supporting

---

1   Wendell Berry, "Two Economies," in *Home Economics* (San Francisco: North Point Press, 1987), 54.

ecosystems that are necessary for holding all the parts together. The problem with selective valuation becomes clear only after the soil erodes from a farm field, the fish begin to die in a lake, or the Cuyahoga River in Ohio catches on fire . . . repeatedly.[2]

In their conversation, Berry and Jackson tried to think of ways to reform the market economy to make it more comprehensive. Had the famous conservation writer Aldo Leopold been part of the conversation, he would have suggested an ecological economy that values things for their contribution to the "biotic community" rather than just human utility. *Eco*nomy and *eco*logy both come from the Greek root *oikos*, which means "household." Leopold would have suggested that we look beyond our own self-interested households and care for the larger household of creation.

But when Berry asked his friend to describe the kind of all-inclusive economy we need, Jackson turned to the Bible rather than to ecology. He smiled for a moment and said, "The Kingdom of God." Jackson was imagining a truly comprehensive economy that takes everything into account and values everything appropriately. The Kingdom of God is precisely this type of economy. God made every part of the creation. God knows the number of hairs on our heads. God notices the fall of every sparrow. God knows every part of the creation and every ecological relationship that sustains it. God also knows the true, or full, value of every plant, animal, river, and mountain. God's economy is truly comprehensive. Everything is included.

Jackson smiled when he said "the Kingdom of God" because he was joking, but in all seriousness. He was joking because he knew that we can't build the Kingdom of God or a human economy that mirrors it. Jackson was perfectly serious, though, because he knew that the creation will fully flourish only when God's comprehensive Kingdom arrives.

Seeking First the Kingdom of God

I think often about Jackson's winsome answer, "the Kingdom of God," as I teach environmental studies courses and as I speak with others about environmental stewardship. The language of stewardship captures

---

2   Erik W. Johnson and Scott Frickel, "Ecological Threat and the Founding of U.S. National Environmental Movement Organizations, 1962–1998," *Social Problems* 58, no. 3 (August 2011): 308.

important aspects of human responsibility for God's creation. It rightly emphasizes the fact that God granted humans authority to serve and till the earth. It rightly identifies humans as stewards or caretakers of the creation on God's behalf. But I worry that we settle for an understanding of stewardship that is too small, too selective, and ultimately too arrogant. What we need is an understanding of stewardship that is truly comprehensive. Our calling is, after all, to steward in a way that reflects God's own love and care for all of creation and that helps to bring about God's Kingdom.

Trying to cultivate sufficient understanding to practice environmental stewardship well (see Rienstra, chapter 8) leads us directly into the frustration that Berry and Jackson faced: it is impossible. There is no way around this problem. God has called us to a responsibility that we cannot, on our own, hope to fulfill. The principle challenge for Christians, I think, is facing this discouraging reality while simultaneously pursuing the work of creation care with joy and gratitude.

To meet this challenge, we need to reimagine stewardship in more humble ways that better address the reality of our situation. We should think of stewardship as seeking first the Kingdom of God, trusting that God's grace covers our failures and that God will complete the good work begun in us by creating a new heavens and a new earth. The idea of stewardship I have in mind is what theologians would call "eschatological stewardship." It is stewardship framed by Christian hope in God's perfect future. Eschatological stewardship doesn't reduce our responsibility today. Instead, it provides the humility and the motivation we need as we wrestle with our limitations and failures as God's stewards.

The good news is that Christians have resources for facing precisely this frustration or challenge. Christians already struggle with biblical demands to "be perfect . . . as [our] heavenly Father is perfect" (Matthew 5:48), and we have developed practices to embrace this pursuit even though we know we cannot succeed on our own. We embrace the pursuit of perfection despite our imperfections in faith, trusting that God will complete the good work begun in us when Christ returns and we see God face-to-face.

The Problem of Finitude . . . and the Response of Humility

Reimagining stewardship requires us to be clear about why humans do not and cannot properly fulfill the call to care for God's creation completely. On the surface, the reasons are obvious. Human stewardship falters because of what Thomas Aquinas once described as "the twofold darkness into which we were born": finitude and sin.[3]

The first and obvious reason we fail is because we are finite and our knowledge is limited. Many of us agree with Aldo Leopold that "a thing is right when it tends to preserve the integrity, stability, and beauty of the biotic community. It is wrong when it tends otherwise."[4] But in our finitude, we rarely know exactly what it will take to preserve creation's integrity, stability, and beauty. Even Leopold expressed frustration that his discipline, ecology, didn't provide enough information for him to live out his moral conviction.[5]

History is replete with examples that highlight the limits of human ecological knowledge that often thwart our best intentions. Consider a case study from the field of forestry management.

More than a century ago, Congress created the U.S. Forest Service to manage the national forests. At the time, private timber companies were laying waste to forests across the United States. Many would buy land and clear-cut the forest, leaving the slash to burn and the soil to erode. By any measure, this was not good environmental stewardship.

The first Forest Service chief, Gifford Pinchot, argued that forest destruction was primarily a moral problem. Companies motivated only by profit were destroying the land. As he saw it, an agency guided by public virtue and the best scientific knowledge would ensure healthy forests. The Forest Service developed a management approach called sustained-yield forestry. Using the best available forest science, managers estimated exactly

---

3 Cornelius Plantinga Jr. and Sue A. Rozeboom, *Discerning the Spirits: A Guide to Thinking about Christian Worship Today* (Grand Rapids, MI: Eerdmands, 2003), 12.
4 Aldo Leopold, *A Sand County Almanac with Essays on Conservation from Found River* (New York: Oxford University Press, 1966), 262.
5 Aldo Leopold, "The Land-Health Concept and Conservation," in *For the Health of the Land: Previously Unpublished Essays and Other Writings*, ed. J. Baird Callicott and Eric T. Freyfogle (Washington, DC: Island Press, 1999), 218–26.

how much lumber grew in a forest each year. They allowed logging companies to harvest only that amount annually. By matching growth rate and harvest rate, the Forest Service promised a "perpetual flow of timber." Essentially, the agency promised to manage the national forests for optimal timber production.

A century later, we can look back and see that things didn't work out as planned. At times, the agency ignored its own management principles. But the deeper problem was that forestry science did not provide a complete understanding of how forests function. For example, the early Forest Service established a policy of full fire suppression in the national forests, because fire destroys valuable lumber. But many of the forests managed by the agency depend on fire for their health. By banishing fire from the national forests, the Forest Service actually decreased the health and productivity of many forests.[6] Aldo Leopold once lamented this pattern in environmental management. Managers often assume, he wrote, that they know "just what makes the [forest] tick, and just what and who is valuable, and what and who is worthless."[7] In reality, he argued, they don't know either, and their arrogance leads to failure.

The problem of finite environmental knowledge isn't limited to scientists and government agencies, however. It is a problem for all of us, even if we don't work directly in land and resource management. In a globalized economy, we buy coffee from Indonesia, bananas from Ecuador, oil from Saudi Arabia, shoes from China, wine from France, chocolate from Belgium, vanilla from Madagascar, and so forth. Historian William Cronon explains that the market economy creates these vast networks of relationships around the globe. It also obscures, or hides, those relationships through market exchanges.[8] As the market economy grows in space and complexity, so does consumer ignorance.

---

6   Paul W. Hirt, *A Conspiracy of Optimism: Management of the National Forests since World War Two* (Lincoln: University of Nebraska Press, 1994).
7   Leopold, *A Sand County Almanac*, 240.
8   William Cronon, *Nature's Metropolis: Chicago and the Great West* (New York: W. W. Norton, 1991).

Christians who want to live in ways that promote the integrity, stability, and beauty of creation face these frustrating limits. We buy products from around the world, and these products have positive and negative impacts on God's creation. At the same time, we can never have complete knowledge of these impacts, and therefore we can never make fully informed decisions. We are and always will be finite creatures.

So how do we live with our finitude and ignorance, whether we are foresters or general consumers? Throwing up our hands in despair and giving up certainly won't help. We can say with confidence that giving up won't improve forests or the global economy. Instead, we need to continue our efforts with a newfound humility, acknowledging that even our best attempts will always require adjustments and improvements as we gain more knowledge.

Think back to the Forest Service. The agency overestimated its predictive knowledge, and forest health declined. Starting in the late 1980s, the Forest Service and other federal agencies adopted a strategy called "adaptive ecosystem management." The new approach reflected two key changes in thinking. First, because new forestry science recognized that complex ecological processes keep forests healthy and productive, the Forest Service committed to protecting whole forest ecosystems rather than just trying to protect a particular resource like timber. Second, the Forest Service changed the way it talked about management. Acknowledging the complexity of forest ecosystems, the Forest Service moved away from a fixed approach to management. In other words, they didn't assume that the best-informed forest plan would get everything right. Forest management, the agency said, should be an adaptive process. Each plan for a forest is like a research hypothesis. The agency *thinks* that a plan will achieve the outcomes it wants. It then tests the plan through management and monitors its efforts to see if they are working. As the agency's goals change, or as certain management practices fail, the Forest Service adjusts its plan accordingly. Management, in this model, is an experimental process or pattern rather than a system of control.

Even for those of us who do not manage forests and farms, the pattern of adaptive ecosystem management is helpful. It suggests an experimental approach to stewardship in our economic and political activity. As with a forest plan or a species recovery plan, we deceive ourselves if we think that we can do enough research and gather enough good knowledge ahead of time to establish the *right* investment plan, the *right* shopping plan, or the *right* lifestyle. We should *expect* to find that a particular socially responsible investment fund is not a perfect filter to ensure that our money preserves rather than destroys parts of God's creation. We should *expect* to find that although our fair-trade coffee improves the lives of some farmers and some coffee plantations, it may also harm others.

We will do better, then, to study our options and make decisions that are provisional and experimental. To be faithful stewards, we *must* act. (See Heun, chapter 1.) Whether volunteering for work on watershed restoration, working to challenge environmental injustices, reducing herbicide use on our lawns, or bringing reusable bags to the store, we have to express our love for God and the creation through action. But we must also see these acts as inherently limited by our finite knowledge and humbly consider opportunities for adaptation. This means listening to new information, talking through options within our communities, and remaining open to revising our practices. In short, we need to be humble.

The Problem of Sin . . . and a Christian Response

Being humble in our creation care, with provisional decision-making and continual revision, may sound difficult, or even exhausting. What can sustain us in our efforts if we must always expect at least partial failure? Indeed, why bother to work so hard if we know we cannot achieve the *right* environmental stewardship? (See the preface.)

Here it is helpful to think about the other darkness into which Aquinas said we are born: sin. Christians have not always given sufficient thought to the challenges of human finitude, at least not as a fundamental Christian issue. However, Christians have for millennia addressed the central problem of human sin. For the remainder of this section, I will explore individual and systemic sin and remind us of the Christian practices to address them. In the following section, I will show how those practices are helpful in thinking about finitude as well.

Christians generally understand sin at an individual level. We are sinful, which means we individually ignore God's call to faithful stewardship. We are inclined to seek first our own individual desires rather than seeking first the Kingdom of God. What is more, our industrial economy encourages this. For the good of the economy, we are encouraged to practice greed, selfishness, pride, envy, and other vices. We are encouraged to fear tomorrow rather than to trust God. It makes much more sense, so we are told, to lay up stores for ourselves here and now rather than to lay up treasures in heaven. In our individual lives, sin is something we struggle with daily and something with which we are all too familiar.

By contrast, Christians have a more difficult time understanding the broader implications of sin, which go beyond individual thoughts and actions. Sin is a principality and power in the creation that distorts what God created good. It is a resounding no that challenges God's loving affirmation. Sin has worked its way into the warp and weave of creation. In other words, it is systemic. Therefore, our industrial economy, our public policy, and our broader culture produce suffering even when we can't identify individual sin as the smoking gun.

In both cases—individual and systemic—the problem of sin can be overwhelmingly discouraging, even for Christians who understand God's love and forgiveness. It can seem utterly discouraging to confess our sin, receive God's forgiveness, turn with a genuine desire to live a faithful, upright life, only to return to sin once again.

Yet Christians have faced this problem with the hope that God is sanctifying us and that God will someday liberate us fully from sin. Said another way, Christians have faced this problem with eschatological hope in the Kingdom of God. And as we live into this hope, we embrace a regular pattern of Christian spiritual discipline, which most churches follow in their weekly service. The primary prayer of confession in the Episcopal Church reads, "Most merciful God, we confess that we have sinned against you in thought, word, and deed, by what we have done, and by what we have left undone. We have not loved you with our whole heart; we have not loved our neighbors as ourselves. We are truly sorry and we humbly repent. For the sake of your Son Jesus Christ, have mercy on us and forgive us; that we may delight in your will, and walk in your ways, to the glory of your Name. Amen."[9]

I would argue that Christians need to embrace this pattern in addressing more than personal sin. We must use it to address the systemic and structural distortions that sin causes in God's creation. We need to confess, for example, that our economy causes enormous harm to people and to the nonhuman creation. It creates wealth for some people, while others go hungry. It yields examples of ecological restoration and yet continues to stimulate utter destruction. Confessing both systemic sins and our complicity in them does not necessarily require that we reject the capitalist market economy. It does require, however, that we acknowledge the very real suffering it causes. We confess. We seek forgiveness. We seek wisdom to navigate economically. We once again buy and sell within the system we know to be broken.

Think about this for a moment longer. Why bother following this pattern of confession, forgiveness, and renewal if we aren't going to get it right? Why not just give up altogether? We don't give up because we have faith, which the author of Hebrews describes as "confidence in what we hope for and assurance about what we do not see" (11:1). We have faith that God will sanctify us in meaningful ways. We have faith that God will give us strength to transform both our individual lives and the economic and political systems in which we live so that they better reflect biblical ideas of justice and equity. But even more importantly, we have faith that Christ's death and resurrection are a seal on God's promise to one day liberate economic systems, political systems, and indeed the whole creation from sin and suffering.

Applying Christian Practices toward Sin to the Problem of Finitude

As we deal with the problem of finitude in our caring for creation, we will find helpful guidance in the practices for dealing with sin that Christians

---

9 *The Book of Common Prayer and Administration of the Sacraments and Other Rites and Ceremonies of the Church Together with the Psalter or Psalms of David* (New York: Oxford University Press, 1990), 360.

have developed over the millennia. Indeed, Christian Environmental Stewardship is limited by both human finitude and human sin. One is simply our limited knowledge and understanding of what it means to care for God's creation, while the other is our tendency to reject God's lordship over the creation, both consciously and unconsciously. While these are distinct problems, they are not always easy to separate. We often fail to recognize our finite knowledge because of our sinful pride. We often fail to grasp knowledge within our reach because we are blinded by sinful desire.

Separating finitude and sin perfectly may not be important, though, because the same practices that Christians have developed for addressing sin can serve as a model for dealing with the problem of finitude in creation care as well. For both finitude and sin, we start by recognizing our limits as finite and sinful creatures. In both cases, we reflect on our actions to see how those limits have caused harm rather than led to the flourishing of the creation. In both cases, we seek wisdom and renewal to care for creation more effectively and faithfully. In both cases, we know that we, on our own, will fail. In both cases, we still move forward, sustained by the hope that God will fulfill our stewardship responsibilities fully in the new heavens and new earth. And in both cases, we express gratitude that we have been invited to participate in that work.

The Episcopal prayer doesn't mention creation care and stewardship specifically, but it certainly applies to them. We confess that we have not loved God with our whole hearts by loving and caring for the creation. We confess that we have not loved our neighbors as ourselves by accumulating wealth and financial security without thought to the environmental degradation that harms our human neighbors. We claim God's promised forgiveness and seek renewal so that we may once again strive to delight in God's will and walk in God's ways more fully by striving yet again to care well for the creation.

Conclusion

At the outset, I proposed that we need to reimagine stewardship as living out the Kingdom of God. I argued that we need an eschatological understanding of stewardship. Like Wes Jackson, I say that with a smile on my face, because I know it is impossible for us. We are finite and sinful, which means that we can never know enough or desire virtue enough to ensure the creation's integrity and stability. But I say that in all seriousness as well, because nothing less than the Kingdom of God will fulfill God's plan for the creation. Humbly cultivating the ancient Christian process of confession and renewal creates the patterns and practices we need to identify our failures and to press on in humble confidence, faith, and hope.

So what exactly is new or different about eschatological stewardship? Is eschatological stewardship a move beyond stewardship? After all, I am still affirming our responsibility to care for God's creation. I am still calling for efforts to manage flourishing forests and to promote just and equitable economies. In some ways, this is what stewardship has always meant. But eschatological stewardship provides an essential posture of humility that we have often lacked. It is stewardship that highlights our limits as finite and sinful people. In doing so, it becomes a stewardship that expects failure or only partial success. And it is a stewardship that provides a way to deal with failures, because it expects continual adjustment and correction.

Eschatological stewardship, I hasten to add, is more than just pietistic stewardship. As the example of adaptive ecosystem management suggests, maintaining a clear-eyed view of human limitations can lead to improved management processes and practices. And eschatological stewardship is, above all, hopeful stewardship in which we seek to learn more about God's creation and God's promises through the successes *and* the failures that flow from our efforts. All the while, we live in faith and hope for God to finish the good work to which we have been called.

Works Cited

Berry, Wendell. "Two Economies." In *Home Economics*, 54–75. San Francisco: North Point Press, 1987.

The Book of Common Prayer and Administration of the Sacraments and Other Rites and Ceremonies of the Church Together with the Psalter or Psalms of David. New York: Oxford University Press, 1990.

Cronon, William. *Nature's Metropolis: Chicago and the Great West*. New York: W. W. Norton, 1991.

Hirt, Paul W. *A Conspiracy of Optimism: Management of the National Forests since World War Two*. Lincoln: University of Nebraska Press, 1994.

Johnson, Erik W., and Scott Frickel. "Ecological Threat and the Founding of US National Environmental Movement Organizations, 1962–1998." *Social Problems* 58, no. 3 (August 2011): 305–29.

Leopold, Aldo. "The Land-Health Concept and Conservation." In *For the Health of the Land: Previously Unpublished Essays and Other Writings*, edited by J. Baird Callicott and Eric T. Freyfogle, 218–26. Washington, DC: Island Press, 1999.

———. *A Sand County Almanac with Essays on Conservation from Found River*. New York: Oxford University Press, 1966.

Plantinga, Cornelius, Jr., and Sue A. Rozeboom. *Discerning the Spirits: A Guide to Thinking about Christian Worship Today*. Grand Rapids, MI: Eerdmans, 2003.

Part Three

———

REORIENTING:
Hopeful Ways Forward

8

WHAT'S THAT?

Naming, Knowing, Delighting, Caring, Suffering

Debra Rienstra

When my daughter Mia was two, we lived next door to a grumpy recluse. We hardly ever saw or spoke to him. In his backyard, adjacent to ours, he kept a dog in a kennel. She was a chocolate lab, and she lived outdoors year-round, despite the sweltering Iowa summers and frigid Iowa winters. On the coldest winter days, the poor dog would bark her misery for hours. Her owner never let her out of the kennel except for once or twice each hunting season. He fed her and, every week or so, sprayed the poop out of her cage with a hose. Dismayed by all this, I called the Humane Society once, but they told me there was nothing they could do. Meanwhile, my tiny daughter Mia was enchanted with the doggie and wanted to visit her every day. Eventually, we learned from another neighbor the dog's name: Penny. Every winter morning we bundled up and made the tiny trek to Penny's kennel so Mia could pat the doggie's nose through the cage wire. In summer, we made the daily pilgrimage in bare feet so Mia could chat with her waggy friend. I could see that Mia sensed Penny's suffering in some basic, childlike way. I don't know whether our ritual visits made a difference to Penny, but I do know that Penny's suffering mattered more to us after we knew her name.

Mia's attentiveness to Penny, despite the creature's unfortunate circumstances, was, of course, completely normal. Little children delight us with their innocent curiosity about the world. They remind us what it feels like to be enchanted with the most common things—a caterpillar creeping across a sidewalk, a kitty licking its paw, an autumn-brown oak leaf crunching underfoot. To learn about the world, children are driven to learn language, compelled by impulses even child development experts don't entirely understand. Little kids pick up words and phrases by imitating older people, and soon they start demanding to know the names of things: "What's that?" they pester. With the guidance of attentive and loving caretakers, children typically learn language with astonishing speed.

God gave humans the gift of language as a powerful and distinctive way for us to manage our relationships with the world. And the ability to use language is one of the most important aspects of our being made in the image of God. (See Heun, chapter 1.) Through language, we echo the way the Creator beholds the world and declares that it is good. But we can also, sadly, use language as a form of dominance and control. In fact, sinful uses of language can lead to distorted relationships with one another, with other creatures, and with all aspects of creation and culture. However, based on Scripture as well as on our experiences of beautiful, attentive, and loving language, it seems that God intended language to draw us into relationships of mutual delight, understanding, and respect.

As this volume demonstrates, the words we choose as we discuss the relationship between humans and the nonhuman creation make a difference. One important problem with the term *stewardship* is the implicit presumption that it is both possible and easy for us to learn what we need to know about the world to steward its natural resources well (as the subtitle of the first edition of *Earthkeeping*[1] put it). (See Skillen, chapter 7.) In other

---

1   Loren Wilkinson, ed., *Earthkeeping: Christian Stewardship of Natural Resources* (Grand Rapids, MI: Eerdmans, 1980).

words, the term *stewardship* can effectively shield us from the ongoing challenge of deeply understanding the world. And without that understanding, we cannot live in healthy kinship with the creation, we cannot fulfill our role as earthkeepers, and we cannot be responsible place-keepers. (See Meyaard-Schaap, chapter 3; Bouma-Prediger, chapter 6; and Bjelland, chapter 13.)

Learning what is needed to steward the nonhuman creation is very difficult, especially because many of us cannot name more than a few of the plants, animals, waters, or landforms around us. Indeed, many of us are so insulated from the nonhuman creation that we hardly speak of it at all. Or we speak of it in simplified, objectifying terms, glossing over our ignorance and obscuring the complexities and intricacies of our world. What we cannot name, we cannot properly see, let alone understand. So as we seek to fulfill our responsibilities toward the creation, we can begin at the beginning: we can learn the names for things. Learning names, we might say, is the first step in creation care. When we begin by learning names, we activate a deeper knowledge that prepares us to receive the gifts of delight, caring, and suffering.

Adam Names the Creatures

In two verses in the Genesis creation narratives, Adam confers names on all the creatures. Why does the Genesis story include this curious detail? And what might Adam's naming of the creatures mean for us today?

Genesis 1 and 2 work in tandem to portray humans as both responsible rulers over and humble servants within the nonhuman creation. (See Bouma-Prediger, chapter 6.) In the Genesis 2 story, the Lord God places the soil-creature in a lush garden and immediately gives him some limits: he may not eat from one of the trees. Other than that, his vocation is to "work/serve" (*abad*) the garden and "take care of / keep" it (*shamar*). Then God declares that Adam should not be doing this work alone. So God forms beasts and birds, also from the soil. Biblical scholar Theodore Hiebert suggests that God's concern here is not so much about loneliness but about the amount of work—earthkeeping—that needs doing. God provides Adam with animals, including domestic animals suited to helping

Adam fulfill his vocation as a worker of the soil. These creatures fill out the ecosystem in which humans, animals, and birds thrive by living together and serving the soil together.[2]

At this point, God brings the animals to Adam so that Adam can name them. This is the first instance in the Bible in which human beings use language. It is a charming moment in which we can imagine God enjoying the suspense. God waits "to see what [Adam] would name them" (Genesis 2:19). Adam is given the freedom to play with language, and God accepts Adam's proposals: "whatever the man called each living creature, that was its name" (v. 19). Some interpreters suggest that Adam's naming of the animals is just another way to "steward" the creation, with implications of power, control, and authority. But I contend that we should understand naming differently: as a loving act.

Taking their cue from earlier biblical commentary, Reformation theologians emphasized Adam's special knowledge and wisdom as he named the animals. Martin Luther imagined that Adam, "as soon as he viewed an animal, came into possession of a knowledge of its entire nature and abilities."[3] Adam could give the animals their "right" names because of this intuitive and profound knowledge. The animals, according to these commentators, were obedient and cooperative. John Calvin remarks that their gentleness would have remained if not for the Fall. When Adam disobeyed God, he lost his original, God-given authority over the animals. Instead, says Calvin, Adam "experienced the ferocity of brute animals against himself. Indeed, while some can be broken with great effort, others always remain untamed, and some inspire us with terror by their fierceness, even when unprovoked."[4]

The point here is not to establish historical facts about God's creation process. Rather, the point is to explore what the story is meant to teach us. In proposing that Adam had profound, innate knowledge of the

---

2   Theodore Hiebert, *The Yahwist's Landscape: Nature and Religion in Early Israel* (New York: Oxford University Press, 1996).

3   John L. Thompson, ed., *Old Testament I: Genesis 1–11*, Reformation Commentary on Scripture, vol. 1 (Downers Grove, IL: InterVarsity Press Academic, 2012), 97.

4   Thompson, *Old Testament I*, 99.

creatures, Reformation theologians offered a fanciful conjecture. But it is a thought-provoking idea. If we imagine Adam beginning with deep knowledge of the other creatures, could his act of naming also be seen as an act of love? His relationship with the creatures, enhanced through naming them, seems to have been characterized by attention and delight. The text allows us to perceive God and Adam together delighting in the creatures. If Hiebert is right, Adam's relationship with the creatures also involved partnership in the vocation of serving the land. Along with his knowledge, then, Adam exhibited attention, respect, delight, and partnership. We might describe these ingredients, blended together, as love and kinship. The moment when Adam named the animals thus suggests the right relationship between humans and fellow creatures: loving kinship. (See Meyaard-Schaap, chapter 3; and Haney, chapter 10.)

In the next section of Genesis 2, God creates a woman from Adam's rib. Here, Hiebert suggests, Adam receives a true companion who can serve as a sexual partner and an equal partner in the cultivating work to which human beings are called.[5] Adam responds to the woman's appearance with an effusion of language. He performs a little poem:

> This is now bone of my bones
>   and flesh of my flesh;
> she shall be called "woman" [isha]
>   for she was taken out of man [ish]. (Genesis 2:23)

Adam makes a pun, connecting the Hebrew words for man and woman. Through this act of naming and language play, Adam establishes a relationship of delight and mutuality with his co-human. In the woman, the soil-creature sees a mirror image of himself. In fact, though I have been referring to the man as "Adam" in the last few paragraphs, this passage actually refers to him only as "the man," *adam*, the soil-creature. Thus, in Genesis 2:23, Adam finds a word for himself and for the woman at the same time: *ish* and *isha*. Their coordinating names signal their relationship

---

5   Hiebert, *The Yahwist's Landscape*, 60.

of mutual regard. (The woman does not get the name Eve until after the Fall account in Genesis 3.) These verses are therefore consistent and continuous with the verses about the animals. In this whole passage, Adam is using language to build relationships characterized by knowledge, delight, and partnership.

The animal-naming story in Genesis might help us better understand our role in the creation by offering an encouraging invitation into the challenges of earthkeeping. Imagining a profoundly knowledgeable pre-Fall Adam suggests to us that the right relationship between humans and the rest of creation is one of deep knowledge for a greater purpose: partnership in a world that gives praise to God. We know that in our fallen state, knowledge comes only slowly and painfully, and it is difficult to care for the earth when there is so much we don't know. (See Skillen, chapter 7.) It is also difficult to care for the earth if we don't have the power to act. (See Heffner, chapter 11; and Bouma, chapter 12.) Unfortunately, returning to a pre-Fall state in which we have profound and innate knowledge of all the creatures is not possible.

However, if we imagine Adam beginning with knowledge and then finding names, perhaps we can work backward, so to speak, by learning names first and letting names lead us toward deeper knowledge, expecting that deeper knowledge will enlarge our capacity for delight in and wise care of the earth. Genesis 2, in other words, reminds us that the slow, painful work of knowledge is redemptive work. As we strive to know, we slowly restore our intended role in creation, and we slowly restore the creation itself.

Naming Leads to Knowledge

Learning names may seem a simple thing, but knowing names is the first step toward seeing a thing at all. Every semester I face classrooms full of new students, and they all blur together for me until I learn their names. I try to do this very quickly because knowing a student's name draws me into relationship with that person. As the semester progresses, I learn more about each student. Eventually, I associate their names not only with their faces but also with their ways of speaking and thinking, a little of their personal stories, and our shared experiences in class. I can teach them better if I know them better, and that starts with learning their names.

The same is true for our nonhuman neighbors. Michigan author Mary Blocksma was prompted to write her 1992 book, *Naming Nature*, when she looked out her window one day and realized she could not identify any of the trees she saw. [6] She considered herself a lover of nature and an educated person, yet her "natural literacy" was desperately lacking. She realized she could not see or know what she could not name. So she decided to learn to identify the common trees, plants, birds, and critters around her as a "gentle, playful way to say hello." [7] Inspired by Blocksma, I have been trying to learn names for years. When my family and I lived in Iowa, I started learning the names for common perennials and annuals: day lilies, irises, peonies, salvia, and lobelia. When we moved into our current home in Michigan, I learned many shrub names: sand plum, red osier dogwood, weigela, and (unfortunately) the perniciously invasive buckthorn. Lately, I have been concentrating on birds: tufted titmouse, red-bellied woodpecker, white-breasted nuthatch. And in honor of our wonderful Michigan lakeshore, I have been learning terms for different kinds of dunes: linear, perched, and parabolic. Now when I walk through my neighborhood, I recognize birds, trees, even shrubs: that is viburnum with its lacy spring poms; that is ninebark with its cascades of chocolat-ey-purple leaves. I encounter my surroundings not as an undifferentiated backdrop for human activity but as a neighborhood of familiar creatures. It is amazing what I never even bothered to notice until I intentionally began learning names.

One of the first benefits of learning names is delight. As a person who loves words, I find names themselves interesting: their sounds, their etymologies, the playful folk wisdom often embedded within. The little wildflower called Dutchman's breeches, for example, does indeed look like tiny pairs of pants on a line. I am focusing my learning on the native landscapes of West Michigan, but the world is full of fascinating names.

---

6   Mary Blocksma, *Naming Nature: A Seasonal Guide for the Amateur Naturalist* (New York: Penguin, 1992).

7   Blocksma, *Naming Nature*, xii.

There is a type of carpet shark that lives near Australia called, wonderfully, the tasselled wobbegong. Robert Macfarlane's book *Landmarks* contains 380 pages of place names in the United Kingdom and Ireland along with explanations derived from the intimate knowledge of people who live attentively on their land: a fell, a flam, and a flan, for example, are all different kinds of wind in certain regions of Scotland.[8] People come up with the most wonderful words for things! These delightful words invite us to return to that childlike sense of the world as a curious and lively place.

Names are the first step toward knowledge, but already we encounter complications. Plant and animal species often have many common names even in one language. All the trees in my field guide have at least two or three alternative names. The red maple, for example, is also called the swamp maple, the water maple, and the soft maple. The system of binomial Latin names established in the late 1700s helps sort out the confusion, as this system clarifies identification across languages and cultures. Common names and Latin binomials together comprise a kind of luggage set, each carrying more pieces of knowledge. The good news is that names lead us down additional paths of curiosity. Why is this little stream called Whiskey Creek? Who named it? I wonder what Native Americans called it? (Answer: local experts I asked had only guesses.) Why is this dragonfly named *Acisoma attenboroughi*? (Answer: to honor David Attenborough.) Names carry scientific and folk wisdom, but they may also contain histories of human conflicts and conquests. Winners of wars get to choose the names of conquered places. And names can be a form of forgetting, or unknowing, especially when new names cover up something lost or conquered. As we explore names, these complexities prompt more questions and invite us to deeper knowledge, slowly unfolding layers of history and complex interrelationships among all created things.

Applied to creation care, being ignorant of names indicates that we lack knowledge about human and nonhuman creatures that inhabit the creation, not to mention the interactions on which they depend. In contrast, by learning the names of the people, creatures, and places that

---

8   Robert Macfarlane, *Landmarks* (New York: Penguin, 2016), 228.

intersect our lives, we enter into the deep and sometimes complicated knowledge that is required for thoughtful caretaking of the creation.

Knowledge Can Lead to Caring

When I learn a name and gain a little knowledge, intricacies and relationships are revealed. And the relationships lead to caring. My daughter and I deepened our relationship with Penny when we learned her name, and we became more concerned for her welfare. We began to care for her.

Knowledge and care enhance each other. As care grows, thirst for knowledge grows too. Eventually, I feel compelled to connect with other people who know more than I do. To help a gorgeous oak leaf hydrangea thrive in my yard, for example, I learned from a landscaper that these woody, effusive wonders like shelter and moderate sun, perhaps up against a house and facing east. I learned that they produce flowers on old growth—careful where you prune! And, like all hydrangeas, they like acidic soil.

Learning the name of, gaining knowledge about, and caring for one shrub in my own yard is relatively easy business, but what about whole ecosystems? Here is where we acknowledge the essential need to join forces in gaining and implementing knowledge. As a professional scientist, my colleague Deanna van Dijk has spent two decades lugging equipment up and down windy dunes to collect and weigh "slugs" of sand. She and her students study the motion of sand on dunes so that we all can learn better how to live in cooperation with their natural movements. I joined Deanna one evening when she put this hard-earned knowledge to work for the board of the Kitchel-Lindquist-Hartger Dunes Preserve near Ferrysburg, Michigan. The board was worried that one of their active dunes was slowly swallowing an educational building. These good people were already quite knowledgeable about dunes, and they cared deeply about managing their problem well. Deanna was able to suggest a number of ways to slow down dune movement. The board's favored suggestion: recycled natural Christmas trees laid horizontally across the dune face.

While we are each individually responsible to acquire knowledge, knowledge building is ultimately a vast, collective project. Every fact we know about river water levels, pheasant populations, and tree diseases required years of careful record-keeping and study by scientists and observers, perhaps generations of them. They get muddy, wet, cold, hot, sunburned, and thoroughly bitten by insects in order to weave small threads into the ever-changing tapestry of human understanding. Scientists are not the only people with extensive knowledge, of course. Good farmers know their acreage and animals intimately. Most hunters and anglers have a rich understanding of and respect for the creatures they hunt and fish, and they care deeply about the ecosystems that help the creatures thrive. Landscapers, garden center workers, and other professional tradespeople often carry encyclopedic knowledge of local plants and microclimates. Some people serve as "citizen scientists," taking water temperature readings and counting frogs or owls. Almost every community has people who work on land use issues, either professionally or as volunteers. Indigenous peoples preserve ancient wisdom about our world, though unfortunately their knowledge is not often consulted or respected. (See Haney, chapter 10). For those of us who wish to learn more, there are wise and willing teachers all around.

To be sure, there are challenges in moving from knowledge to caring. One difficult part can be combining all the different kinds of knowledge together to form a complete picture. Both Deanna van Dijk and my friend Tim Van Deelen, a wildlife biologist, have described to me their frustrations with "piecemeal" scientific study. Scientific funding systems and scientific processes tend to favor smaller, particularized studies. When many scientists are doing different kinds of studies, building useful, shared understanding takes a long time and much cooperation. Meanwhile, mistrust, crossed motivations, and differing priorities can mar relationships among experts. Two groups of experts, say farmers and ecologists, might disagree strongly about whether it is advisable to allow fertilizer runoff into a river, for example.

Even worse, the combination of human finitude and human hubris can lead us to think we know more than we actually do. (See Skillen, chapter 7.) We repeatedly prove the adage "a little knowledge can be a dangerous thing" when our well-meaning attempts at creation care go all wrong. The book *The Death and Life of the Great Lakes* by Dan Egan outlines a number of misguided attempts to "steward" resources in the Great Lakes region. For instance, American settlers traveling west in the nineteenth century dreaded crossing the fearsome, vast Great Black Swamp that covered much of northern Ohio. In the second half of the nineteenth century, settlers in nearby communities decided to drain the swamp. This seemed like an excellent idea because it would allow new settlers to cross Ohio much more easily, and it would provide good farmland for people who settled in Ohio. Indeed, the drained soil was amazingly rich and productive. Eventually, however, Ohioans realized that the vast wetland had served as a "kidney" for Lake Erie, filtering water from the entire watershed and keeping Lake Erie's waters fresh and full of fish. Without the swamp, Lake Erie has become chronically sick. For more than a century, the lake has been overloaded with runoff from the entire region, including sewage, farm and industrial wastes, and heavy loads of fertilizer. As a result, Lake Erie has been wracked with pollution and toxic algae blooms for decades.[9]

Moving from knowledge to care, admittedly, is no easy task. Our complex and differing human motivations and priorities combined with the sheer amount of labor required make gathering and combining knowledge difficult. When we do this work well, however, we come to marvel at the intricate complexity, the thousands of interconnections within and among ecosystems and indeed across the entire planet. We can move from names to knowledge to purposeful and beneficial caring for the creation.

Caring Leads to Suffering

If we seek, as part of our human vocation, to gain deep knowledge about the creation, we must also accept the pain that accompanies caring. When naming leads to knowing and knowing leads to caring, caring will eventually lead to suffering. My little daughter delighted in Penny the dog, but she also worried, because she had come to care about this fellow creature. Similarly, I often rejoice in the beautiful turquoise hue of Lake

---

9   Dan Egan, *The Death and Life of the Great Lakes* (New York: W. W. Norton, 2018), 212–44.

Michigan. But now that I know more about Lake Michigan ecology, I also lament the ravishingly clear water, because invasive quagga mussels have devoured so much of the life-giving plankton. Richard Powers's novel *The Overstory* draws the reader into this kind of grief through the stories of several characters who learn about timber companies clear-cutting trees in the Pacific Northwest. The characters become eco-activists and get in trouble for their activism. Apart from personal troubles, what grieves them most is that they now understand intimately what is lost when even a single old-growth California redwood is cut.[10] Grief, it seems, is an inevitable result of the redemptive knowledge to which we are called as human beings. Once we start investing in knowledge of the world, we begin to see the suffering of creation more clearly. Environmental scholars and writers often cite the famous line from Aldo Leopold: "One of the penalties of an ecological education is that one lives alone in a world of wounds."[11] Very quickly, deeper knowledge will bring us up against climate change and species extinction, and we will shoulder the burden of collective grief. We learn to lament. (See Heun, chapter 1; and Heffner, chapter 11.)

It might seem easier not to bother. Those of us living comfortable lives might prefer to enjoy our comforts and avoid the grief. But grief is good. It means we have come into meaningful relationship. In light of the ecological crises to which this book responds, our redemptive assignment is more urgent than ever. Each of us needs to join in the project of learning names, gaining knowledge, caring, and suffering if we are to fulfill our calling as God's image bearers and work toward justice and flourishing for "all creatures here below." Knowledge is difficult and complicated, but ignorance is dangerous and irresponsible. All of us must take responsibility to learn not only about plants, animals, and habitats but also about the human systems that damage our world and the human systems that help to heal. If I had been braver, maybe I could have learned about city ordinances and worked with the local Humane Society and made more of

---

10 Richard Powers, *The Overstory: A Novel* (New York: W. W. Norton, 2018).

11 Aldo Leopold, *Round River: From the Journals of Aldo Leopold*, ed. Luna B. Leopold (New York: Oxford University Press, 1993), 165.

a difference for Penny. Instead, I just minded my own business. None of us can simply mind our own business now. The more we know, the more we realize there is no such thing as "our own business." We are all in this together, the entire creation.

Humility and Limits

Entering into a knowledgeable and loving relationship with the non-human creation leads us into delight in addition to suffering. If we can endure the suffering, we may find within it the gifts of wonder and humility. Foreword writer Bill McKibben calls Job 38–41 "the first and greatest piece of nature writing in the Western tradition." [12] After Job cries out to God in his suffering, God at last responds. "Where were you when I laid the earth's foundation?" "Do you know when the mountain goats give birth?" "Does the eagle soar at your command?" God goes on for four full chapters, painting a vast picture of the wild world far beyond Job's understanding. This "whirlwind" of God's words overwhelms Job with humility. The glory and terror of the world, the vast scale of it, the deep time of God's perspective—it's all too much. "I put my hand over my mouth," Job says (Job 40:4).

Even with our best efforts, our human knowledge will always be limited, both individually and collectively. There are mysteries beyond the boundaries of all human language. Nevertheless, we are both individually and collectively responsible. (See Bouma, chapter 12.) And the simplest place to begin is right where we are, learning the names of plants, animals, and landforms around us. We can read books. We can get involved with local restoration and ecology projects. We can use less energy. We can befriend local experts in fields of knowledge that most interest us. We can learn alongside our children. We can share the knowledge and expertise we might already have. We can encourage students to become experts. These simple practices are critical expressions of our human vocation to name, know, delight, care, and suffer.

---

12 Bill McKibben, "Bill McKibben Dartmouth Baccalaureate Address," June 11, 2011, http://www.dartmouth.edu/~commence/news/speeches/2011/mckibben.html. (He has said this in similar terms in many other places.)

The poet Mary Oliver writes in her beloved poem "The Messenger" that her work as a poet is to love the world. That work, she writes, is about "standing still and learning to be astonished," [13] which requires a posture of gratitude. Similarly, our work is to find our way into the delight and mutual respect that Adam had for the creatures he named, the delight and curiosity of an innocent child. That work is risky, because it may lead to the suffering that comes with caring. But it is necessary work on our way to a doxology of love and praise.

Works Cited

Blocksma, Mary. *Naming Nature: A Seasonal Guide for the Amateur Naturalist.* New York: Penguin, 1992.

Egan, Dan. *The Death and Life of the Great Lakes.* New York: W. W. Norton, 2018.

Hiebert, Theodore. *The Yahwist's Landscape: Nature and Religion in Early Israel.* New York: Oxford University Press, 1996.

Leopold, Aldo. *Round River: From the Journals of Aldo Leopold.* Edited by Luna B. Leopold. New York: Oxford University Press, 1993.

Macfarlane, Robert. *Landmarks.* New York: Penguin, 2016.

McKibben, Bill. "Bill McKibben Dartmouth Baccalaureate Address," June 11, 2011. http://www.dartmouth.edu/~commence/news/speeches/2011/mckibben.html.

Oliver, Mary. "The Messenger." In *Thirst: New Poems.* Boston: Beacon Press, 2006.

Powers, Richard. *The Overstory: A Novel.* New York: W. W. Norton, 2018.

Thompson, John L., ed. *Old Testament I: Genesis 1–11.* Reformation Commentary on Scripture, vol. 1. Downers Grove, IL: InterVarsity Press Academic, 2012.

Wilkinson, Loren, ed. *Earthkeeping: Christian Stewardship of Natural Resources.* Grand Rapids, MI: Eerdmans, 1980.

---

13 Mary Oliver, "The Messenger," in *Thirst: New Poems* (Boston: Beacon Press, 2006), 1.

REIMAGINING OUR KINSHIP
WITH ANIMALS

Matthew C. Halteman and Megan Halteman Zwart

S ocial media offers no shortage of quizzes and optical illusions to puzzle over. Consider this commonly shared image.

The idea is to count the number of animals you can find. For most people, four animals appear immediately—the elephant, donkey, dog, and cat. Perhaps the attentive among us will also notice the mouse beneath the cat. However, for those of us who have seen our fair share of social media memes, we know that five animals cannot be the final answer. Sure enough, it turns out that with careful inspection, sixteen animals can be spotted. Though these other animals are there all along, they are hiding in plain sight.[1]

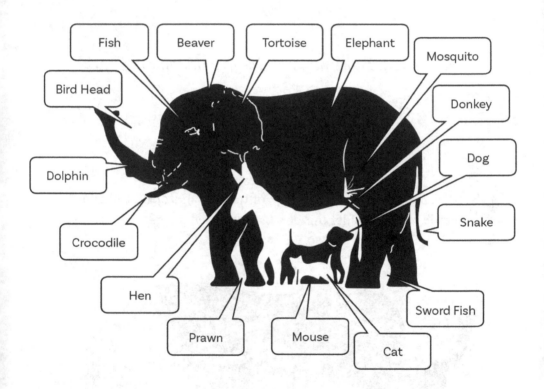

This clever meme offers a trivial example of how a shift in perspective can enable something previously invisible to become suddenly obvious. But such shifts in perspective can occur in more dramatic and transformational ways as well.

---

1   This image appears to have first been posted on Facebook in 2016. The editors have been unable to locate the original designer, and the image has been redrawn for this volume.

In this volume, for instance, we invite readers into a new frame of reference that brings environmental racism into view. (See Heffner, chapter 11.) We highlight human dependence on God's nonhuman creatures by showing how our (literally invisible) microbial gut bacteria enable us to digest our daily bread. (See Al-Attas Bradford, chapter 5.)

In this chapter, we invite readers to shift their perspectives, putting animals at center stage, even though this means confronting the many consequences of our current treatment of animals. We suggest that to care for creation, human beings must learn to see animals as fellow creatures, not just resources. We must also change our consumer habits to reflect this new vision. We hope that learning to *see* animals differently might inspire readers to *think*, *feel*, and *act* differently toward animals too.

The sad truth is that humankind's treatment of animals as mere resources to be stewarded for consumption has a big, negative impact on creation. Because we are so defensive of these practices, both individually and as a culture, it is easy to remain naïve or willfully ignorant of their impact. Being less defensive of ourselves and more curious about animals can promote important changes in our attitudes and actions that can have a big, positive impact on creation. But before we consider the drawbacks of seeing animals as resources and the benefits of seeing them as fellow creatures, let's take a look at how such a shift in perspective might play out in real life.

A Transformation of Vision

Imagine a college student, Jasmin, who has grown up with dogs in her family home. These dogs are deeply loved, spoiled, given costly medical attention when necessary, and have their own Christmas stockings. They are generally considered by everyone to be members of the family.

During college, Jasmin finds herself in an environmental studies class that visits a sustainable farm to learn about prairie restoration, wastewater treatment, and wind power. While visiting the farm, Jasmin falls in love with the peaceful surroundings, the beauty of the land, and especially the animals on the farm.

She returns outside of class hours to help Farmer Marie feed the animals, trim the goats' hooves, and weed the vegetables. All the while, baby goats nip at Jasmin's heels. She stops to check on Betsy the milk cow, who is about to deliver a calf. She gets to know several other animals on the farm by name too, including a friendly, mischievous goat named Freckles and a flamboyant rooster named Rocky.

One day when Jasmin visits, she is excited to see that Betsy's calf has arrived. Betsy nuzzles the calf and keeps him close by her side, becoming protective of the calf when Jasmin approaches. When Farmer Marie emerges from the barn, Jasmin congratulates her on the new addition to her farm. Marie thanks Jasmin and says, "We hoped she'd have a girl so we could expand our dairy herd, but since it's a boy, at least we can count on a freezer full of veal for our Christmas dinner!"

Jasmin finds this comment unexpectedly jarring. There are few people in her life she admires more than Farmer Marie. Marie is clearly a deeply caring person who sees farming as a God-given vocation, regularly professes her love for her animals, and seems committed to showing that care in practice. Moreover, Jasmin has eaten veal herself at least a dozen times, and beef is a mainstay of her diet. So it's not as if Farmer Marie's comment conveys any new, much less shocking, information.

And yet somehow her relationship with Farmer Marie's animals has led her to see animals used for farming in a different light. Her natural response has been to relate to these animals more like she relates to her dogs at home and less like she relates to her lunch. Suddenly, she sees things differently and feels downright alarmed later in the day when she and Farmer Marie find that Freckles the goat has a severe infection and needs medical treatment. Farmer Marie remarks with noticeable regret that the visit from the veterinarian would cost more than Freckles' market value, and so sadly it makes more sense to euthanize him than to pay for an expensive course of treatment.

Jasmin feels conflicted. Though she understands Farmer Marie's predicament and believes that Marie's lament is genuine, she suddenly finds this calculation upsetting. She is bewildered, too, that just weeks ago, she probably wouldn't have cared much about the fate of a sick goat. But now that she has direct personal experience of goats as unique individuals—similar to her experience of her beloved dogs as individuals—the idea that a creature like Freckles could be reduced so casually to a mere economic resource is deeply troubling to her.

Jasmin cares more about Freckles' suffering because she knows his name. (See Rienstra, chapter 8.) To Jasmin, Freckles is no longer just *something* to be bought, stewarded, and sold but *someone* with personal, creaturely dignity and moral worth. Jasmin is achieving a deeper understanding of both herself and Freckles, discovering a fellow earthling with moral standing beyond her instrumental relationship to him as merely future food. (See Joldersma, chapter 4.)

What Jasmin is experiencing is similar to what happens when you look more closely at the elephant optical illusion. She was previously attentive to a number of animals in her life. The dogs and cats that lived in her house and slept at the foot of her bed, for instance, appeared clearly to her from the outset as individuals with desires and preferences, worthy of moral consideration, medical care, and daily attention and affection. But the interests of animals on the farm were invisible to her, even though on some level she knew they had physiology, cognitive capabilities, and moral standing similar to those of the companion animals in her home. She hasn't necessarily gained any new information through her visits to the farm, but the way she views this information has shifted and snapped into perspective in a new way. What was previously hiding in plain sight—the intimate bond between Betsy and her calf, the self-assured swagger of Rocky the rooster, Freckles' interest in continuing to enjoy his life—is now plainly evident and indeed even glaringly obvious to her.

From Transformed *Seeing* to Transformed *Being*

Jasmin's transformed vision of animals used for farming begins primarily as a new way of *seeing* the world. But it doesn't take Jasmin long to realize how intimately connected this new way of seeing is to new ways of *being* in the world. She starts noticing subtle changes in the way she goes about her daily life. At the snack table backstage at play practice, she finds herself passing on the ham sandwiches and choosing a veggie sub instead. In English class, she elects to write a persuasive speech defending stronger animal welfare laws in agriculture, and in biology class, she decides to forgo dissecting a pig in favor of using a computer simulation.

When her brothers start making bacon jokes in front of a vegetarian family at church, she silences them with a subtle side-eye and explains why she was upset on the ride home. And at the cast party on closing night, Jasmin not only chooses vegetarian pizza but also explains to one of her friends what has motivated the switch. *Where did this confidence come from?* she wonders to herself. Three months ago, she was grabbing the last slice of meat-lovers pizza and wouldn't have dreamt of making waves with her friends over this issue.

Much to her surprise, Jasmin is not only *seeing* animals used for farming in a new light but also *engaging with* them in her daily life in ways that reinforce and clarify these recent revelations and motivate and embolden her to pursue further progress. Her new vision is naturally giving rise to adjustments and changes in her behavior. With each new action, the vision becomes just a little clearer, less threatening, and more approachable. As the vision is incrementally clarified, new behaviors become easier and easier to try. Jasmin is becoming less and less defensive of the views about animals she grew up with and more and more curious about where her newfound animal consciousness might lead her.

One day, a few months later, she comes across an article with a startling headline on a classmate's social media feed. The headline reads, "Veganism Is 'Single Biggest Way' to Reduce Our Environmental Impact on Planet."[2] A year earlier she would have ignored or dismissed the article. But this year she reads on with interest: "Avoiding meat and dairy could reduce your carbon footprint from food by nearly three-quarters."

Given that popular science journalism is often sensationalized, Jasmin traces the article back to the peer-reviewed research on which it was based. It turns out that the research was published in the prestigious academic

---

2 Olivia Petter, "Veganism Is 'Single Biggest Way' to Reduce Our Environmental Impact on Planet, Study Finds," *Independent*, June 1, 2018, https://www.independent.co.uk/life-style /health-and-families/veganism-environmental-impact-planet-reduced-plant-based -diet-humans-study-a8378631.html.

journal *Science* by two professors from the University of Oxford who "consolidated data covering five environmental indicators; 38,700 farms; and 1,600 processors, packaging types, and retailers."[3] Jasmin knows better than to believe that any single study is definitive, but this experience feels like a turning point. From now on, she is not just going to pass on the occasional slice of pepperoni pizza. She is resolved to eat less meat, experiment more with plant-based foods, and see where things go from there.

Seeking Transformation through Openness to Experience

Jasmin's experience illustrates that to see clearly what is hiding in plain sight and to begin living out these new revelations requires two things. First, she needs a *transformation of vision* so that she can see animals as valuable individuals. Second, she needs a *transformation of practice* so that her daily actions match her new vision.

To clarify how these transformations work, let's further investigate the idea of something hiding in plain sight. Why do some things appear evident to us from the outset and other things fail to appear until a jarring experience brings them into relief? Our ability to see some connections and miss others has a great deal to do with our background experiences and beliefs. What we have been taught and have experienced in the past primes us to pay special attention to experiences that confirm our expectations and to respond defensively to, downplay, or dismiss experiences that contradict our expectations. The background beliefs that give rise to our expectations are set early on by shaping institutions such as the family, religion, and culture.

For instance, in Jasmin's home, there was no contradiction on Christmas morning between stuffing a stocking for the family dog with one hand and snacking on bacon with the other. She was aware from trips to petting zoos and basic science classes that dogs and pigs are similar in many ways. But Jasmin never thought to question the different treatment they received because it was so common and widespread. And even if she had experienced a passing concern that this behavior was inconsistent,

---

3   J. Poore and T. Nemecek, "Reducing Food's Environmental Impacts through Producers and Consumers," *Science* 360, no. 6392 (June 1, 2018): 987–92.

she would have reassured herself with the religious teaching that human beings have "dominion" over animals. She always took this to mean that animals are here for human use.

Furthermore, she trusts her teachers, parents, church leaders, and mentors like Farmer Marie as moral authorities in her life. None of them have seemed overly concerned about these inconsistencies. Without the intervention of a transformative experience such as coming to know Betsy the cow and Freckles the goat, her background beliefs and experiences would likely have offered enough moral and spiritual cover for her to dismiss any creeping doubts about her Christmas morning routine of celebrating with her dog while eating a pig.

Such background beliefs and experiences condition us to notice certain things and miss others. But then what explains cases in which we have truly jarring experiences that shake or even transform our previous beliefs? And what should we do in these cases? Jarring experiences are unsettling, but they perform an invaluable service to us in the pursuit of becoming good knowers and thoughtful moral agents.

When we experience something that feels jarring, this uneasy feeling is good evidence that there is cognitive dissonance at work. By cognitive dissonance, we mean a mismatch among our beliefs, attitudes, and actions. This mismatch occurs if we believe or value one thing but act in a way that suggests we believe the opposite. For instance, if we believe that all human beings are made in the image of God but we harass and bully those who are different from us, we should feel unsettled about this inconsistency. If we want to live lives in which our beliefs and values are consistent with our actions, as we assume Christians generally should, we must remain attentive to these jarring experiences. They are clear red flags to help us notice and respond to cognitive dissonance.

Swapping Curiosity for Defensiveness

An important first step for making invisible creatures visible, then, is becoming aware of experiences that are jarring and noting them as red flags. But there is a second step that is equally important: turning away from the defensive feelings that often arise after such jarring experiences toward curiosity about where the experience might lead. The process of feeling unsettled in the wake of a new experience or reflection is uncomfortable. We human beings have a strong internal pull to remain comfortable, even complacent. Familiar habits are difficult to overcome, even for otherwise curious and engaged individuals. Our natural response is to get defensive, which could shut down the important process of investigating our beliefs to root out the inconsistencies causing the cognitive dissonance. Defensiveness is a natural response, but it closes one off from learning from a range of experiences. While defensiveness in response to a new, jarring experience closes us off, curiosity opens us up to being tutored by new experiences.

So let's rewind to the immediate aftermath of Jasmin's jarring experience on the farm. She is uncomfortable with Farmer Marie's attitude toward eating Betsy's calf for Christmas dinner and toward reducing Freckles to market value. She is also somewhat confused by it, since Farmer Marie seems genuinely to care about her animals. Jasmin can't help but think to herself that this kind of inconsistency is also operational in her own bacon-fueled Christmas morning routine. Jasmin immediately experiences a familiar defensiveness rise in her gut, and the onslaught of replies comes easily at first. She is just being a bleeding heart, ascribing human attributes to animals. Sure, our treatment of animals in industrial farms is troublesome, but animals were given to us for food. And Farmer Marie's animals seem happy here on the farm until their deaths. Jasmin didn't set up the system, and animals are going to be raised and slaughtered whether she participates or not, so it is not her problem.

In the past, Jasmin might have been content to let these defensive arguments win the day, short-circuiting her thought process and soothing her concern. But what if Jasmin doesn't let these knee-jerk defensive replies have the final say? What if she notes the defensiveness but moves past it to curiosity? What will she do next in such a case?

If Jasmin is open to following her curiosity to a truly transformed vision, she will not shrink from new experiences that are initially uncomfortable.

On the contrary, she will seek out these jarring experiences, knowing that they can give rise to confidence-inspiring actions. New, bold actions may lead her to yet more jarring experiences, but she will be open to these as well. That is how transformation works: there is always something more to be uncovered. In Jasmine's case, her curiosity will lead her to pay closer attention to the interests and behaviors of the animals on the farm. She will investigate more about their biology, psychology, and cognitive capabilities. In the process, she will be continually surprised at how much they have in common with human beings. As her vision transforms, she will naturally and automatically be nudged in the direction of adopting new behaviors.

Though Jasmin's vision is beginning to change, and her actions are changing too, the behaviors she has newly adopted may feel tedious or ineffective at first. Over time, though, her sense of authenticity will grow, and in fact, the behaviors will end up opening new avenues of awareness. For instance, at first, Jasmin's newfound concern for animals applies only to those land animals that resemble her family pets. However, on a subsequent family visit to an aquarium, Jasmin sees the sea animals through a new lens. She is moved to investigate further the environmental destruction of their habitats at the hands of human beings and to learn more about their abilities to forge relationships, make memories, and anticipate the future. At home, she notes a wasp nest in a tree outside and wonders how she previously was able to see only a nuisance in what now appears as a unique wonder of engineering.

Jasmin is especially surprised to realize that as her actions continue to transform, so does her vision. She is particularly taken aback at how these lifestyle changes have reinvigorated her faith. When this process of transformation first began, she had to admit to feeling a little alienated from certain people at church who seemed skeptical of her new commitments. She even worried that maybe she was straying from a Christian vision of the human-animal relationship.

These worries prompted her to investigate further. She soon discovered Christian theologians such as Nekeisha Alayna Alexis, David Clough, and Sarah Withrow King (whose work we recommend in appendix 2). These perspectives gave her the tools to return to the Bible with new eyes, prepared to see something wonderful hiding in plain sight that is often overlooked: the Bible tells of God's deep love for nonhuman creatures, and it shows God's deep desire to restore relationships between all species. This harmony between human and nonhuman animals is described in the Genesis creation story (Genesis 1:20–31). It is anticipated in Isaiah's promise of the wolf and the lamb lying down together (Isaiah 11:6–9). It is clear in Paul's testimony that Christ's power will reconcile all creation to God (Colossians 1:19–20).

For the first time, Jasmin understands that God's human and nonhuman creatures fundamentally belong together. The strong bond that unites them is more like a loving family relationship than an instrumental relationship between a steward and a resource. The word *kinship* captures the nature of this bond. (See Meyaard-Schaap, chapter 3.) Jasmin is confident that she wouldn't have been as receptive to understanding other creatures as part of God's family if she were still thinking of them and treating them like mere resources to be stewarded. And she is encouraged by the thought that her new behaviors are not only consistent with the Christian vision but also opening her to a richer, broader, more coherent understanding of it.

If we look at Jasmin's experience through a lens of defensiveness, her transformation may feel exhausting, and we might be moved to get defensive ourselves. You might even be tempted to stop reading this chapter to escape what seems like a spiraling process of tedious moral self-judgment that threatens not only your breakfast bacon but also most aspects of your consumer life. But note that this response is born of defensiveness, not curiosity, and that Jasmin's experience of the process need not be seen as tedious, judgmental, and filled with deprivation. On the contrary, led by curiosity and nourished by the comfort of moving toward consistency of belief and action, she actually experiences joy rather than deprivation. She doesn't need to make every change (or any change) overnight. She just needs to move slowly, deliberately, and joyfully toward a transformed vision of the world, and living in light of this transformed vision, in turn, inspires her to take increasingly transformative actions.

What she is doing is letting curiosity be her tutor and resisting defensiveness, allowing a transformation to occur at the level of her vision *and* her actions. These are not separate processes but rather a feedback loop in which Jasmin's behaviors expand her imagination and her imagination motivates new actions. In other words, *seeing* anew leads to *being* anew. New behaviors open the way to deeper insight, which prompts new behaviors, and so on.

As a finite, imperfect human being, Jasmin should expect to experience challenges and setbacks. There may be some robust dialogue, disagreement, and even social awkwardness with others in her community who are differently experienced and have different talents, gifts, and callings. Her efforts will never be perfect. But as long as Jasmin is motivated by a desire to see God's world more clearly and to investigate the ways in which her entrenched attitudes and behaviors can obscure her vision, she will continue to be engaged in this process of transformation.

From Personal Transformation to a Transformed Creation

Let's not lose sight of the fact that Jasmin is not the only one who stands to benefit from seeking a transformed relationship to God's nonhuman creatures. Our food system and the meat-heavy standard American diet contribute massively to the environmental crisis we now face. (See the introduction.)

We currently raise and kill almost ten billion land animals annually in the United States so that Americans can eat nearly three times the global average of meat per person per year (100 kg). Feeding these animals requires huge amounts of oil, land, and water to grow grain. The animals themselves produce unsustainable amounts of manure and greenhouse gases. Processing so many animals at a profit means that underpaid laborers must work in dangerous conditions. Further, this often-exploited workforce is disproportionately made up of minorities. Eating this many animals correlates with the rise of preventable diseases estimated to cost $314 billion a year in health care.[4] Meanwhile, as Jasmin discovered,

---

4 Modified versions of this paragraph appear in Matthew C. Halteman, "Eating Toward Shalom: Why Food Ethics Matters for the 21st-Century Church," *Banner*, February 19, 2018. https://www.thebanner.org/features/2018/02/eating-toward-shalom-why-food-ethics-matters-for-the-21st-century-church; and Andrew Chignell, Terence Cuneo, and Matthew C. Halteman, eds., *Philosophy Comes to Dinner: Arguments about the Ethics of Eating* (New York: Routledge, 2016), 1.

strong evidence suggests that a plant-based diet is the single most effective way for someone to reduce their negative environmental impact.

But even though we all stand to gain from reimagining our kinship with animals, we should recognize that some of us have a greater responsibility to do so. Those of us who enjoy the privilege of food autonomy—the freedom to choose from a variety of healthy foods we can afford—will have more flexibility to modify our diets. We should point out that people of goodwill disagree about how we should eat, even after reimagining our relationship to animals. More concretely, our fellowship halls will likely contain a mix of omnivores, vegetarians, and vegans even after everyone in the room has given some thought to these questions. Even so, we maintain that people who are able should strongly consider eating much less meat and many more plants. We see this intentional approach to eating as a powerful way to care for the creation in a twenty-first-century American context.

If we reimagine and transform our relationship to animals, then, all of creation stands to benefit. In particular, a journey like Jasmin's should move us *away* from viewing nonhuman creatures as resources for human use and *toward* envisioning ourselves as parts of a whole creation, called to build kinship with our fellow creatures.[5]

Works Cited

Chignell, Andrew, Terence Cuneo, and Matthew C. Halteman, eds. *Philosophy Comes to Dinner: Arguments about the Ethics of Eating*. New York: Routledge, 2016.

Halteman, Matthew C. *Compassionate Eating as Care of Creation*. Washington, DC: Humane Society of the United States, 2010.

---

5   This chapter draws on and extends some ideas that the authors developed previously in "Philosophy as Therapy for Recovering (Unrestrained) Omnivores," in *Philosophy Comes to Dinner: Arguments about the Ethics of Eating*, ed. Andrew Chignell, Terence Cuneo, and Matthew C. Halteman (New York: Routledge, 2016), 129–47. We are grateful to the Humane Society of the United States for permission to repurpose some material from Matthew C. Halteman, *Compassionate Eating as Care of Creation* (Washington, DC: Humane Society of the United States, 2010) and to the *Banner* for permission to repurpose some material from Matthew C. Halteman, "Eating Toward Shalom: Why Food Ethics Matters for the 21st-Century Church," *Banner*, February 19, 2018. https://www.thebanner.org/features/2018/02/eating-toward-shalom-why-food-ethics-matters-for-the-21st-century-church.

———. "Eating Toward Shalom: Why Food Ethics Matters for the 21st-Century Church." *Banner*, February 19, 2018. https://www.thebanner.org/features/2018/02/ eating-toward-shalom-why-food-ethics-matters-for-the-21st-century-church.

Petter, Olivia. "Veganism Is 'Single Biggest Way' to Reduce Our Environmental Impact on Planet, Study Finds." *Independent*, June 1, 2018. https://www.independent .co.uk/life-style/health-and-families/veganism-environmental-impact-planet -reduced-plant-based-diet-humans-study-a8378631.html.

Poore, J., and T. Nemecek. "Reducing Food's Environmental Impacts through Producers and Consumers." *Science* 360, no. 6392 (June 1, 2018): 987–92.

A New Worldview

Becky Roselius Haney

The Fault in Our Worldview

In *The Worst Hard Time: The Untold Story of Those Who Survived the Great American Dust Bowl*, journalist Timothy Egan describes the human tragedy that resulted from the massive ecological and economic disaster that occurred in the 1930s. In contrast to John Steinbeck, who tells the story of migrants who *left* the Dust Bowl in *The Grapes of Wrath*,[1] Egan tells the stories of the homesteaders who stayed. The compelling stories of people who lived through the Dust Bowl, and the illumination of the forces that caused it, reveal a fatal flaw in the predominant belief of that time: that human ingenuity can conquer any problem that nature presents. This mind-set led people to believe that they could use land, water, and other natural resources however they wished and invent their way out of negative side effects. "If nature is out of whack, then we'll fight with everything we got, they said at town meetings."[2]

---

1 John Steinbeck, *The Grapes of Wrath* (New York: Modern Library, 1939).
2 Timothy Egan, *The Worst Hard Time: The Untold Story of Those Who Survived the Great American Dust Bowl*, 1st Mariner Books ed. (Boston: Houghton Mifflin, 2006), 8.

The Dust Bowl was sparked by a recurring natural drought but was a man-made disaster. "Some environmental catastrophes are nature's work . . . The Dust Bowl, in contrast, was the inevitable outcome of a culture that deliberately, self-consciously, set itself that task of dominating and exploiting the land for all it was worth."[3] When farmers and ranchers looked over the open western plains dotted with sparse buffalo grass, they saw an empty wasteland waiting for human hands. Over the next four decades, they worked diligently to transform the rolling grasslands into neat, productive squares of wheat and alfalfa. Then, during the First World War, the government put pressure on farmers to produce more wheat, even guaranteeing the farmers an irresistible price of $2 per bushel.[4] The invention of the mechanized tractor increased agricultural productivity, making farming even more enticing. "In the 1830s, it took fifty-eight hours of work to plant and harvest a single acre. By 1930, it took only three hours for the same job."[5] Settlers uprooted the buffalo grass, tilled the virgin topsoil, and created hundreds of thousands of highly productive agricultural acres. This work often resulted in eye-popping financial gains. "The self-described wheat queen of Kansas, Ida Watkins, told everyone she made a profit of $75,000 on her two thousand acres of bony soil in 1926—bigger than the salary of any baseball player but Babe Ruth, more money than the president of the United States made."[6]

Even before the fantastic fortunes of the 1920s appeared, settlers had been drawn to the Great Plains to start a new life on the land. God-fearing farming families diligently bent to the perceived task of improving the land and their lives, providing food for many others in the process. From the settlers' perspective, the earth and its resources were meant to be used to support and enhance the quality of life for humans. However, the land, grass, and water of the plains had not been sitting idle, waiting to be put to use before the settlers arrived. The ecosystems were actively

---

3 Donald Worster, *Dust Bowl: The Southern Plains in the 1930s*, 25th ann. ed. (New York: Oxford University Press, 2004), 4.
4 Egan, *The Worst Hard Time*, 43.
5 Egan, *The Worst Hard Time*, 47.
6 Egan, *The Worst Hard Time*, 44.

participating in the joyful celebration of praise to which the creation is predisposed. In particular, the sparse clumps of buffalo grass that made the prairie look barren served a central role in the prairie ecosystem. Extensive root systems anchored the topsoil during times of drought, and dense cellular leaf structures provided rich fodder for the large mammals of that region.[7]

For centuries, the indigenous people inhabiting the land had understood the importance of buffalo grass to the prairie ecosystem. They understood the interdependency of all things. They kept the scale of their farms and settlements appropriate to the capacity of the land. Their human systems and the surrounding natural systems worked in harmony to survive many of the recurring drought seasons. "The Pueblo Indians have succeeded, in a few localities, and by a unique method, in raising maize without irrigation. The yield is too meagre to tempt the white man to follow their example, and for his use the region is agricultural only where it can be watered artificially," wrote John Wesley Powell.[8]

In contrast to the indigenous peoples, the new settlers could not imagine that the scale of their production could outstrip the capacity of the land. The land was providing families with incomes eight times or more that of a Ford factory worker. "People had been farming since Biblical times, and never had any nation set out to produce so much grain on ground that suggested otherwise. If the farmers of the High Plains were laying the foundation for a time bomb that would shatter the natural world, any voices that implied such a thing were muted."[9] The bomb exploded in 1931, the beginning of a decade of drought. Over 100 million acres of land were rendered barren. Hundreds of children and elderly died from dust-related pneumonia. Most homesteads were abandoned. No family emerged unscathed. Even by 1938, over 850 million tons of dirt continued to blow away from the Great Plains each year.[10]

---

7 Egan, *The Worst Hard Time*, 25.
8 John Wesley Powell, *Report on the Lands of the Arid Region of the United States, with a More Detailed Account of the Land of Utah. With Maps*, 2nd ed. (Washington, DC: Government Printing Office, 1879), 56,
9 Egan, *The Worst Hard Time*, 43.
10 Worster, *Dust Bowl*, 29.

Human ingenuity and backbreaking work initiated a booming economy. But the human economy could not endure because it had been created with too little regard for the ecological context within which it was embedded. Wholesale removal of the dominant buffalo grass and intense farming techniques were successful for several decades, but mechanized farming ultimately brought about the destruction of families, the economy, and the surrounding lands when drought returned. Without an informed understanding of how human and natural systems interrelate, the best intentions of ingenuity and hard work actually undermined the viability of an economy and the ecosystems on which it depended.

Today, we still fail to understand the interdependence of human and natural systems. On an even grander scale than the Dust Bowl, human activity is outstripping the capacity of the nonhuman creation to absorb the wastes from our energy-hungry economy. Pollution (including atmospheric carbon) is considered to be an isolated problem that can be solved by human ingenuity. But new inventions take time and money to create, so the economy must keep growing to provide the means to solve the problem that economic growth created in the first place.

A New Worldview

The prevailing Western worldview, including a traditional understanding of Christian Environmental Stewardship, divides the creation into human and nonhuman parts. This worldview ignores interdependent relationships between human and nonhuman parts of creation and considers humans to be independent managers over creation. We need a new worldview. These critical errors must be corrected. Humans should understand themselves as active participants within the creation and learn to live in affirming kinship with it. (See Meyaard-Schaap, chapter 3.) Acknowledging our interdependence with the nonhuman creation is necessary for the true flourishing of all creation.

If a faulty worldview contributes to environmental degradation, how might an improved worldview prevent it? One example is found in the same, albeit unlikely, place described above: the Dust Bowl. Forty years before the Dust Bowl, a few early settlers had just begun farming the land and raising cattle. Another natural drought occurred in the region, creating a mini dust bowl that nearly wiped them out. Their experience prompted the government to seriously consider an innovative but radical settlement plan proposed by Major John Wesley Powell.

Powell was a renowned geologist and celebrated leader of the first expedition to explore a landscape that included the area known today as the Grand Canyon. A few years before farmers began settling the Southwest in earnest, Powell published his 1879 *Report on the Lands of the Arid Regions of the United States*. Powell explained that the official approach to development (160-acre sections) would fail in this landscape. Instead, homestead boundaries and the scale of the communities should be carefully planned in advance. The size of farms and ranches should be based on the volume of water available from infrequent springs and streams. Small, interdependent communities, rather than isolated, self-sufficient farms, should be given collective responsibility for managing the water sources around which they were organized.[11] Powell's plan was based on a worldview in which settlers lived in community and in harmony with the land.

Unfortunately, Powell's plan was ignored. There was no patience for taking the time to learn how best to settle these new lands that had vastly different landscapes with vastly different climates from the East. In the rush to settle the land, the government carved out homestead parcels of land using the same approach that had been used in the humid East. The pattern of land use reflected the human-centered assumption that abundant quantities of land were ready and available to meet the demands of a growing population. Had Powell's approach been widely adopted, it very likely would have prevented the Dust Bowl and would have contributed to sustainable, flourishing communities.

Learning from the Past

How did Powell develop a proposal that was so different from the conventional wisdom of his time? Powell was a geologist who led expeditions to map the geography of the region. Powell was also an ethnologist, dedicated

---

11 Wallace Stegner, *Beyond the Hundredth Meridian: John Wesley Powell and the Second Opening of the West* (New York: Penguin, 1992), 226–27.

to learning the indigenous languages and cultures of the region. He lived among the Ute and Paiute peoples for several years. He became a trusted interpreter for the tribes and learned a great deal from them. A compelling 1871 photograph shows a relaxed Powell talking comfortably with Tau-gu, chief of the Paiute Nation in the Grand Canyon. Based on wisdom gained through generations of intimate knowledge of the land, the Utes, Paiutes, and other indigenous groups had learned to live in dynamic interdependence with the land. Powell most likely observed firsthand what Kat Anderson's revealing and extensive study of California's indigenous peoples confirms: "human cultures that established intimate relationships with plants and animals time and again informed and dictated the elements of harvest and management, and these practices eventually led to some measure of ecological harmony."[12]

Powell's experiences and a worldview informed by living in kinship with indigenous peoples led him to propose his "radical" approach to economic growth and development. Powell knew that people needed to take time to understand the creation and how to live carefully within it. He himself undertook extensive scientific studies to provide future settlers with knowledge of the land. Powell's surveys were meant to introduce the unfamiliar land to the new settlers and to suggest boundaries for farms and ranches. Powell's plan was based on a deliberate pace and a slow scale of economic growth that would allow the human and the nonhuman creation to flourish together over the long term. "Powell would proffer a wholly new outlook by claiming that Americans needed to listen not only to their hearts, pocketbooks, and deep aspirations, but to what the land itself and the climate would tell them."[13] Powell understood that the best way to care for the creation is to know it intimately. (See Rienstra, chapter 8.) He knew that we need to live in ways that recognize and celebrate our kinship with the creation. (See Meyaard-Schaap, chapter 3.)

---

12 M. Kat Anderson, *Tending the Wild: Native American Knowledge and the Management of California's Natural Resources* (Berkeley: University of California Press, 2005), 127.

13 John F. Ross, *The Promise of the Grand Canyon: John Wesley Powell's Perilous Journey and His Vision for the American West* (New York: Viking, 2018), 4.

Living out Powell's understanding of the interdependent relationship between human and nonhuman systems would have required patience, humility, and the acceptance of limits. Powell's plan and the worldview on which it was based were rejected because his geographic surveys, necessary for determining how best to apportion the land, would take too long to complete. Settlers, land developers, and politicians wanted to start mechanized farming as soon as possible. Settlers were ready to move their families and start their new lives. Railroad owners were ready to extend their networks. People in positions of political and economic power wanted to maintain and increase that power. So Powell's stern warning fell on deaf ears. Instead of learning how to live in harmony with the new land, settlers transformed the nonhuman creation into profit-making farms as quickly as possible. This new human worldview was imposed on the nonhuman creation with the assumption that hard work, human ingenuity, and grit would be more than sufficient to overcome any consequences that might arise.

To Powell's peers and the eager settlers, postponing development to learn how to live in kinship with the land seemed unnecessary at best and a damaging step backward at worst. Powell's plan was dismissed, even with the devastation of the earlier drought still within living memory. Thus, among the many causes of the Dust Bowl, we must include pride, willful ignorance, convenience, and impatience.

Similarly, powerful societies today refuse to accept the reality of climate change. The underlying condition then as today is a lack of humility in relation to the nonhuman creation. The settlers' attitudes toward the land did not change, even as they watched their world abruptly dry up and blow away. Jared Diamond's *Collapse: How Societies Choose to Fail or Succeed* presents even more case studies of past societies that failed to recognize the interdependence between human and nonhuman creation and ultimately failed economically, socially, and ecologically. Today's society, however, has knowledge of the past, advanced medical technology, and a greater technical ability to respond to problems as they arise than past societies.[14] But, as Diamond points out, the ability to respond does not

---

14 Jared Diamond, *Collapse: How Societies Choose to Fail or Succeed*, rev. ed. (New York: Penguin, 2011), 8.

necessarily provide the will to respond. "A society's responses depend on its political, economic and social institutions and on its cultural values."[15]

Western society lacks the will, not the ability, to respond to wicked social problems such as climate change. John Ross draws parallels between the Dust Bowl and today in describing this lack of will. Ross explains that Powell sought to remind the settlers and the politicians that we live in relationship with the creation and must adopt an attitude of humility in our relationship with the land. "It was not then, and not today, an easy message for Americans to hear," Ross writes.[16] One hundred years of experience and accumulation of scientific knowledge have passed since Powell pleaded for humility. In that time, even as our scientific knowledge of the biophysical interdependence between the human and the nonhuman creation has grown, we have moved even further away from an attitude of humility. In the technologically sophisticated twenty-first century, we are even less convinced that we live in kinship with the creation. Surrounded by streams of constant information, waves of automation, and mountains of concrete skyscrapers, we see living in kinship with the creation as a romantic or primitive notion. Nonetheless, all human societies—even technologically advanced ones—are interdependently reliant on the nonhuman creation. (See Bjelland, chapter 13.) Will we, and Western society as a whole, finally begin to respond in humility to issues such as climate change before we encounter another "Dust Bowl"?

Hopeful Alternatives

Although the window of opportunity is closing, there may still be time to change the global trajectory regarding environmental degradation and climate change. One of the hopeful ways forward lies hidden in plain sight among the lifeways of indigenous peoples. Kat Anderson shares in detail how indigenous peoples past and present live in relationship with the nonhuman creation. In her conclusion, she states, "A society's view of humans' place in nature shapes collective behavior toward other species.

---

15 Diamond, *Collapse*, 14.
16 Ross, *The Promise of the Grand Canyon*, 337.

The *kincentric* worldview of California Indians, wherein plants and animals are seen as blood relatives, fostered responsible treatment of other species because it established that they had an equal standing in the world and in fact had much to teach humans."[17]

Even today, we observe modern indigenous peoples living in interdependent relationship with the nonhuman creation. For example, the Menominee Nation of northern Wisconsin owns several enterprises, including the logging industry of their 235,000 acres of timber lands. In the late 1800s, the Menominee were restricted to a small, low-quality portion of their original lands. They have cultivated the forest since that time, and it has yielded over one-half billion board feet of lumber for their economy. Because Menominee timber harvesting is done carefully and sustainably, the forest is even more vibrant and diverse today than when they started, with over thirty tree species, 58,000 individual trees, and a host of other plants, insects, birds, and mammals supported by these trees.[18] In satellite images, the lush green "postage stamp" of the Menominee Forest stands out because it is surrounded by the sandy remains of clear-cutting.

The areas surrounding the Menominee Nation were originally vibrant, dense mixed hardwood forests. These areas were sold to lumber companies by the government in the late 1800s. Similar to what happened in the southwestern United States prior to the Dust Bowl, new towns sprouted up overnight, timber-related businesses grew rapidly, and the local economy boomed. But within sixty years, thousands of acres of forest lands were rendered tree-less, the booming economy dried up, and the population dispersed. The state of Wisconsin sold those barren expanses at a deep discount to farmers, hoping they could transform the land into productive agriculture. But it was too late. The clear-cutting techniques that had generated the greatest and quickest profit had left the land sandy and barren. Many of those lands are still barren today, healing slowly even in ecological time.

---

17 Anderson, *Tending the Wild*, 362 (emphasis added).
18 Christopher and Barbara Johnson, "Menominee Forest Keepers," American Forests, April 27, 2012, https://www.americanforests.org/magazine/article/menominee-forest-keepers/.

The contrast between the Menominee Forest and the surrounding areas illustrates how different worldviews play out either favorably or detrimentally on the social and ecological landscape. The Menominee Forest and the people who live in relationship with it have experienced slow and steady flourishing, while the societies in the surrounding areas experienced feast-and-famine economic oscillations. At first, the slow and steady growth of the Menominee economy was ridiculed by outsiders, derided as the result of laziness and incompetence. Yet the Menominee people and their worldview have stood the test of time. They have continued to thrive as a nation in an interdependent relationship with their small parcel of land.

Today, the Menominee apply the latest science to their harvesting techniques. Their technology is modern, but the scale of their economy is purposefully restrained by their relationship with the land. Their cultural heritage informs their business practices, as evidenced by their land ethic, which is proudly displayed on the homepage of their timber business: "Start with the rising sun and work toward the setting sun, but take only the mature trees, the sick trees, and the trees that have fallen. When you reach the end of the reservation, turn and cut from the setting sun to the rising sun and the trees will last forever.—Chief Oshkosh, Menominee Nation."[19] The forests have financial value, yes, but equally important is their environmental, cultural, and spiritual value. Similar to the success of other contemporary indigenous tribes, the success of the Menominee economy is the result of a worldview that has protected the ecological integrity of the portion of creation on which their economy depends.

A second hopeful alternative lies within the creative planning undertaken in rapidly growing urban areas, such as Curitiba, Brazil. From 1940 to 1960, Curitiba's population more than doubled, and the chaotic growth pattern that emerged mirrored that of the rest of Brazil. The city became clogged with cars and hemmed in by favelas (unregulated housing neighborhoods). In the 1970s, however, a group of young architects with a new approach that emphasized the interdependence of the human and the

---

19 Menominee Tribal Enterprises, accessed February 2, 2019, www.mtewood.com/.

nonhuman creation rose to prominence.[20] To win over the skeptical business leaders of Curitiba, these architects refashioned the large downtown as a pedestrian mall. The unexpected benefits of a more organic center were convincing. The visionary leaders went on to build an elaborate bus system that is used by 85 percent of Curitiba's residents today.[21] The city was eventually transformed to balance the built environment with the natural environment. Within the city, there are over fifty square meters of green space per person, as opposed to two square meters per person in cities such as Buenos Aires. The city residents divert 70 percent of their garbage from the landfill toward recycling and other uses. Curitiba's path to living in harmony with the nonhuman creation is one of many hopeful alternatives. Steven Moore's book, *Alternative Routes to the Sustainable City: Austin, Curitiba, and Frankfurt,* tells the story of two other global cities that are redesigning their infrastructure as they grow. All three cities are quite different in terms of political structure, but what they have in common is a "regime of sustainability" that fostered ongoing public conversation about sustainability. [22] Both the leaders and the citizens of these cities are aware of how intimately human well-being depends on creational well-being.

Conclusion

We need a widespread rediscovery and a fresh awareness of how intimately human well-being depends on creational well-being. A Christian Environmental Stewardship paradigm that assumes that humans are independent from the creation is unlikely to lead to long-term flourishing. In contrast, a kinship worldview is embedded within Scripture and Christian theology, as several other chapters illustrate. Thus, Christian environmental stewards should take a step back to gain perspective on our unquestioning acceptance of the Western worldview that values economic gain above all

---

20 David Adler, "Story of Cities #37: How Radical Ideas Turned Curitiba into Brazil's 'Green Capital,'" *Guardian,* May 6, 2016, https://www.theguardian.com/cities/2016/may/06/story-of-cities-37-mayor-jaime-lerner-curitiba-brazil-green-capital-global-icon.

21 Adler, "Story of Cities #37."

22 Steven A. Moore, *Alternative Routes to the Sustainable City: Austin, Curitiba, and Frankfurt* (Lanham, MD: Lexington Books, 2007), 13.

else. Separating human enterprises from the nonhuman creation and prioritizing human enterprises over the nonhuman creation end poorly for all involved. We have the opportunity to choose a better way, and Christians are especially equipped to do so. We profess a Savior who set aside personal interests and laid down his own life for the reconciliation of all things (Colossians 1). As his followers, we have the opportunity to speak boldly and live prophetically to advance an alternative worldview that promotes creational well-being in balance with personal economic gain. We have the opportunity to live actively in ways that illumine a rediscovered kinship with the creation.

Works Cited

Adler, David. "Story of Cities #37: How Radical Ideas Turned Curitiba into Brazil's 'Green Capital.'" *Guardian*, May 6, 2016. https://www.theguardian.com/cities/2016/may/06/story-of-cities-37-mayor-jaime-lerner-curitiba-brazil-green-capital-global-icon.

Anderson, M. Kat. *Tending the Wild: Native American Knowledge and the Management of California's Natural Resources.* Berkeley: University of California Press, 2005.

Diamond, Jared. *Collapse: How Societies Choose to Fail or Succeed.* Rev. ed. New York: Penguin, 2011.

Egan, Timothy. *The Worst Hard Time: The Untold Story of Those Who Survived the Great American Dust Bowl.* 1st Mariner Books ed. Boston: Houghton Mifflin, 2006.

Johnson, Christopher, and Barbara Johnson. "Menominee Forest Keepers." *American Forests*, April 27, 2012. https://www.americanforests.org/magazine/article/menominee-forest-keepers/.

Menominee Tribal Enterprises. Accessed February 2, 2019. www.mtewood.com/.

Moore, Steven A. *Alternative Routes to the Sustainable City: Austin, Curitiba, and Frankfurt.* Lanham, MD: Lexington Books, 2007.

Powell, John Wesley. *Report on the Lands of the Arid Region of the United States, with a More Detailed Account of the Land of Utah. With Maps.* 2nd ed. Washington, DC: Government Printing Office, 1879. DOI: 10.3133/70039240.

Ross, John F. *The Promise of the Grand Canyon: John Wesley Powell's Perilous Journey and His Vision for the American West.* New York: Viking, 2018.

Stegner, Wallace. *Beyond the Hundredth Meridian: John Wesley Powell and the Second Opening of the West.* New York: Penguin, 1992.

Worster, Donald. *Dust Bowl: The Southern Plains in the 1930s.* 25th ann. ed. New York: Oxford University Press, 2004.

Making Visible the Invisible:

Environmental Racism

Gail Gunst Heffner

My surprise caught my attention. A small group of us were walking along a highly industrialized section of Plaster Creek in the downstream reaches of its watershed. We were noting that the creek looks different there compared to other sections—more channelized, lots of broken concrete, steeply cut banks. We were talking about Plaster Creek's label as the most contaminated urban waterway in West Michigan. Because of high bacteria concentration, the creek is often deemed unsafe for even partial body contact, making it hazardous for wading or swimming.

As we were walking, we rounded a bend to see two people fishing! I didn't expect to see them. I didn't expect to find anyone interacting with the water along this section of the creek. They appeared to be a grandfather and his young grandson relishing a quiet moment together—one generation teaching a skill to the other. It could have been a scene from a classic American childhood. But they were *fishing in Plaster Creek*.

In that moment, I made a number of assumptions. I assumed this pair lived near the creek because they were African American and African American communities are prevalent in this part of the city. I assumed they were low-income because the man was fishing rather than working on a weekday. And I assumed they did not know the creek was contaminated with high levels of *E. coli* and other bacterial pollutants. I knew they were putting themselves at risk, and I felt an internal tension. Do I speak up and say something about the contaminated creek? Do I interrupt their quiet time together with disturbing information?

In the instant that my mind wrestled with whether to speak up or remain silent to allow them privacy, I also knew this was not an isolated incident. People are drawn to water—to its sights and sounds, to the way it reflects light and creates shadows, to its cool feel on the skin. In the Bible, water is intended as both a provision and a delight. Psalm 46 reminds us that "there is a river whose streams make glad the city of God" (v. 4). Yet here was a river that brings harm.

Observing firsthand the surprising sight of the boy and his grandfather woke me up to what had been invisible before. (See Halteman and Zwart, chapter 9.) Some people, particularly many black and brown people, do not enjoy the benefits of a vibrant, healthy place to live. People like me—white, educated, and middle-class—who do have the privilege of living in healthy places, often don't realize this privilege has not been available to everyone. Witnessing with my own eyes people who live in my city enjoying the calm and beauty of the flowing water, without adequate knowledge of how this might put them in harm's way, made the issue more real. It put a face on the reality that people of color in the United States are disproportionately impacted by environmental degradation. And it made me ask new questions: How did this urban creek become so degraded? Why are some neighborhoods safer, cleaner, and more desirable than others? Why do black and brown people experience more environmental risks than white people in the United States? Searching for answers to these and other such questions drove my curiosity and motivated me to learn more. (See Rienstra, chapter 8.)

While the literature on Christian Environmental Stewardship (CES) is important and necessary for understanding our responsibility as humans to care for the nonhuman creation, I have come to believe that CES is not sufficient to properly articulate all that is at stake. Much that has been written and spoken about CES makes no mention of the social constructs of race. Statements are made about stewardship that assume a common experience for all people and their interactions with the creation. Ignoring the influence of race and assuming common experiences lead to inequitable protection against environmental harm and inadequate representation when environmental decisions are made. This is environmental racism.

In the rest of this chapter, I will describe how we have come to this situation, describe environmental racism in more detail, and suggest some steps to overcome it.

Christian Environmental Stewardship Overlooks Systemic Racism

In 1967, historian Lynn White Jr. argued that the ecological crisis is the result of an anthropocentric Christianity in which human beings see themselves as being above nature.[1] White's article launched decades of responses that continue to this day. For more than forty years, the Christian Environmental Stewardship framework has encouraged Christians to protect and conserve resources, to limit greed and self-interest, and to think beyond the present to what future generations might need to survive and thrive. Numerous writers have agreed with White that anthropocentrism and objectification of the nonhuman creation are problematic. (See Al-Attas Bradford, chapter 5.) Some writers contend that ecological degradation is partly caused by the failure to recognize creation as a gift that has value beyond human usefulness.[2] (See Joldersma, chapter 4; and Warners, chapter 14.)

One insightful critique of White comes from theologian Kiara Jorgenson: "With five short pages in a scientific journal, Lynn White Jr. brought to the limelight the nexus of ecology and Christianity, *devoid of constructive*

---

1 Lynn White Jr., "The Historical Roots of Our Ecologic Crisis," *Science* 155, no. 3767 (March 10, 1967): 1203–7.
2 See the writings of Steven Bouma-Prediger, Bill McKibben, Brian Walsh, Wendell Berry, Loren Wilkinson, and Norman Wirzba, among others.

attention to race, shaping conversation for decades to follow up until our present day."[3] Jorgenson further acknowledges a weakness in much of the current Protestant theological reflection on ecology and environmental stewardship: because the conversation has been shaped predominantly by white male theologians and biblical scholars whose own lived experience is distant from the lived experience of people of color, race continues to be ignored. "The Protestant environmental movement has undervalued fertile grounds of lived experience and related sites of creative theological production, most notably created by communities of ethnic diversity."[4] Christians who take seriously the biblical commands to care for the earth and to care for our brothers and sisters must confront and correct this oversight. We can begin to do so by understanding the environmental impacts of systemic racism.

Environmental Racism and Injustice

Sociologists argue that racism is more than individual, personal prejudice. Racism is also the collective misuse of power that results in diminished life opportunities for particular racial groups. Some societies, such as the United States, are *organized* with racial hierarchies that inequitably allocate economic, social, and political rewards along racial lines.

Societies organized with racial hierarchies of superiority and inferiority create unequal opportunities and unequal life experiences without those who experience racial advantage even being aware of it.[5] Racialized societies also lead to unequal environmental protection and risk. Numerous research findings have documented that, in the United States, people of color and those in economically impoverished communities are exposed to greater environmental hazards in their homes, in their neighborhoods, and in their workplaces.[6] Both unequal opportunity and

---

3   Kiara Jorgenson, "White Blight and the Legacy of Protestant Ecotheology," *Word & World* 38, no. 2 (Spring 2018): 181 (emphasis added), https://wordandworld.luthersem.edu /content/pdfs/38-2_1968/38-2_Jorgenson.pdf.

4   Jorgenson, "White Blight and the Legacy of Protestant Ecotheology," 187.

5   Eduardo Bonilla-Silva, *White Supremacy and Racism in the Post–Civil Rights Era* (Boulder, CO: Lynne Rienner Publishers, 2001), 75.

6   Robert D. Bullard and Glenn S. Johnson, "Environmental Justice: Grassroots Activism and Its Impact on Public Policy Decision Making," *Journal of Social Issues* 56, no. 3 (2000): 555.

unequal environmental protection are examples of historically specific racism,[7] which leads to environmental injustice. Christians need to pay special attention to those who have borne a disproportionate share of environmental hazards and risks over time.

Land use patterns and policy-making are often tools of systemic racism, and they can produce racial and environmental inequality. When siting a landfill, city planners often choose land that is less expensive and less desirable—often land that is closer to where people of color live. Robert Bullard has documented, for example, that Houston, a city with five hundred neighborhoods, had no zoning laws, even as late as 2005. This created an erratic land use pattern in which city government and private industry "targeted Houston's black neighborhoods for landfills, incinerators, garbage dumps, and garbage transfer stations."[8] Bullard has detailed that public policy decisions authorizing construction of industrial companies and waste facilities often affect neighborhoods of people without political or economic clout. The people who are most affected have not been involved in the decision-making process and essentially have no voice to make things better. (See Bouma, chapter 12). Because these environmental threats have been invisible to and thus ignored by many white people in American society, many whites don't notice these threats as environmental injustice.

To summarize, environmental racism is twofold: the unequal protection against environmental harm and the exclusion of people of color from environmental decision-making that affects their communities. Ethical and political questions need to be raised about whose priorities dominate when decisions are being made about policies that impact the state of the environment. Whose suffering is acknowledged, and whose is ignored? Whose preferences count, and who is missing from the conversation?

Environmental Justice

Beginning in the late 1980s (shortly after the CES literature emerged), people of color and other marginalized people groups in the United States

---

7   Bonilla-Silva, *White Supremacy and Racism in the Post–Civil Rights Era*, 44–46.
8   Robert D. Bullard, ed., *The Quest for Environmental Justice: Human Rights and the Politics of Pollution* (San Francisco: Sierra Club Books, 2005), 44.

began to organize to confront the environmental threats they were facing. A movement advocating for environmental justice arose. In contrast to environmental racism, environmental justice is defined as "the fair treatment and meaningful involvement of all people regardless of race, color, national origin, or income with respect to the development, implementation, and enforcement of environmental laws, regulations, and policies."[9] No group of people should bear a disproportionate share of negative environmental risks or consequences. Environmental benefits and burdens should be shared equitably. Environmental justice also means that the people most affected by environmental threats or risks are able to make their voices heard and can share in decision-making that impacts their lives and communities. Too often people of color are not taken seriously when they speak up about ecological health and sustainability. The environmental justice movement attempts to uncover the underlying assumptions that contribute to and produce differential exposure and unequal protection.[10]

Why Dealing with Environmental Racism Is Difficult

Part of the problem in addressing environmental injustice is that it is too easy to focus merely on our own self-interest and to disregard dangerous situations others may face. One consequence of our human limitations is that we can't hold too many things in mind at the same time. (See Skillen, chapter 7.) If we are focusing on what is closest at hand, usually our own interests, it is easy to overlook the concerns of others.

Human limitations have implications for understanding the magnitude of environmental injustice. Very few Americans have any concept of how their decisions, actions, or behaviors can impact positively (or negatively) those around them. Two examples illustrate. First, American homeowners typically pay no attention to rain water. Few realize that rain water picks up contaminants as it pours off roofs, driveways, sidewalks,

---

9 Bullard, *The Quest for Environmental Justice*, 4.
10 For an extensive history of the environmental justice movement and its successes, see Dorceta E. Taylor, *Toxic Communities: Environmental Racism, Industrial Pollution, and Residential Mobility* (New York: New York University Press, 2014); and Robert D. Bullard, *Unequal Protection: Environmental Justice and Communities of Color* (San Francisco: Sierra Club Books, 1994).

and streets and flows into storm sewers, through which it is conveyed to local streams and creeks. But what happens upstream affects people who live downstream, oftentimes low-income communities of color. Second, when residents discard garbage, it is out of sight and out of mind. Yet garbage goes to a landfill, where it impacts those who live nearby, as documented by many environmental justice scholars.[11] Most residents have a lack of awareness of upstream-downstream connections. Beyond mere awareness is also the unwillingness to make moral choices or to take moral action to care for those living downstream.

Environmental justice becomes a question of whose interests count. How should decisions be made that take into account the interests of all people, not just the wealthy or the powerful? What will *prompt* people to consider the interests of others to be as important as their own? What will *provoke* people to exercise self-restraint for the common good? What will *persuade* people to take moral action to bring about environmental justice?

Recognition—Empathy—Lament—Restoration

I suggest that answering the above questions involves several steps. First, all people must recognize the reality of environmental racism. Next, privileged people must develop empathy for and learn from the people most affected by environmental injustice. Then privileged people must admit and lament complicity in the formation and perpetuation of environmental injustice. Finally, restorative action must occur.

Noticing the environmental degradation perpetrated on communities of color is an important beginning. The environmental impacts caused by systemic racism need to be recognized and acknowledged before they can be changed. However, neither recognition nor acknowledgment is enough to motivate needed change.

Privileged people need to have empathic encounters with nonprivileged people, to feel what they feel, to experience what they experience.

---

11 See Robert D. Bullard, *Dumping in Dixie: Race, Class, and Environmental Quality*, 3rd ed. (Boulder, CO: Westview Press, 2000); and Dorceta E. Taylor, *The Environment and the People in American Cities: Disorder, Inequality, and Social Change* (Durham, NC: Duke University Press, 2009).

White people and people of color need to experience each other's spaces, to listen to each other, to uncover barriers, to name injustice. Empathy has the potential to wake the privileged to what has been invisible to them. But for empathy to arise, people who may not typically "see" each other need to encounter each other in a space of mutual learning and respect. Those people in American society who have been falsely deemed as superior and have been given opportunities to acquire wealth and power need to have direct interactions with those in American society who have been falsely deemed as inferior and have been deprived access to wealth and power. We need occasions for those who have been ignored or excluded and those who have reaped the benefits of systemic racism to find solidarity. We need occasions—in our schools, our neighborhoods, our churches—for white people and people of color to genuinely encounter each other and experience the reality that their futures are in fact linked. Like my encounter with the boy and his grandfather, shared experiences between victims and beneficiaries of environmental racism can foster a sense of empathy.

Empathy can lead to lament—for the arrogance and self-satisfaction of privilege, for complacency and self-interest, for not considering the needs of other people and other creatures, and for failing to act when environmental injustice is apparent. Historically, there has been an absence of lament for environmental racism. Yet true, honest lament can be a motivating force for change. Lament can arise from grief for harm done to land, to water, and to people of color near and far. Lament prompted by empathic encounters can lead white people to work together with people of color to rebuild broken places. In retrospect, I wish I had spoken to the boy and his grandfather to invite them into the work being done to restore Plaster Creek. In lament, what began as mere recognition can be transformed into a commitment to take action. (See Heun, chapter 1.)

When empathy leads to lament and lament leads to the conviction that change is needed, Christians are challenged to put faith into intentional action to bring restoration. Because one aspect of environmental racism has been the exclusion of people of color from decision-making that affects communities of color, one way to initiate restoration is for decision-makers (many of whom historically have been white people) to learn from leaders of color and enable them to determine directions that will lead to restoration. People of color must occupy leadership roles when solutions are being considered and implemented. And white leaders need to listen and submit to leaders of color when restorative action is deliberated.

Two examples follow that showcase how environmental justice is fostered by recognition, empathy, lament, and restoration.

In Michigan, people of color are providing leadership to confront lead poisoning, an explicit example of environmental racism in their communities. Much has been written about the lead poisoning faced by residents in low-income communities of color in Flint.[12] The public outrage has been widespread and important. However, since 2015, Grand Rapids has reported the highest levels of lead poisoning and has had the largest number of children with elevated blood lead levels in the state of Michigan.[13] Lead poisoning can affect all racial groups and income levels, but low-income communities of color are disproportionately impacted by it. Recently, a group of parents with at-risk children organized to take action in Grand Rapids. Parents for Healthy Homes (PHH) calls attention to the environmental risks faced by local communities of color, and currently members are focusing on compelling city and county officials to require building inspections to ensure that a building is lead-free before it can be rented. Because there has never been such an inspection policy in place for rental properties, renters are at higher risk for lead exposure. Parents for Healthy Homes is an example of people of color recognizing a problem, providing leadership that will foster environmental justice, and fighting for policy change to safeguard children.

Young people also deserve opportunities to learn about environmental injustice and to develop eyes to recognize where it exists in their own

12 Yanan Wang, "In Flint, Mich., There's So Much Lead in Children's Blood that a State of Emergency Is Declared," *Washington Post*, December 15, 2015, https://www.washingtonpost.com/news/morning-mix/wp/2015/12/15/toxic-water-soaring-lead-levels-in-childrens-blood-create-state-of-emergency-in-flint-mich/?noredirect=on&utm_term=.e082757d40bd.

13 Dana Chicklas, "Data Shows Even Higher Lead Poisoning in Kids in West Michigan than Flint," *Fox 17 News*, January 4, 2016, https://fox17online.com/2016/01/04/data-shows-even-higher-lead-poisoning-in-kids-in-west-michigan-than-flint/.

communities. One hopeful example is a summer Green Team program in which high school youth learn about watershed restoration in West Michigan. Plaster Creek Stewards, working to return health and beauty to a highly degraded urban waterway, created the Green Team to introduce urban youth to environmental problems in their watershed through educational sessions and hands-on experience. Recently, the Green Team program expanded to include students from the Rogue River watershed, whose residents tend to be white, more suburban, and wealthier compared to Plaster Creek watershed residents. The young people from these two very different watersheds learn and work side by side. They make upstream and downstream connections as they practice how to care for their local waterways. Cross-cultural friendships have formed, and empathy and understanding are growing. And perhaps most important, Green Team members are undertaking tangible restorative action together.[14] The Green Team program provides occasions for young people to experience solidarity with one another, recognizing what they have in common despite their differences. (See Groenendyk, chapter 2 and Meyaard-Schaap, chapter 3.)

Christian Environmental Stewardship could be strengthened if people acknowledged the impact of race on human interaction with the creation. No one people group has all the answers to effective creation care, but all groups have something to contribute. Empathic encounters between people from different racial groups will help Christians recognize mutuality and interdependence. Empathy calls us to wake up to what has been invisible in the past and commit to taking action to promote environmental justice. African American theologian James Cone argues, "Only when white[s] realize that a fight against racism is a fight for *their* humanity will we be able to create a coalition of blacks, whites, and other people of color in the struggle to save the earth."[15] Christians interested in the work of reconciliation—reconciling people to God, to each other, and to the

---

14 David Warners and Gail Heffner, "Plaster Creek Stewards Summer Green Team to Train Youth in Watershed Restoration," *Rapidian*, June 3, 2014, https://therapidian.org/placematters -learning-doing-plaster-creek-stewards-summer-green-team-trains-youth-watershed -restoration.

15 James H. Cone, "Whose Earth Is It Anyway?" *Cross Currents* 50, nos. 1–2, (2000): 44–45.

earth—need to develop eyes to see what environmental racism has done, the honesty to lament its damage, the humility to learn from leaders of color, and the courage to collaborate in reimagining a way forward that brings healing and restoration for all the creation.

Works Cited

Bonilla-Silva, Eduardo. *White Supremacy and Racism in the Post–Civil Rights Era.* Boulder, CO: Lynne Rienner Publishers, 2001.

Bullard, Robert D. *Dumping in Dixie: Race, Class, and Environmental Quality.* 3rd ed. Boulder, CO: Westview Press, 2000.

———, ed. *The Quest for Environmental Justice: Human Rights and the Politics of Pollution.* San Francisco: Sierra Club Books, 2005.

———. *Unequal Protection: Environmental Justice and Communities of Color.* San Francisco: Sierra Club Books, 1994.

Bullard, Robert D., and Glenn S. Johnson. "Environmental Justice: Grassroots Activism and Its Impact on Public Policy Decision Making." *Journal of Social Issues* 56, no. 3 (2000): 555–78.

Chicklas, Dana. "Data Shows Even Higher Lead Poisoning in Kids in West Michigan than Flint." *Fox 17 News,* January 4, 2016. https://fox17online.com/2016/01/04/ data-shows-even-higher-lead-poisoning-in-kids-in-west-michigan-than-flint/.

Cone, James H. "Whose Earth Is It Anyway?" *Cross Currents* 50, nos. 1–2 (2000): 36–46.

Jorgenson, Kiara. "White Blight and the Legacy of Protestant Ecotheology." *Word & World* 38, no. 2 (Spring 2018): 180–89.

Taylor, Dorceta E. *The Environment and the People in American Cities: Disorder, Inequality, and Social Change.* Durham, NC: Duke University Press, 2009.

———. *Toxic Communities: Environmental Racism, Industrial Pollution, and Residential Mobility.* New York: New York University Press, 2014.

Wang, Yanan. "In Flint, Mich., There's So Much Lead in Children's Blood that a State of Emergency Is Declared." *Washington Post,* December 15, 2015. https:// www.washingtonpost.com/news/morning-mix/wp/2015/12/15/toxic-water -soaring-lead-levels-in-childrens-blood-create-state-of-emergency-in-flint-mich /?noredirect=on&utm_term=.e082757d40bd.

Warners, David, and Gail Heffner. "Plaster Creek Stewards Summer Green Team to Train Youth in Watershed Restoration." *Rapidian,* June 3, 2014. https://therapidian .org/placematters-learning-doing-plaster-creek-stewards-summer-green-team -trains-youth-watershed-restoration.

White, Lynn, Jr. "The Historical Roots of Our Ecologic Crisis." *Science* 155, no. 3767 (March 10, 1967): 1203–7.

WHO CAN BE A STEWARD?

Dietrich Bouma

E ven before we reached the Anamalai Tiger Reserve, we saw elephants. The students, my Indian colleagues, and I observed quietly
as three females of varying sizes encircled a small male "tusker"
fifty meters from our vehicle. Apparently undisturbed by us, the elephants
slowly ambled among the towering bamboo stands, eating vegetation and
tossing soil on their sun-speckled backs.

It wouldn't be our last animal sighting as we ascended the lush moun-
tainside toward the town of Valparai. We watched Nilgiri tahrs (endemic
mountain goats) traverse rocky outcroppings, Nilgiri langurs (endemic
monkeys) lounge on tree branches, and a mountain hawk-eagle survey
the landscape with piercing eyes, looking for prey. At our lunch spot one
thousand meters above the plains below, we watched a troupe of thirty
bonnet macaques emerge on the horizon. They fanned out across the
asphalt road, an alpha male leading the group directly toward us. Defense-
less, I clutched my chapati and dal. But the monkeys walked fearlessly
through our small crowd to the fig trees beyond. They owned the place.

As our vehicle eased over the mountain crest, the hairpin turns of the
road began to flatten, bob, and weave instead. Everything else changed too.

The towering broad-leaved evergreen and deciduous trees evaporated. The blue sky emerged. A monochrome landscape replaced the diverse color palette of tropical trees. A carpet of compact, flat-topped shrubs spread before us, glistening green and bright like a well-manicured lawn after rain.

We had reached the plantations. A patchwork of tea trees made an endless soccer-ball-like pattern on the landscape. Lone, slim silver oaks planted thirty meters apart provided the precise dose of shade for the sun-drenched trees. Each hexagonal plant nestled next to its neighbors in the optimal use of space. Their perfectly geometric arrangement echoed the large businesses, international markets, and economic metrics that engineered the fields before us.

Tea Labor

The majestic ascent and orderly tea-covered landscape of southwestern India is mesmerizing. But what captures my attention on each visit to Valparai are the tea laborors. Harvesting tea requires human power, and the engine of Indian tea plantations is poor Indian workers. Dressed in conspicuously bright, full-length clothes, they tend waist-high tea trees for meager wages.

In the early morning, they leave their small, estate-owned shacks and gather at the entrance to the estate-provided compound. They load into estate-owned vehicles that will carry them to the fields where they pluck leaf buds (the top three leaves only), apply dangerous pesticides, cart precious leaves, and trim the branches to keep the paths navigable. While they work, the laborers watch for harmful elephants, wild boars, and leopards that may stray into the fields. At the end of the day, the estate's trucks bring the laborers back to their one-bedroom shacks on the estate's compound. What free time laborers have can be spent at the estate-provided grocery stall. In exchange for a job they desperately need, a tea laborer's life is given to the plantation.

These days tea estates must recruit workers, and most come from thousands of kilometers away. They have little formal education and hail from India's low-income northeastern states of Odisha, Jharkhand, and Assam. The economics dictate this arrangement. Northeastern laborers will work for comparatively lower daily wages than laborers from other parts of India. The promise of higher wages and other perks attracts individuals and families to the tea estates, where they surrender much of their personal freedom.

Preaching on Environmental Stewardship

Each time I venture to Valparai to teach an undergraduate field course for local and North American students, my Indian colleagues ask the same question. On Saturday evening, after they obtain the consent of the pastor of the local church where we will worship, I get a knock on my hotel door. I am asked to deliver the sermon the next day. The thought of giving a sermon always makes me quiver. I feel inadequate to the task. I have no formal ministry training. And Indian pastors and priests memorize their sermons and deliver them flawlessly.

This year the circumstances accompanying the request were slightly different. I was asked to preach in a laborers' church on a tea plantation compound. I was also asked, perhaps to allay my obvious discomfort, "Maybe you could preach a sermon on Christian Environmental Stewardship (CES)?"

I perked up at the suggestion. I know enough Bible passages and stories to give a sermon on CES. And I give regular devotions on the topic throughout my course. On top of that, this tea plantation is in the middle of one of the world's biodiversity hotspots, the Western Ghats. Asian elephant, Bengal tiger, great Indian hornbill, and king cobra meander, roam, fly, and slither through these forests. An eye-popping number of species call it home: 139 mammals; 508 birds; 334 butterflies; 179 amphibians, including many found nowhere else; 288 freshwater fish; and 7,402 flowering plants.[1] If there ever was a place to preach about CES, this was it.

After I accepted the suggestion, I considered the congregants to whom I would be preaching. (See Groenendyk, chapter 2.) Then it struck me: there could not be a *less* appropriate topic for this particular audience. Even if I convicted them of their responsibility to care for the environment

---

1   "Western Ghats, India," World Wide Fund for Nature (WWF), 2019, http://wwf.panda.org /knowledge_hub/where_we_work/western_ghats/.

within which they lived and worked, they had no means by which to act on their convictions. The plantation estate owns everything around them. It dictates everything in their lives. The tea laborers have no agency to be stewards.

Society doesn't enable tea laborers to live out their calling to care for the earth. They work land not managed by them. They live on land and in shacks not owned by them. They eat few foods that they grow themselves. They purchase food from a store with few options stocked by their employer. They lack the ability to vote for people to represent their interests. They live in one of the most biodiverse places on the planet, yet they have been stripped of their ability to care for the land, water, and creatures around them. They do as they are told or as they are allowed by the tea estate.

The laborers have come to this position out of their poverty. Their dire economic circumstances deprive them of the power to participate in one of our God-given commands, to care for "the fish in the sea and the birds in the sky and . . . every living creature that moves on the ground" (Genesis 1:28). Thinking further, I realized they weren't alone. Many people, often those who are closest to land and water and who would know how best to care for the creation, have little power to do so. Unfortunately, the paradigm of Christian Environmental Stewardship is mute on this point.

Who Gets to Be a Steward?

The paradigm of CES correctly emphasizes that the call to care for the earth extends to all people based on God's commands to the first humans.[2] Every person is connected to the earth. Our food, shelter, and clothing all come from the earth. Every part of the built environment in which we live, work, and play comes from or is part of the earth. Indeed, we are earthlings. (See Joldersma, chapter 4.) The creation sustains us, and we all rely on it. We are embedded in local ecosystems and global cycles. We are part of food webs and nutrient cycles that tie us to all other creatures and nonliving elements of the earth. We are part of the biosphere. As such, we

---

2   Genesis 1:26; 1:28; 2:15.

bear responsibility for the ways that our actions contribute to sustaining the biosphere or lead to its unraveling. We *all* must care for creation. The earth is a commons, reliant on and relied upon by us all.

However, CES has a significant shortcoming: it has individualistic undertones (see the introduction) that emphasize personal responsibility for the piece of the creation that each person controls. CES implicitly assumes that individuals *have* control of a piece of creation. It assumes that individuals *can* exercise their personal responsibility. (For the Valparai tea laborers, both assumptions are false.) CES overlooks the collective nature of caring for the earth if we are to do it well. It ignores questions about which people can and should be involved with creation care. Consequently, CES does not fully appreciate the social relationships and power dynamics that mediate humanity's relationship with the nonhuman creation. A fuller understanding of our Christian call to care for the earth needs greater emphasis on both (1) our collective (as opposed to individual) responsibility to care for the earth and (2) removing the barriers that prohibit so many people from acting on this responsibility.

Agency Is Foundational

Before encountering tea laborers in Valparai, I had thought that caring for the earth required three things: passion, knowledge, and skills. Passion originates from having a love for the creation and a biblical and theological understanding of why God loves the creation. Knowledge comes from studying science and learning about the intricacies of the creation. Skills come from learning about the techniques we can use to preserve, conserve, sustain, manage, or restore the creation.

But the workers in Valparai reveal that passion, knowledge, and skills are not enough. The plantation laborers are knowledgeable, skilled, and thoughtful caretakers. Before becoming laborers, many lived on, worked, and cared for land their families owned for generations. Their traditional knowledge and skills are proved through time, grounded in place, and sustained by dependency on the land. Yet the laborers leave behind traditional ways to pursue a better economic life for their families. In so doing, they relinquish power to care for the land. To restore their role as caretakers of creation, they require something more foundational than passion, knowledge, and skills. They require agency. Without agency, their passion, knowledge, and skills have nowhere to go.

Who Are Disempowered?

If everyone is meant to participate in caring for the earth, it is important to identify those who are unable to do so. The tea laborers in Valparai are not alone in lacking agency to care for the earth. Over one million tea plantation workers pluck leaves in India's south and northeast states under similar or worse conditions.[3] Worldwide, the International Labour Organization estimates that there are 16.3 million migrant workers,[4] both long term as in Valparai and short term in many other places. However, disempowerment extends far beyond agricultural laborers beholden to the corporations for whom they work.

Many rural, landless households and displaced indigenous peoples also lack agency. Rural, landless people are often poor, ostracized, and disenfranchised. Landesa, an organization that strengthens land rights for women and poor households, estimates that there are hundreds of millions of landless people worldwide, and most of them are in rural areas.[5] The causes of landlessness include colonial policies (such as land seizures) and social structures (such as the caste system). Furthermore, tens of millions of indigenous peoples have been displaced from their ancestral homes to create protected conservation areas.[6] Throughout the centuries, indigenous peoples had developed practices that allowed them to live sustainably within the ecosystems found within their territories. (See Haney,

---

3   Jayaseelan Raj, "The Hidden Injuries of Caste: South Indian Tea Workers and Economic Crisis," Open Democracy, last modified June 29, 2015, https://www.opendemocracy .net/beyondslavery/jayaseelan-raj/hidden-injuries-of-caste-south-indian-tea-workers -and-economic-crisis.

4   ILO Labour Migration Branch & ILO Department of Statistics, *ILO Global Estimates on International Migrant Workers: Results and Methodology* (Geneva: International Labor Organization, 2018), 5, https://www.ilo.org/wcmsp5/groups/public/---dgreports/---dcomm /documents/publication/wcms_436343.pdf.

5   "Landlessness Is Not Forever," Landesa: Rural Development Institute, last modified March 9, 2011, https://www.landesa.org/landlessness-is-not-forever/.

6   Arun Agrawal and Kent Redford, "Conservation and Displacement: An Overview," *Conservation & Society* 7, no. 1 (2009): 1–10.

chapter 10.) Perversely, their ability to coexist with nonhuman creatures has lead to high levels of biodiversity and makes their land worthy of protection, which, ironically, justifies their displacement. For example, indigenous groups down the road from the tea plantation I visited have been systematically moved from their lands to create the Nilgiri Biore-serve for tigers, elephants, and biodiversity generally.

Not all examples are so extreme. Disempowerment is a matter of degree. As noted earlier, our relationship with the earth involves multiple areas of our lives (food, shelter, transportation) and multiple scales (local, state, regional, federal, and international). The multifaceted character of our relationship with the social and natural world means that people can be empowered in one area and disempowered in another. The tea plan-tation workers in Valparai lack agency to care for the land. But a person living at the federal poverty line in the United States may have little agency to make decisions about nutrition due to urban food deserts.

Social forces (economic, political, sociological, or psychological) often prevent people from participating in caring for our earthly commons. Eco-nomic forces can lead members of already poor households to take jobs that minimize agency, like the tea plantation workers in Valparai. Eco-nomic factors can also reinforce poverty within households through unjust compensation for labor. Lack of income limits choices and hence power.

Political forces can limit voices in public decision-making. For exam-ple, a person may be overlooked to participate on a committee or unjustly prevented from voting because they come from a certain ethnic group, family, or income level.

Sociological forces can reinforce social expectations and behaviors that discourage or limit participation. For example, a person born into a lower social class and lacking a strong educational background may be fearful of, or not even consider, participating on an environmental task force.

Lastly, psychological forces can reinforce debilitating stereotypes, feel-ings of lack of self-worth, or lack of belief in oneself. A person who doubts their abilities or intentions (due to race, gender, or social class) might hes-itate to add their voice to discussions about the ways we should care for the creation.

As a rule of thumb, those who lack agency for earthkeeping are disempowered in other areas of civic life too. Power relationships can be interpersonal, but more often they are structural. Race, gender, educational status, socioeconomic status, and familial status can all dictate who has earthkeeping agency and who does not.

Disempowerment based on gender and race is widespread in North American environmental organizations, government agencies, and foundations. Dorceta Taylor, a professor at the University of Michigan, analyzed each of these sectors for diversity in 2014.[7] She found that while women have made strides in leadership positions and entering the environmental workforce, they still lag far behind men in sitting on environmental boards and occupying leadership positions. The lack of minorities in environmental institutions is even more stark. Ethnic minorities and multirace individuals make up 38 percent of the US population but only 16 percent of the staff positions and less than 12 percent of the leadership positions in environmental organizations.[8] There are many reasons for these statistics, but the strongest driver lies in the history of structural racism and sexism in the United States. (See Heffner, chapter 11.) After reading Taylor's report, I have often asked myself, "Who is sitting at the (boardroom, staff, community meeting) table?" when a specific environmental issue arises. The answer indicates who has agency.

Expanding Christian Environmental Stewardship

The Christian responsibility to serve and protect the earth may better be understood as Christian commons care. Emphasizing our planet as a commons is an important step. But our understanding of the commons needs to expand to include both the social and the ecological, both the communal and the personal. When it does, we can add social and communal building blocks to the foundation of Christian Environmental Stewardship.

---

7   Dorceta E. Taylor, "The State of Diversity in Environmental Organizations," Green 2.0, July 2014, http://orgs.law.harvard.edu/els/files/2014/02/FullReport_Green2.0_FINALReduced Size.pdf.
8   Taylor, "The State of Diversity," 4.

Christians need to care for one another to ensure that we can be effective collectively in caring for our planet. One way we can care for one another is to pay attention to who has agency and who does not in environmental decision-making. Who controls financial and environmental resources? How are resources distributed? How are decisions made? Whose preferences count? (See Heffner, chapter 11.) Once we understand these power dynamics, Christians should find ways to relink disempowered people to commons caretaking. Those who have agency should identify, involve, listen to, and strengthen those who don't.

Case Study in Empowerment

An outstanding example of expanded agency is the community forestry program in Nepal. Ten years ago, I traveled to Nepal to study how climate change was affecting local communities. I spent much of my time with community forest user groups, organizations of local households who collectively manage and care for a local forest. The Nepali government started taking possession of forest lands from individuals and communities in 1957. Common wisdom at the time was that governments could best manage forests for the public good. (See Skillen, chapter 7.) However, the Forest Department did not have the capacity to manage all of Nepal's forests, and lax enforcement of laws led to deforestation. To correct these failures, the Nepali government implemented a national community forestry program in 1988. Since then, hundreds of community forest user groups have been formed each year.

The community forest user groups are democratic: all households participate and vote on decisions. They have an elected board that leads the group, and a woman from the community must be the chair or vice chair. This requirement is sensible, for women often know the forest most intimately. They travel regularly to the forest to collect firewood, fodder, and leaf bedding as they cook for their families and care for the household livestock. From my observations, women are also the primary responders to forest fires. Because men often migrate for work, women play an outsized and critical role in the community and in forest protection.

Under the community forestry program, each community forest user group writes a five-year management plan for their forest with the technical support of the Nepali Forest Department. The management plans outline what and how much can be collected from the forest: firewood for cooking, grasses to feed livestock, leaves for livestock to sleep on, medicinal plants, and more. The groups may decide to protect areas around streams to safeguard water sources. They may also set aside certain parts of the land for restoration, if deemed necessary.

Community forest user groups collectively police their forests to prevent theft. Policing is often done with forest guards hired from within the community. Social pressures provide additional enforcement: a local person caught stealing would bring embarrassment and potential backlash from the community. Reputations are on the line.

All community forest user groups I visited were fascinating and filled me with hope, but the Godawari Kunda group stood out. Their 350-hectare forest is thirty minutes outside the capital of Kathmandu. The elders in the village have records documenting sustainable care for their forest commons stretching back two hundred years, with one exception. In 1973, the Nepali government took control of this forest on behalf of the Nepali Army. The Army clear-cut the forest in five years, then vacated. The forest took sixteen years to begin to regenerate.

Godawari households first formed their community forest user group in 1995. They appoint an eleven-person board and hold annual meetings to determine how to care for their forest. Membership is comprised of different castes and ethnic groups. The first board included a female vice chair and a number of other women in leadership.

The forest products that Godawari households collect make significant contributions to their lives. They save money on food for domesticated animals, fuel for cooking, and timber for building. The community forest user group itself receives revenue from selling forest products and uses those funds to offset school fees for lower-income households and to purchase electricity for the entire community. Because they have protected a stream with vegetation, they can sell some of the water to their local government.

The group has built relationships with conservation organizations as well. They documented over three hundred species of birds, which led to a partnership with the organization Birds of Nepal. They have cataloged a wide variety of creatures, including leopards, jackals, and wild boars.

Godawari Kunda (and Nepal's community forestry program as a whole) is an example of moving from a lack of agency to empowerment. Together, the community forest user group members work to serve and protect their local forest. The community is reempowered as a whole, and the group creates space for historically marginalized people to have a voice in group decision-making.

What might a similar transformation from powerlessness to empowerment look like for the tea plantation workers in Valparai? Perhaps tea corporations could be converted into cooperatives in which workers share ownership and contribute to decision-making about the direction of the company. Perhaps policies could better support rural and peasant farmers in India so that they can stay on family lands that they know so well.

Finally, what about environmental issues in our own backyards and local communities? Who has agency to address them? Who does not? When we develop answers to these questions, we live into a hopeful future of a shared, earthly commons to which all participants bring gifts of faith, experience, and insight to address critical, complex issues with the fullness they require.

Works Cited

Agrawal, Arun, and Kent Redford. "Conservation and Displacement: An Overview." *Conservation & Society* 7, no. 1 (2009): 1–10. http://www.jstor.org/stable /26392956.

ILO Labour Migration Branch & ILO Department of Statistics. *ILO Global Estimates on International Migrant Workers: Results and Methodology*. Geneva: International Labor Organization, 2018. https://www.ilo.org/wcmsp5/groups/public /---dgreports/---dcomm/documents/publication/wcms_436343.pdf.

"Landlessness Is Not Forever." Landesa: Rural Development Institute. Last modified March 9, 2011. https://www.landesa.org/landlessness-is-not-forever/.

Raj, Jayaseelan. "The Hidden Injuries of Caste: South Indian Tea Workers and Economic Crisis." Open Democracy. Last modified June 29, 2015. https://www .opendemocracy.net/beyondslavery/jayaseelan-raj/hidden-injuries-of-caste -south-indian-tea-workers-and-economic-crisis.

Taylor, Dorceta E. "The State of Diversity in Environmental Organizations." Green 2.0, July 2014. http://orgs.law.harvard.edu/els/files/2014/02/FullReport_Green2.0 _FINALReducedSize.pdf.

"Western Ghats, India." World Wide Fund for Nature (WWF), 2019. http://wwf .panda.org/knowledge_hub/where_we_work/western_ghats/.

13

FROM STEWARDSHIP TO PLACE-MAKING AND PLACE-KEEPING

Mark D. Bjelland

My backpack was packed and stored beneath my bed. Inside was my sleeping bag, pup tent, poncho, pocketknife, and official Boy Scout canteen. Each item was precious and carefully considered. Every dollar from every lawn I mowed and every sidewalk I shoveled went toward camping supplies. I didn't have plans for any upcoming trips. But I kept my backpack ready, just in case. I felt trapped in the city and dreamed of escape. The books I read were a mix of nature writing and how-to books on wilderness living, edible wild plants, and backpacking. I hoarded my mom's copies of *Mother Earth News*. My mom, dad, stepdad, and stepmom were all Midwest farm kids who had ended up, reluctantly, in Chicago or Minneapolis. At age twelve, I was a new Christian and learning to pray. I remember sitting at an overlook one day, praying that God would rescue me from the city and set me free to live in the wild. I scoured the classified ads, looking for a job in the north woods for my stepdad, who worked for the Minneapolis Housing and Rehabilitation Authority.

Slowly, my attitudes began to change. My church youth group became a community where I felt a sense of belonging. My youth leader taught us to explore the city. He took us on scavenger hunts in downtown alleys and spelunking beneath city streets. He introduced us to worship with black churches, where the music and the preaching stirred something deep within me. I fell in love with my city and its people, its history, its problems, its parks, its ghettos, its decrepit mills, and its hilltop mansions. At university, where I started as a civil engineer, I found myself working on transportation, flood control, and environmental cleanup projects to better my hometown. I volunteered with my neighborhood organization and served on city commissions. In short, I learned to love and care for a place that was not my ideal but was the place that over time had become my home.

Although it is tempting to associate environmental stewardship with living on a solar-powered organic farm far from city lights or doing ecological research in a pristine cloud forest, most of us should focus on the streets, fields, neighborhoods, watersheds, towns, and cities where we live. These places are where both environmental problems and solutions are to be found. These are the places with real neighbors we are called to love. Stewardship needs to begin at home, not in some distant, untouched environment, and it should be reimagined as a call to faithful place-making and place-keeping.

Place and Environment in the Scriptures

Over the past forty years, evangelical Protestants have published a number of important books on environmental stewardship. Authors Loren Wilkinson, Calvin DeWitt, and Steven Bouma-Prediger each frequently return to the first chapters of Genesis in search of a biblical vision of what it means to be human and how we should relate to the rest of the created world.[1] Their works of theological reimagination have been done in the shadow of Lynn White Jr.'s influential thesis, which claims that the roots of the

---

1 Loren Wilkinson, ed., *Earthkeeping in the Nineties: Stewardship of Creation*, rev. ed. (Grand Rapids: Eerdmans, 1991); Calvin DeWitt, *Caring for Creation: Responsible Stewardship of God's Handiwork* (Grand Rapids: Baker, 1998); and Steven Bouma-Prediger, *For the Beauty of the Earth: A Christian Vision for Creation Care* (Grand Rapids: Baker, 2001).

contemporary ecological crisis are to be found in the Judeo-Christian ethic of dominion. White traced Western ecological destruction back to God's charge to the first humans in Genesis 1:26–28 to exercise dominion over and subdue the earth.[2] Wilkinson, DeWitt, and Bouma-Prediger reject White's interpretation of Genesis 1 as a license for domination. Drawing on the second creation narrative found in Genesis 2, these authors reinterpret dominion as a call to responsible caretaking in service to creation. (See Joldersma, chapter 4; and Bouma-Prediger, chapter 6.) Where the NIV translated Genesis 2:15 as a divine mandate to the first human "to work . . . and take care of" the Garden of Eden, these authors shift the emphasis to a call to *abad* (serve) and *shamar* (keep) the garden of creation.

While the Christian Environmental Stewardship paradigm awakened new biblical insights and inspired important acts of creation care, it failed to reconcile the stewardship mandate in Genesis 2 with the cultural mandate in Genesis 1. The first chapter of Genesis emphasizes that humans are created in the image of God, blessed, and assigned the tasks of filling the earth and ruling over the creation (dominion). (See Bouma-Prediger, chapter 6.) In the second chapter of Genesis, the first humans are tasked with serving the creation to encourage its flourishing (stewardship). Perhaps the hesitation of some Christians to fully embrace environmental stewardship can be traced to unresolved tensions between dominion and stewardship or between affirming the uniqueness of humans and affirming the value of the nonhuman creation. (See Meyaard-Schaap, chapter 3.) Thus, many Christians have rightly wondered how creation care relates to the great commandment to love God and our neighbor. The concept of place offers a path forward because places contain both human and nonhuman elements, social relationships, and ecological relationships. Places integrate all aspects of creation.

Places matter in Scripture because both the created order and physical embodiment are gifts from God. (See Warners, chapter 14.) Places provide a setting for the flourishing of both human and nonhuman life. As such, they are central to the biblical vision of shalom. The biblical narrative

---

2 Lynn White Jr., "The Historical Roots of Our Ecologic Crisis," *Science* 155, no. 3767 (March 10, 1967): 1203–7.

begins with God creating a place—the Garden of Eden. The Garden of Eden was a focus of divine and human care, a place of embedded relationships where the first humans enjoyed intimate fellowship with each other and with the nonhuman world and where God walked and spoke with them. The story of the Jewish people is intimately connected to the gift of place— the Promised Land. Biblical history ends with God creating another type of place—the garden city of the New Jerusalem. The author of Revelation uses all his descriptive power to describe this place, which is so beautiful, so wonderful, so pure and good that it is beyond all imagining. Using the conceptual framework of place, we can put the two creation narratives together, the stewardship and the cultural mandates. Taken together, Genesis 1 and 2 present a call to build and to tend, to fill up and to protect the various corners of the earth where God has placed us. In short, the first two chapters of Genesis issue a call to both place-making and place-keeping.

Seeing the World through the Lens of Place

The concept of place, as elaborated within cultural geography, is rich with insights for ethical engagement with God's world. In everyday terms, the word *place* is often used interchangeably with *space*. But in geographic usage, a space is simply a set of geographic coordinates, whereas a place is a location that has become meaningful through human habitation. Spaces become places through human experience and attention. For a New Yorker, the Midwest might be "flyover country," that is, a space of little interest or value. But for someone who has lived long in the Midwest and developed strong connections to neighbors and the land, the space is transformed into a meaningful place.

Each place is unique because it assembles three elements: (1) a material setting, (2) a set of social relationships, and (3) lived experiences that impart personal and shared meanings.[3] In architecture and urban

---

3   This definition represents a synthesis of the following: Yi-Fu Tuan, *Topophilia: A Study of Environmental Perception, Attitudes, and Values* (Englewood Cliffs, NJ: Prentice-Hall, 1974); John A. Agnew, *Place and Politics: The Geographical Mediation of State and Society* (Boston: Allen & Unwin, 1987); Doreen B. Massey, *Space, Place, and Gender* (Minneapolis: University of Minnesota Press, 1994); and Robert David Sack, *Homo Geographicus: A Framework for Action, Awareness, and Moral Concern* (Baltimore: Johns Hopkins University Press, 1997).

planning, place-*making* refers to creating high-profile public places such as Chicago's Millennium Park, while place-*keeping* refers to the care and maintenance of such spaces. Going beyond their technical usage, we should think of place-making as all the ways that humans turn a location (or a space) into a place—by naming its features, tilling the soil, harvesting trees, planting gardens, building cities, and so forth. (See Rienstra, chapter 8; and Haney, chapter 10.) Place-keeping, then, simply refers to all the ways we care for our place—by visiting neighbors, picking up trash, protecting a stream, painting a house, attending a community meeting, and the like. (See Heffner, chapter 11.) Place-making and place-keeping encompass more of the breadth of Scripture than stewardship. We engage in place-making and place-keeping when we fill the earth, when we preserve God's creation, and when we love our neighbors.

Beyond Dualisms and Dichotomies

I have taught many classes with "earth," "environment," or "nature" in their titles. Yet when it comes to living faithfully as God's stewards, I suggest we rethink our relationship to God's creation in terms of place rather than environment, earth, nature, or wilderness. Compared to terms such as *environment* and *nature*, the concept of place gives us humans a specific location to stand and a meaningful role to play. The problem with the terms *environment* and *nature* is that they are both based on dualisms that divide and separate humans from the nonhuman world.

The term *environment* is defined as that which is outside an organism. Scholarship on human-environment relationships has tread two well-worn paths. The first, environmental determinism, dominated anthropology and geography in the early twentieth century. Environmental determinism considered the environment to be the controlling force, shaping cultural evolution. The second path heads in the opposite direction of environmental determinism. It arose in the late twentieth century as we began to recognize the widespread human destruction of earth systems. Contemporary scholarship in geography and environmental studies focuses on humans' impact on the environment, construed in overwhelmingly negative terms.

175

The term *nature* contains a similar dualism, finding its meaning in opposition to culture. But when nature is understood as the absence of human culture, can humans and their works ever be natural? We think of beaver lodges as natural but houses and office buildings as unnatural. Environmentalists often remind us that we are part of nature and admonish us to redesign our buildings and landscapes so they better fit into the natural world. But thinking in terms of the nature/culture dichotomy traps us. If we are part of nature, then whatever we do is natural. A beaver doesn't have to decide to act natural or to fit better into nature.

Nowhere is this opposition between nature and culture more pronounced than in the concept of wilderness, which deeply influenced the environmental movement and inspired my childhood imagination. Modern ideas of wilderness are largely indebted to the Romantic movement, which embraced pristine nature as the antidote to a corrupt culture and civilization. As enshrined in law by the US Wilderness Act of 1964, wilderness is defined as a pristine environment "untrammeled by man, where man himself is a visitor who does not remain."[4] The language of the Wilderness Act reflects a culture alienated from God's creation, for it sees the human presence only as a contaminating influence.

My family tries to take a canoe trip in the Boundary Waters Canoe Area Wilderness each summer. We sweat and strain across wind-swept lakes and rocky portages, imitating the work of indigenous peoples and voyageurs of old. The wilderness ideal privileges play over work and the interests of white-collar urban professionals like myself over working-class loggers or miners whose opportunity for income is curtailed in wilderness areas. As if privileging one social class over another were not enough of a problem, the wilderness ideal gives us an excuse for neglecting the places in our everyday lives—the towns, cities, and suburbs we call home.

Embracing People and Cities

Thinking in terms of place helps us resist the low view of humanity that continues to lurk in the environmental movement. It is common in

---

4   Wilderness Act, Public Law 88-577, 16 U.S. C. 1131-1136 (1964), https://www.nps.gov
     /subjects/wilderness/upload/1964-Wilderness-Act.pdf.

environmental circles to hear humans described as a weed species. Some environmental scholars suggest that if our job is to steward the creation, then we should start by reducing our numbers.[5] Once when an academic colleague announced that she was pregnant with twins, the founder of her college's environmental studies program shot back, "Well, I sure hope you'll stop after this pregnancy." No excitement. No congratulations. Just an insensitive comment from a zero-population growth advocate. After all, if the earth and its ecosystems are tainted by the human presence, wouldn't it be better if most humans just disappeared? But seeing the earth through a place framework is to acknowledge that we humans are not a weed species. God has placed us here, and it is people who choose how to turn a space into a place, imbuing it with life, human initiative, memory, and meaning. In praise, the mountains and hills burst into song, the trees of the fields clap their hands, and the heavens declare the glory of God. But humans have a unique role to play in helping to voice, through prayer, song, poetry, or art, each place's praise of the Creator.

The nature/culture dichotomy has tended to shape a view of urban and industrialized places as fallen and less worthy of care. A towering oak in an ecosystem preserve is somehow perceived to be more beautiful than one on a city street. But there is an expansiveness to the concept of place that allows us to speak of place-keeping in all kinds of settings. A place may be an old-growth forest or a city square surrounded by high-rise buildings and buzzing with human activity. Place-keeping is equally applicable in the Costa Rican rainforest and the scarred industrial landscapes of Flint, Michigan. If we view the world through the lens of place instead of nature or environment, we are more likely to consider urban places as equally important as rural or wild places.

Humans, like other species, adapt to and transform their environment, and villages, towns, and cities are the typical human habitat. When Loren Wilkinson's *Earthkeeping* was published in 1980, the world's urban population was 1.5 billion. The world's cities are now home to 4 billion people

---

5   Gene Wunderlich, "Evolution of the Stewardship Idea in American Country Life," *Journal of Agricultural and Environmental Ethics* 17 (2004): 89.

and will capture virtually all of the world's future population growth so that by 2050 they will house 6.7 billion people. Cities are perhaps humanity's greatest invention and contribute in myriad ways to human flourishing. With their transit systems and density of goods and services, cities offer the possibility of living with much less impact on the planet.[6] But most cities do not live up to their potential, possibly because we see them as unnatural and therefore less worthy of care.

Embracing the Interplay of Humans and Nonhumans

One of the key features of a place is its material setting, which is a blend of human and nonhuman elements. Even in a designated wilderness, cultural elements are present. A wilderness area exists because of rules, management policies, and mapped boundaries. Conversely, the first of the three dimensions of place (material setting) offers a reminder of our inescapable connections to the material world. The world is far more than a social construction. Even in an urban center where the works of humans dominate, there are nonhuman systems and creatures all operating in their own way. Biodiversity hotspots exist in urban areas right in the shadow of freeways, high-rises, and heavy industrial zones.[7] The world's most livable cities celebrate this interplay of the human and the nonhuman. For example, Berlin, Germany's capital and largest city, has integrated biodiversity conservation into its urban planning and has some of the most diverse and dense bird populations in the entire country.[8]

Within a place framework, we don't need to purify the wilderness by ignoring or erasing cultural traces the way that the Romanticism-tinged wilderness preservation movement has done. The myth of the pristine American wilderness has long prevented scientists and environmentalists from seeing the extent to which New World landscapes were modified

---

6 David Owen, *Green Metropolis: Why Living Smaller, Living Closer, and Driving Less Are the Keys to Sustainability* (New York: Riverhead Books, 2009).

7 Michael L. Rosenzweig, *Win-Win Ecology: How the Earth's Species Can Survive in the Midst of Human Enterprise* (New York: Oxford University Press, 2003).

8 Jens Lachmund, *Greening Berlin: The Co-Production of Science, Politics, and Urban Nature* (Cambridge, MA: MIT Press, 2013).

by indigenous peoples.[9] John Muir, the founder of the Sierra Club, wrote beautiful prose in praise of natural beauty but was disgusted by the indigenous tribes in Yosemite Valley and encouraged their removal.[10] In park after park, the idealized notion of wilderness in which "man is a mere visitor" has led to expulsions of long-term users and residents.[11] At Isle Royale National Park, this idea meant relocating the Scandinavian American fishing community and burning their cabins and boathouses. At Glacier National Park, it meant treating the Blackfoot tribe's legal hunting rights as illegal poaching. And in the developing world, it means displacing subsistence hunting/gathering or agricultural societies in the name of preserving a pristine material setting.[12]

Place-Making in Action

A place framework also anticipates that human work can restore and improve God's creation. (See the introduction.) In Boston, Frederick Law Olmsted's design for the Fens and Riverway restored a highly polluted and flood-prone landscape by implementing functional drainage and a rich habitat. It has become a wonderfully enjoyable emerald necklace running through the heart of the city. Today, visitors and residents enjoy the beautiful waterways and woodlands, unaware of the extensive human role in their creation. Olmsted's shortcoming was to conceal his engineering so well that today's visitors miss this example of place-making and landscape improvement.[13]

---

9 Charles C. Mann, *1491: New Revelations of the Americas before Columbus* (New York: Knopf, 2005); and William Cronon, *Changes in the Land: Indians, Colonists, and the Ecology of New England* (New York: Hill and Wang, 1983).

10 Mark David Spence, *Dispossessing the Wilderness: Indian Removal and the Making of the National Parks* (New York: Oxford University Press, 2001).

11 Karl Jocoby, *Crimes against Nature: Squatters, Poachers, Thieves, and the Hidden History of American Conservation* (Berkeley: University of California Press, 2001).

12 Stan Stevens, *Indigenous Peoples, National Parks, and Protected Areas: A New Paradigm Linking Conservation, Culture, and Rights* (Tucson Basin: University of Arizona Press, 2014); and Alexander Zaitchik, "How Conservation Became Colonialism," *Foreign Policy* (July 16, 2018): 58–63.

13 Anne Whiston Spirn, "Constructing Nature: The Legacy of Fredrick Law Olmsted," in *Uncommon Ground: Rethinking the Human Place in Nature*, ed. William Cronon (New York: W. W. Norton, 1996), 91–113.

In the Amazon Basin and several other tropical forest regions around the world, *terra preta* soils are islands of high fertility amid typically low-nutrient tropical soils. Terra preta soils are dark black and are the product of millennia of pre-Columbian human habitation. Regular additions of biochar—biomass charred in smoldering fires—produced soils that store large amounts of carbon and nutrients. These human-influenced soils, with their high fertility and ability to remove carbon from the atmosphere, date back seven thousand years and yet are valuable models for twenty-first-century sustainable agriculture.[14]

Connecting the Social and the Ecological

A place framework encompasses the social dimensions to our dwelling on the earth. It anticipates the sustainable development paradigm that broadens the focus of environmental thinking to a triple bottom line of ecological, economic, and social sustainability. Social dimensions are important, because it is insufficient for me to care for God's creation on my own through recycling, gardening, and restoring native plants. My impacts on the earth are mediated by economic and political systems beyond my direct control. (See Skillen, chapter 7; and Bouma, chapter 12.) Similarly, I cannot create a good place by myself. Others must be involved. Place-making and place-keeping are inherently socio-political-economic projects that involve legislation, city planning, transportation system operations, municipal government operations, and community building as much as individual efforts. Environmental action is often shaped by ecological and economic considerations, at the expense of its social dimensions. But all too often the social aspects of environmental problems are the more difficult to overcome. The concept of place has the benefit of incorporating the social dimensions of environmental action.

When we focus our stewardship on an environment that is outside of us, we tend to separate ecological issues from social issues. But places are mixtures of peoples and environments that contain both human and

---

14 Bruno Glaser, "Prehistorically Modified Soils of Central Amazonia: A Model for Sustainable Agriculture in the Twenty-first Century," *Philosophical Transactions—Royal Society of London, Biological Sciences* 362, no. 1478 (2007): 187–96.

nonhuman elements. The interweaving of the social and the environmental means, for example, that the quality of one's local environment is often connected to one's socioeconomic status. The most desirable and most pristine environments are often controlled by the rich, and "protection of nature" is sometimes used as a strategy for excluding the poor.[15] Meanwhile, pollution and the negative effects of climate change are disproportionately visited upon the poor. (See Heffner, chapter 11.)

Place Matters

When I was an environmental consultant, time and time again, our pollution cleanup projects took us to the poorest neighborhoods. Yet our mandate was to address the "environmental" problems rather than the poverty, joblessness, or blight that shocked us when visiting these places. When I take my sustainable communities class on a Chicago field trip, we detour through the industrial heart of Gary, East Chicago, and Whiting, Indiana. The sheer scale of heavy industrial pipelines, steel mills, oil refineries, and derelict factories overwhelms the students. One student commented that the barren industrial landscape made him think of Chernobyl. In the middle of all this overpowering industry, we enter a quiet residential area of modest houses. We stop at the West Calumet public housing complex on 151st Street. It was built atop the closed USS Lead Smelter that was later designated as a national toxic Superfund site. Recent testing of local children showed that many of those under age six, three-quarters of whom were African American, had dangerously high blood lead levels. The residents were recently moved out, and soil contamination in nearby yards is being addressed. But the purpose of our visit is to wrestle with the bigger questions. Why, I ask, was housing for society's poorest residents built atop a former lead smelter? Paying attention to the actual places where people live, work, and play is a starting point for expanding our understanding of the stewardship responsibility and beginning to work toward environmental justice. (See Heffner, chapter 11.)

---

15 James S. and Nancy G. Duncan, *Landscapes of Privilege: The Politics of the Aesthetic in an American Suburb* (London: Routledge, 2003).

Places come in all sizes, from a comfortable living room to the entire planet. What size of place is most appropriate for our work of stewardship? *Earthkeeping* is an excellent term that summarizes the Genesis 2 mandate. (See Bouma-Prediger, chapter 6.) But "earth" conjures satellite images of the big blue marble, not the everyday worlds we inhabit. Earth is beyond the scope of care and comprehension for most of us. But our earthkeeping can begin close to home with place-making and place-keeping in the locations where we live, work, and play. These are the places where, hopefully, we feel a sense of attachment, have a degree of control, and exercise personal responsibility. Our calling is to live God's shalom in our houses, gardens, streets, and neighborhoods, not just in wild, beautiful, or exotic landscapes. In short, we need to see the world through the lens of place so that we can begin to live faithfully in our places and learn to care for all their dimensions—soils, plants, animals, parks, buildings, neighborhoods, and people.

Works Cited

Agnew, John A. *Place and Politics: The Geographical Mediation of State and Society.* Boston: Allen & Unwin, 1987.

Bouma-Prediger, Steven. *For the Beauty of the Earth: A Christian Vision for Creation Care.* Grand Rapids, MI: Baker, 2001.

Cronon, William. *Changes in the Land: Indians, Colonists, and the Ecology of New England.* New York: Hill and Wang, 1983.

DeWitt, Calvin. *Caring for Creation: Responsible Stewardship of God's Handiwork.* Grand Rapids, MI: Baker, 1998.

Duncan, James S., and Nancy G. Duncan. *Landscapes of Privilege: The Politics of the Aesthetic in an American Suburb.* London: Routledge, 2003.

Glaser, Bruno. "Prehistorically Modified Soils of Central Amazonia: A Model for Sustainable Agriculture in the Twenty-first Century." *Philosophical Transactions—Royal Society of London, Biological Sciences* 362, no. 1478 (2007): 187–96.

Jocoby, Karl. *Crimes against Nature: Squatters, Poachers, Thieves, and the Hidden History of American Conservation.* Berkeley: University of California Press, 2001.

Lachmund, Jens. *Greening Berlin: The Co-Production of Science, Politics, and Urban Nature.* Cambridge, MA: MIT Press, 2013.

Mann, Charles C. *1491: New Revelations of the Americas before Columbus.* New York: Knopf, 2005.

Massey, Doreen B. *Space, Place, and Gender*. Minneapolis, MN: University of Minnesota Press, 1994.

Owen, David. *Green Metropolis: Why Living Smaller, Living Closer, and Driving Less Are the Keys to Sustainability*. New York: Riverhead Books, 2009.

Rosenzweig, Michael L. *Win-Win Ecology: How the Earth's Species Can Survive in the Midst of Human Enterprise*. New York: Oxford University Press, 2003.

Sack, Robert David. *Homo Geographicus: A Framework for Action, Awareness, and Moral Concern*. Baltimore: Johns Hopkins University Press, 1997.

Spence, Mark David. *Dispossessing the Wilderness: Indian Removal and the Making of the National Parks*. New York: Oxford University Press, 2001.

Spirn, Anne Whiston. "Constructing Nature: The Legacy of Fredrick Law Olmsted." In *Uncommon Ground: Rethinking the Human Place in Nature*, edited by William Cronon, 91–113. New York: W. W. Norton, 1996.

Stevens, Stan. *Indigenous Peoples, National Parks, and Protected Areas: A New Paradigm Linking Conservation, Culture, and Rights*. Tucson Basin: University of Arizona Press, 2014.

Tuan, Yi-Fu. *Topophilia: A Study of Environmental Perception, Attitudes, and Values*. Englewood Cliffs, NJ: Prentice-Hall, 1974.

White, Lynn, Jr. "The Historical Roots of Our Ecologic Crisis." *Science* 155, no. 3767 (March 10, 1967): 1203–7.

Wilderness Act. Public Law 88-577, 16 U.S.C. 1131-1136 (1964). https://www.nps.gov/subjects/wilderness/upload/1964-Wilderness-Act.pdf.

Wilkinson, Loren, ed. *Earthkeeping in the Nineties: Stewardship of Creation*. Rev. ed. Grand Rapids, MI: Eerdmans, 1991.

Wunderlich, Gene. "Evolution of the Stewardship Idea in American Country Life." *Journal of Agricultural and Environmental Ethics* 17 (2004): 77–91.

Zaitchik, Alexander. "How Conservation Became Colonialism." *Foreign Policy* (July 16, 2018): 58–63.

14

Walking through
a World of Gifts

David Paul Warners

Larry's Gift

Larry and I have been friends since high school. We have similar family backgrounds, a shared history, and mutual admiration. To this day, we have serious conversations and hearty laughter, often within the same ten minutes. Larry has several interesting hobbies, one of which is beekeeping. He has a few hives in his backyard that generate a modest amount of honey each year. The bees have really captivated Larry, and he has taught himself a great deal about their biology. He invests significant time and energy doing what he can to promote their health and well-being.

Each fall Larry comes to our house to bring a precious gift: a quart of honey. This year, after thanking him and chatting about my daughter's high school bowling team (which Larry is coaching), I set his gift on the shelf in our cupboard. It sat next to a jar of store-bought honey. As we moved through this winter, making tea, granola, and other foods that need honey, we repeatedly faced the decision—should we use Larry's honey or should we use the store-bought honey?

The decision is not neutral. I know that Larry does not have many bees and his gift to us represents a significant portion of the year's harvest. I also know the time and energy and thought and care needed to keep his bees healthy and productive. There is rich irony in the fact that we value Larry's honey (which we received for free) more highly than the jar of store-bought honey (for which we spent hard-earned dollars). Larry's honey is a gift. The store-bought honey is a commodity. Gifts, as opposed to commodities, are personal; they are reflections of the giver, and they celebrate and strengthen relationships. So each time we need honey and open the cupboard door, we ask ourselves, "Is this particular need worthy of the gift that Larry gave?"

The honey we received from Larry is like the student prototypes described by Matthew Heun in chapter 1. Just as the students spent themselves on their prototypes, Larry spends himself on the bees, and the bees spend themselves making honey. To pour the gift of honey down the drain would be incredibly disrespectful. We would never do such a thing! Instead, Larry's gift is something we cherish, appreciate, and use sparingly. We are reminded of Larry—his good heart, quirky habits, and generous spirit—each time we use the gifted honey. To us, the gift is an expression of the giver. The gift is precious to us, because its giver is precious to us.

Cultivating Gratitude

Robin Wall Kimmerer, an author and scientist, reminds us that "how we think about our relationship to the living world matters deeply."[1] One of the themes that emerges from this book is that our relationship with the living world is not healthy. We have not been thinking about the creation properly, which results in actions that are improper as well. We have been thinking too highly of ourselves and too lowly of the rest of the creation (See Al-Attas Bradford, chapter 5.) We have not been cognizant enough

---

1   Robin Wall Kimmerer, "Reclaiming the Honorable Harvest," TEDx Talks, August 18, 2012, https://www.youtube.com/watch?v=Lz1vgfZ3etE.

that the creation includes urban spaces and the animals we eat. (See Bjelland, chapter 13 and Halteman and Zwart, chapter 9.) And we have not recognized how injustice can result from the way we treat creation. (See Heffner, chapter 11; and Bouma, chapter 12.) We have become way too good at casually smashing prototypes. (See Heun, chapter 1.) Our relationship with the creation needs to be reconciled.

A sober cataloguing of the damage we have caused is a necessary first step in the reconciliation process. Acknowledging that we are changing the climate, that we are causing rapid species loss, that we are polluting streams and air and land and oceans leads us to the second important step—lament. What we have done and are doing to the nonhuman creation ought to make us deeply sad. When we avoid thinking about these uncomfortable, painful realities, we choose to remain irreconciled. Recognizing our complicity and lamenting what we have done are critical steps in the healing process. And yet lament is not an end point but rather a source of inspiration for finding new ways of thinking better and acting better and doing better by the creation and the Creator. Willis Jenkins says that we "must let the morbid catalog pierce hearts and darken souls. Then they [the pierced hearts and darkened souls] can offer the healing salve that brings from those wounds a transforming hope—not a hope that forgets lostness and ruin, but a practical hope that replants in the midst of it."[2]

Another theme that emerges from the chapters in this book is a recognition of how intimately connected we are to the nonhuman creation. Symbiotic stewardship and kinship with the nonhuman creation are phrases some of our authors use to describe that connection (See Al-Attas Bradford, chapter 5; Meyaard-Schaap, chapter 3; and Haney, chapter 10.) Our inescapable embeddedness within creation can lead us to see ourselves as earthlings whose responsibility is to be earthkeepers and place makers. (See Joldersma, chapter 4; Bouma-Prediger, chapter 6; and Bjelland, chapter 13.) Emerging from lament into a reconciled relationship

---

2 Willis J. Jenkins, *Ecologies of Grace: Environmental Ethics and Christian Theology* (New York: Oxford University Press, 2008), 233.

with the nonhuman creation will be enlivening. Reconciled relationships are deeply meaningful because the emerging commitment to live into a new and better future comes out of the brokenness of the past.

In this chapter, I want to add some final thoughts about living into that better, reconciled future. I propose that we learn to cultivate an awareness that the world is richly populated with good gifts. And I believe that recognizing the world as being filled with gifts and learning to receive these gifts well will change the way we live our lives. My proposal is shaped by the Reformed theological context in which I work and think and share ideas with colleagues, among whom are the other chapter writers of this book. These thoughts are also consistent with Willis Jenkins' depiction of Reformed Christianity's emphasis on living lives of gratitude to the Creator for the creation.[3]

A Gift-Laden World

There is much to gain by shifting the focus from "being good stewards of creation" to "living gratefully in a world of gifts." Instead of imagining the nonhuman creation as something outside ourselves that we have been called to care for, we understand ourselves as living among and surrounded by so many good gifts. And this world of gifts not only blesses and nurtures us but also blesses and nurtures everything else too, in an intertwined interdependence of species and soil and climate and atoms and ecosystems and . . . goodness. Furthermore, this gift-laden world has been provided and is sustained by a generous, loving Creator who cherishes and takes great pleasure in the gifts (Job 38–41; Psalms 147–150; Luke 12:22–34). The longing of the Creator is that every aspect of creation would flourish, together.

Since the word *gift* has many subtle meanings, a brief explanation is needed at this point. In a consumer culture, giving gifts is too often simplified as a purchase, followed by a transferal of ownership. Ownership is then conceived as having control: "Now it is mine and I can do with it as I please." But this transferal of ownership is not part of what I mean by

---

3 Jenkins, *Ecologies of Grace*, 81–82.

"gift," and several authors in this volume have highlighted the problems that arise when the nonhuman creation is considered in this way. (See the introduction; Joldersma, chapter 4; and Haney, chapter 10.) Furthermore, gifts are sometimes used as deceptive tools to manipulate or coerce a recipient, which in anthropological literature is referred to as agonistic giving.[4] Such ulterior motives associated with gift giving should not cloud this discussion. The kind of gift to which I am referring is something completely undeserved. It is offered with forethought and intention by a giver who cares deeply for the recipient and who delights in the giving. The gift surprises its recipient and thereafter becomes cherished.

Responding to a Gift-Laden World

In *Braiding Sweetgrass*, Kimmerer explores the varied dynamics of gift giving as practiced within her Anishinaabe culture. She describes their understanding of "gift" and how the receiver is to respond. "A gift comes to you through no action of your own, free, having moved toward you without your beckoning. It is not a reward; you cannot earn it, or call it to you, or even deserve it. And yet it appears. Your only role is to be open-eyed and present."[5] Being open-eyed and present is an appropriate way to start as we consider what it means to live in a world of gifts. But I would like to use a few brief stories to expand this posture in four additional directions: reciprocity, restraint, relationship building, and remembrance.

Reciprocity. When a gift is given and received well, it elicits a desire by the recipient to reciprocate. Larry's gift of honey spurred my mind to remember the containers of garden tomatoes and peppers we had preserved in our freezer earlier in the fall. Larry and I both love to cook, but he doesn't garden as much as I do, so I offered and he gladly received some of our frozen produce. His gift motivated me to give in return. Accounts of gift-giving economies among indigenous communities describe how

---

4   C. Mayet and Karen J. Pine, "The Psychology of Gift Exchange," *Internal Report* (Hertfordshire, UK: University of Hertfordshire, 2010), https://karenpine.com/wp-content/uploads/2011/07/The-Psychology-of-Gift-Exchange.pdf.

5   Robin Wall Kimmerer, *Braiding Sweetgrass: Indigenous Wisdom, Scientific Knowledge, and the Teaching of Plants* (Minneapolis, MN: Milkweed Editions, 2013), 23–24.

gifts, once received, are intended to be shared by the recipient. In this way, gifts that are given within the context of a community foster a communal sense of generosity. To receive a gift is inspiration to give a gift. Recognizing that we live in a world of gifts that sustain, delight, and bless us each day of our lives will cultivate grateful hearts and generous spirits.

When we realize that the nonhuman creation is full of gifts and this realization inspires us to reciprocate, what might we do? How can we gratefully give gifts back to creation? There is no prescription that will fit every reader, but here are a few ideas. Consider composting. The creation blesses you with good food; in response, you can mix kitchen scraps with yard waste and generate an excellent soil. The soil can then be used in your garden or to top dress your lawn, thus reducing or eliminating the need for commercial fertilizers. Another way to give back might be to purchase food that is grown locally or organically, or if you eat animal products, be sure they come from animals that are cared for well. You could leave your car home and use public transportation. Cultivate a habit of using reusable, earth-friendly grocery bags. Reduce the amount of meat in your diet. Carry a plastic bottle past as many garbage cans as it takes until you find a recycling container. Many good resources provide numerous additional suggestions—the possibilities are almost endless. The point is that these activities may take extra time or extra money; they may be inconvenient. But that is the nature of a gift: to give a gift is to extend oneself for the sake of the recipient. Grateful reciprocity is the proper response when living in a world of gifts, even though it is seldom the most efficient or cost-effective option.

Restraint. Realizing that the nonhuman creation's gifts are meant for others as well as ourselves should give us great pause as we think about how to use (or not to use) the gifts. A member of my department at Calvin is a gourmet baker. It is a pretty special day when he brings baked goods and sets them in our office. Although the offerings he brings are unbelievably tasty, and something I really love, I take only my share because I want to make sure others are able to enjoy them too. These gifts are given not just for me but for everyone in our department. It would be dishonorable to the giver and to my fellow department members if I were to take so much that the gifts were not able to bless everyone as they were intended to do.

When we come to appreciate our kinship with the rest of the non-human creation, along with God's deep care and concern for all God has made, we will understand that creation's gifts were not intended just for us.[6] Indeed, this truth is spelled out clearly in Genesis 1:29–30, where God gives seed-bearing plants and fruit-bearing trees not only to Adam and Eve but also to "all the beasts of the earth and all the birds in the sky and all the creatures that move along the ground—everything that has the breath of life in it." As earthlings, we share the earth with nonhuman creation; God's gifts are intended for all of them as well as for us. Hoarding gifts for ourselves dishonors both the gifts and the Giver. Hoarding gifts for ourselves also disrespects the others for whom the gifts were intended. When we learn to properly fit our lives into the broader creation, God's gifts will be able to bless all those they were intended to bless.

Relationship building. A third important outcome of gift giving and gift receiving is that relationships become strengthened. Modern anthropological research has identified gift giving as an important first step in establishing trust between individuals.[7] Kimmerer explains that "gifts from the earth or from each other establish a particular relationship, an obligation of sorts to give, to receive, and to reciprocate. . . . A gift establishes a feeling-bond."[8] Recognizing that we live in a world of gifts will help us develop that kind of feeling-bond with the nonhuman creation, and it will strengthen our relationship with the Creator. As we learn to increasingly appreciate the ways the nonhuman creation sustains and blesses us, respond by giving back reciprocally, and cultivate the virtue of restraint, our relationship with the nonhuman creation and with the Creator will grow stronger. Gift giving and gift receiving knit us into relationships, humble us with a richer appreciation for our interconnected dependence on others, and tune our hearts outward, away from ourselves.

---

6   Gretel Van Wieren, *Restored to Earth* (Washington, DC: Georgetown University Press, 2013), 74–75.

7   Martin Mathews, "Gift Giving, Reciprocity and the Creation of Trust," *Journal of Trust Research* 7, no. 1 (February 13, 2017): 90–106, DOI: 10.1080/21515581.2017.1286597.

8   Kimmerer, *Braiding Sweetgrass*, 25–26.

Both research on gift-giving cultures and personal accounts highlight that gift giving benefits not only the recipient but also the giver.[9] The act of giving enables the giver to feel generous and valuable. Since gifts received inspire further giving, a positive feedback dynamic can arise that builds a tone of generosity within gift-giving networks. These networks are important for acknowledging, affirming, and enriching social bonds. In this way, the giving of gifts can build caring and resilient communities. One simple yet tangible way this happens within a church is with church potlucks. The gifts of food that are brought to a potluck are offered and shared, and through the giving and receiving of these gifts, relationships are strengthened. Being inspired to give back to the creation once we have recognized the gifts it provides for us will draw us into a closer relationship with the nonhuman creation, with the Creator, and with one another. Andrew Light highlights that "when people participate in a volunteer restoration, they are doing something good for their community both by helping to deliver an ecosystem service and also by helping to pull together the civic fabric of their home."[10] Gift giving builds affection, reverence, and thankfulness for places and for communities.[11]

Remembrance. A final aspect of gift giving is that when a good gift is given, the gift itself elicits recollection of the giver long after the gift has been received. My dear great-aunt Georgia passed away over a decade ago. Aunt Georgia was an artist—she painted and sketched, and she also made quilts. Our family has a lovely quilt that was made by Aunt Georgia. The pattern is simple and bright, yet the colors and shapes and lines fit together in ways that only an artist could imagine. In fact, they fit together in ways that only Aunt Georgia could bring about. Aunt Georgia gifted this quilt to our family, and even though she literally handed it over to us, telling us she wanted us to have it, we still refer to this gift as "Aunt Georgia's quilt."

---

9   Mayet and Pine, "The Psychology of Gift Exchange."

10 Andrew Light, "Ecological Citizenship: The Democratic Promise of Restoration," in *The Humane Metropolis: People and Nature in the 21st-Century City*, ed. R. Platt (Amherst: University of Massachusetts Press, 2005), 176–89.

11 Jeannette Armstrong, "Indigenous Knowledge and Gift Giving: Living in Community," in *Women and the Gift Economy: A Radically Different Worldview Is Possible*, ed. Genevieve Vaughan (Toronto: Inanna Publications and Education, 2007), 41–49.

The gift means so much to us because of its beauty, because of the beauty of its giver, and because so much of her was invested in it. And we honor her in the way we care for the quilt and in the grateful thoughts we have of her when the quilt keeps us warm on snowy winter nights.

Consider a forest that instead of being viewed as a resource, or even as an ecosystem that we are called to steward, is understood to be a gift that has been offered by a generous and loving Giver who delights in this forest gift. Similar to how the quilt in some way is still Aunt Georgia's quilt, the gifted forest is still God's forest, and through this recognition, we are inspired to care for it well. If we decide to use the gift, we make sure that we use it carefully, in ways that honor the Giver and in ways that allow the gift to continue to bless others, not just other people but also other creatures, streams, the climate, as the gift was intended to do. (See Haney, chapter 10.) We will respond to the creation differently if we learn to view it as a gift.

Remembering the Giver helps us remember that in terms of ultimate ownership, everything truly does still belong to God. There is a sense in which a painting by Georgia O'Keefe, because she created it, will always belong to O'Keefe regardless of who may be curating it. The blurred lines of ownership that result when a creator generously gives gifts is also depicted in Scripture. God is portrayed as giving plants, land, food, wine, shelter, and so much more, yet in Psalm 24:1, we are reminded that "the earth is the LORD's, and everything in it, the world, and all who live in it." We acknowledge the same mystery when we speak of Christ's incarnation as God's gift of salvation for the world. Christ remains God, but he also becomes our gift. All this reminds us that we live in a world of gifts that belongs, wholly and completely, to God.

Moving Forward

Recognizing that daily we are walking through a world of gifts will cause us to move carefully, to live mindfully, and to consider what we can do in response. Viewing the creation as filled with gifts informs our answer to the question that was raised in the preface: "How shall we live?" How shall we faithfully live out our lives in grateful ways that will protect, enhance, and restore God's broken yet beloved world? This is the challenge we face, and it is a challenge that holds great relevance for future generations of people and other creatures who will also be living out their lives in a world of gifts. Those generations should be able to expect that God's good gifts will have been preserved or even enhanced, not depleted by those who have come before them. May the lives we live in God's good creation today protect the praise of hearts and mouths and wings and petals of those generations yet to come.

"We are dreaming of a time when the land might give thanks for the people."[12]

Works Cited

Armstrong, Jeannette. "Indigenous Knowledge and Gift Giving: Living in Community." In *Women and the Gift Economy: A Radically Different Worldview Is Possible*, edited by Genevieve Vaughan, 41–49. Toronto: Inanna Publications and Education, 2007.

Jenkins, Willis J. *Ecologies of Grace: Environmental Ethics and Christian Theology.* New York: Oxford University Press, 2008.

Kimmerer, Robin Wall. *Braiding Sweetgrass: Indigenous Wisdom, Scientific Knowledge, and the Teaching of Plants* Minneapolis, MN: Milkweed Editions, 2013.

———. "Reclaiming the Honorable Harvest." TEDx Talks, August 18, 2012. https://www.youtube.com/watch?v=Lz1vgfZ3etE.

Light, Andrew. "Ecological Citizenship: The Democratic Promise of Restoration." In *The Humane Metropolis: People and Nature in the 21st-Century City*, edited by R. Platt, 176–89. Amherst: University of Massachusetts Press, 2005.

Mathews, Martin. "Gift Giving, Reciprocity and the Creation of Trust." *Journal of Trust Research* 7, no. 1 (February 13, 2017): 90–106. DOI: 10.1080/21515581.2017.1286597.

Mayet, C., and Karen J. Pine. "The Psychology of Gift Exchange." *Internal Report.* Hertfordshire, UK: University of Hertfordshire, 2010. https://karenpine.com/wp-content/uploads/2011/07/The-Psychology-of-Gift-Exchange.pdf.

Van Wieren, Gretel. *Restored to Earth: Christianity, Environmental Ethics, and Ecological Restoration.* Washington, DC: Georgetown University Press, 2013.

---

12 Kimmerer, *Braiding Sweetgrass*, 263.

AFTERWORD

Loren Wilkinson (with Eugene Dykema and Cal DeWitt)

W e who worked on "stewardship" forty years ago are grateful for this collection of essays that so thoughtfully continues the hard work of understanding what the Christian gospel implies about the human place and role in creation. We are also grateful to the Calvin Center for Christian Scholarship (CCCS) for supporting this project—and for giving us the chance to begin the work a long time ago.

Our work in 1977–78 was the first project undertaken by the CCCS. And like *Beyond Stewardship*, it too was very much a team effort. Sadly, Calvin faculty Peter DeVos in philosophy and Vern Ehlers in physics are no longer with us. Eugene Dykema is retired from the economics department at George Fox University. Cal DeWitt, the University of Wisconsin biologist in our group, remains very active in thinking, writing, and teaching about creation care and has published an important defense of stewardship as a *dynamic* concept.[1] I have discussed *Beyond Stewardship* with both Eugene and Cal, and it has been a pleasure for us to work

---

1 See Calvin B. DeWitt, "Stewardship: Responding Dynamically to the Consequences of Human Action in the World," in *Environmental Stewardship*, ed. R. J. Berry (Edinburgh: T&T Clark, 2006), 145–58. Cal's essay comes out of a conference on the issue of stewardship at Windsor Castle in 2001. One of the participants was James Lovelock, one of the most highly respected critics of the idea of stewardship. After the conference, he said he would withdraw his criticism if the term meant what Cal describes.

together again, however briefly, on this afterword. (In what follows, when I say "we," I include them.)

Since we first met in 1977, both the values and the dangers of the idea of stewardship have become clearer. One value is reflected in the fact that the term *stewardship* has now become widely used in the secular environmental community. Editor David Warners, for example, mentions his involvement with Plaster Creek *Stewards* in his community. In my community, British Columbia's Gulf Islands, land use decisions are handled by the Islands Trust, which draws on the concept of stewardship to explain its mandate—and gives an annual "Stewardship Award." (Not all islanders welcome the idea of stewardship because it challenges the fiction of absolute ownership, and some islanders complain that stewardship is a socialist idea, a kind of expropriation.) In any case, the term is now widespread in environmentalist circles, and we couldn't take it back even if we wanted to. Our challenge is rather to purge stewardship of its dangerous meanings. For that task, these essays are a great resource.

Unfortunately, stewardship can be a dangerous idea (as we can be a dangerous species!). It can lead us (as many of these essays helpfully point out) to exaggerate our knowledge, our wisdom, and our power. James Lovelock, whose scientific work led to the idea of the earth as *Gaia*, a self-regulating organism on which human life depends completely, observed in 2006 that "the humanist concept of sustainable development and the Christian concept of stewardship are flawed by unconscious hubris. We have neither the knowledge nor the capacity to achieve them. We are no more qualified to be the stewards or developers of the earth than are goats to be gardeners."[2]

Arne Naess, a Norwegian philosopher, argued similarly in an influential paper published shortly before our first CCCS project.[3] He distinguished between "shallow environmentalism" and "deep ecology." The essays in this volume rightly call us to move beyond "shallow environmentalism,"

---

2   James Lovelock, *The Revenge of Gaia: Earth's Climate Crisis and the Fate of Humanity* (New York: Basic Books, 2006), 137.

3   Arne Naess, "The shallow and the deep, long-range ecology movement. A summary." *Inquiry: An Interdisciplinary Journal of Philosophy* 16 (1973): 95-100.

which assumes that our knowledge is adequate to fix any environmental problem through improvements in our technology. What he meant by "deep ecology" is nothing less than a religious change. The religion he outlined is a form of Buddhism, characterized by a "biocentric equality" and a redefinition of "self" to include our unity with all things. These *Beyond Stewardship* essays, however, even in their criticism of stewardship, do so within a very different context: that being made in the image of God calls us to the vocation of *care*.

Bron Taylor, in his important book *Dark Green Religion*,[4] is also dismissive of the idea of stewardship. He describes a worldwide emerging "Green Religion," a kind of biocentric pantheism in which we participate in a cosmic, evolving divinity. Taylor would call himself a *former* Christian. He read the original *Earthkeeping* with appreciation but has concluded that all such attempts at Christian Environmental Stewardship are part of a superficial and inadequate greening of religion. He believes that those who care about the health of the planet must abandon the idea of stewardship entirely—along with Christianity and belief in a God who is other than the universe.

The "beyond" in *Beyond Stewardship* can mean two quite different things. It can mean closing the door on a flawed and dangerous idea and leaving it behind. (For Naess and Taylor, that means leaving theism behind. The authors of these essays certainly don't condone that.) But "beyond" can also mean working within an idea, removing its flaws, and building on it. Back in 1977, we already knew that we needed to go beyond the trivialization of the idea of stewardship, which was evident then (as it is now) in its limitation to churchly appeals for tithing or, in early forms of what has since become a toxic strain in contemporary American politics, the idea that stewardship means simply "wise use," crassly calculated.

Any activity of human care for the nonhuman creation (whatever one's belief) has three aspects, which are unavoidable. The first is the fact that (as many of these essays point out) we are part of a gracious gift that is

---

4   Bron Taylor, *Dark Green Religion: Nature Spirituality and the Planetary Future* (Berkeley and Los Angeles: University of California Press, 2010).

also a mystery. It is a mistake to think it belongs to us. The second is that, like every other living thing, we have to *use* this gift in order to live. The third is the most problematic: we human beings have a unique status in the creation, whether we understand it as "creation" or simply as "nature." I was privileged many years ago to attend the 1992 Earth Summit in Rio. To me, the most striking thing about that vast international conference about the health of the planet was that *only humans* attended! It was a profoundly—but unavoidably—*anthropocentric* conference.

Thus, something like stewardship is part of the human makeup. On the one hand, we have a unique capacity to use—and misuse—the non-human creation. On the other, we have a unique capacity to honor and love it. Both Eugene and I have been influenced by the magisterial work of British psychiatrist Iain McGilchrist, *The Master and His Emissary: The Divided Brain and the Making of the Western World*.[5] He points out that part of our kinship with birds and animals is a divided brain, both parts of which are essential. One half simplifies and quantifies for the purpose of use; the other is open to the surprising and the new, for the purpose of empathy and love. McGilchrist's main argument is that, in humans, this capacity for empathy is the true master. However, that other (essential!) part of us that quantifies the world into "resources" keeps trying to usurp the more empathic mastery. These two essential human tendencies, and their relation to each other, underlie this discussion about stewardship—both our apologetics for the term and these essays, which thoughtfully critique it. Though those of us who worked on *Earthkeeping* think the word itself still has value, we deeply respect and appreciate those contributors to this book who are using different words and models for how we humans should think about ourselves and our relationship with the rest of creation.

"Stewardship of natural resources" was the topic Calvin College gave us to work on back in 1977. The use of the word *resources* should have set off alarm bells about how deeply we are conditioned to view the creation

---

5   Iain McGilchrist, *The Master and His Emissary: The Divided Brain and the Making of the Western World* (New Haven: Yale University Press, 2009).

as something to use rather than to care for, but it didn't. The decade of the 1980s made us wiser. When we met again to work on a revision, the first thing we noticed was how glaringly narrow it was to call the earth simply a "resource." So the second edition had the better subtitle "Stewardship of *Creation*."

But we kept the word *stewardship* and still (even after reading all these perceptive essays) would defend it, for two good reasons. The first we discussed above: the word is now used by much of the secular public to speak of environmental concerns. The concept of stewardship is a reminder (unpleasant to some) that we are not absolute owners of anything but hold it in trust. In answer to the question "In trust for *what* or *whom*?" this secular use of the term gets a bit vague. The land itself? Our children? Future generations? The biosphere? Trying to answer such questions takes people out of their philosophical comfort zone, which is a good thing.

Which leads to our second reason for defending the word. Today, the concern for "ecological restoration" is worldwide, and that activity is sometimes spoken of as stewardship.[6] The unavoidably anthropocentric word seems to match the problem of "novel ecosystems," in what is increasingly spoken of as "the Anthropocene": an era in which we must acknowledge that human activity has irretrievably changed the world, usually for the worse. Ecosystems can't exactly be "restored." But they might need to be "stewarded" to try to repair the damage. Unfortunately, neither restoration nor stewardship are value-free concepts, and science by itself doesn't give us our values. Both concepts are deeply anthropocentric, and, as we have seen, many reject them for that reason. As many of the articles in this collection rightly point out, we don't know nearly enough to be stewards for the vast complexity of the biosphere. But without questioning the reality of our kinship with other creatures, or the fact that we "individuals" are really communities of billions of microbes, we also seem to be the only species with a guilty conscience. The concept of

---

6   See, for example, Timothy R. Seastedt, Katharine N. Suding, and F. Stuart Chapin III, "Ecosystem Stewardship as a Framework for Conservation in a Directionally Changing World," in *Novel Ecosystems: Intervening in the New Ecological World Order*, ed. Richard J. Hobbs, Eric S. Higgs, and Carol M. Hall (Hoboken, NJ: Wiley-Blackwell, 2013), 326–33.

stewardship helps us think about both the curse and the blessing of our peculiar status of being human.

Clearly, stewardship poses questions that verge on the theological for everyone, Christian or not. What does restoration mean? Why are we humans concerned about it? Why does nothing else in nature have this concern? What are we, anyway?

These essays hold many good warnings about the dangers in the *misuse* of the term: that it can encourage an I-it relationship; that it can too easily be subverted by capitalism; that it can be too individualistic; that it can encourage us to neglect our embeddedness in the rest of the creation. But these dangers are not intrinsically a part of stewardship. They are dangers (as McGilchrist's analysis makes clear) in all our relationships: the need to view another creature as simply a resource *can* "master" our ability to view that creature as an object of our love and care. Changing the language we use will not necessarily eliminate that danger.

These essays call for enriched imaginations, broader vision—and faithful hearts. Such hearts are necessary if we are to practice both the use of things (which we must) and their care and keeping. New concepts and words may help, but new seed thrown on stony soil will yield no better harvest. Our hearts need to change.

Perhaps *earthkeeping*, the main word in the title of our book on stewardship, helps point to the source of that needed change of heart. In a sense, it too goes "beyond" stewardship—but remains rooted within it. In 1979, as the publication date of that book approached, we knew we needed something catchier than the ponderous title *Christian Stewardship of Natural Resources*. I mentioned to my wife, Mary Ruth, the possibility of *Oikos*. She said that was a really dumb idea: few would know what it meant. I argued that since it is the Greek word for "home" or "household" and is the root for *economy* (a word that in the New Testament is usually translated "stewardship"), *Oikos* would be a good name. *Oikos* is also the root for the newer word *ecology*. It brings these big and distant concepts home: both words suggest a planetary housekeeping. She was still not convinced. But that homey word *housekeeping* suggested something to her: "What about 'earthkeeping'?" she said.

The word *earthkeeping* helps us also recover the deeper roots of both "economy" and "ecology" in the whole "ecumene" (another word with *oikos* at its core). Whatever "dominion" means in Genesis 1:28, it has to be understood in terms of the "keeping" of Genesis 2:15. As Steven Bouma-Prediger points out in this book, *keep* is the same word that is used in the Aaronic blessing: "The LORD bless you and keep you." Implicitly, we are to *keep* one another, and the creation, as God *keeps* us. The entire biblical story can be seen as God's long lesson to humanity about what true keeping means. God's keeping of us took him to the cross, and through the cross and resurrection, we are invited into the whole "household" of the triune, incarnate Creator.

That was what we began to learn in the first Calvin Center for Christian Scholarship project on creation care, and we are grateful for the way these essays continue to invite us into that "beyond" of God's Kingdom.

Works Cited

DeWitt, Calvin B. "Stewardship: Responding Dynamically to the Consequences of Human Action in the World." In *Environmental Stewardship*, edited by R. J. Berry, 145–58. Edinburgh: T&T Clark, 2006.

Lovelock, James. *The Revenge of Gaia: Earth's Climate Crisis and the Fate of Humanity*. New York: Basic Books, 2006.

McGilchrist, Iain. *The Master and His Emissary: The Divided Brain and the Making of the Western World*. New Haven: Yale University Press, 2009.

Naess, Arne. "The shallow and the deep, long-range ecology movement. A summary." *Inquiry: An Interdisciplinary Journal of Philosophy* 16 (1973): 95-100.

Seastedt, Timothy R., Katharine N. Suding, and F. Stuart Chapin III. "Ecosystem Stewardship as a Framework for Conservation in a Directionally Changing World." In *Novel Ecosystems: Intervening in the New Ecological World Order*, edited by Richard J. Hobbs, Eric S. Higgs, and Carol M. Hall, 326–33. Hoboken, NJ: Wiley-Blackwell, 2013.

Taylor, Bron. *Dark Green Religion: Nature Spirituality and the Planetary Future*. Berkeley and Los Angeles: University of California Press, 2010

Postlude: No More Room

Gabrielle Eisma, Leah Knoor, and Hannah Riffell

The inspiration for "No More Room" was a presentation by Dr. David Paul Warners at Calvin College during our January 2019 DCM (Developing a Christian Mind) course "Truth and Reconciliation: The Artist Response I." Dr. Warners spoke of creation as a gift, valued not because it was bought or earned but because God is the gift Giver. As grateful recipients of such a gift, we designed a children's book for our end-of-term project to inspire future generations to protect and preserve the nonhuman creation. In DCM, we were challenged to consider our calling as Christians to restore justice and our ability as artists to use our work for this restoration. Through the words of Dr. Warners and by further exploring the effects of environmental injustice, we came to the undeniable conclusion that creation care is a fundamental Christian calling; it is not optional. However, the call to sustainability is a call not only to environmental stewardship and beyond but also to acknowledge our interdependence with the nonhuman creation. In his speech "Why, as Christians, We Must Oppose Racism," South African archbishop Desmond Tutu says that "we are made to live in a delicate network of interdependence with one another, with God, and with the rest of God's creation." We hoped to reflect these words in our own book, because the truth is that we depend on the earth for resources, beauty, shelter, and nourishment, and the earth depends on us for protection, care, and appreciation. Often dismissed as an injustice not quite worth correcting, the irresponsible treatment of the gift of creation can cause irreparable harm. Frightened and saddened by the looming threats of habitat loss, poaching, pollution, and the ultimate prospect of mass extinction, we made this book to explain to children why so many once-beloved creatures are severely reduced in number or no longer on the earth—there is no more room. A taste of our book can be found in the next two pages. Follow the link to enjoy the fully illustrated text, intended to both bring you delight, just as God delights in the creation, and challenge you to take up the charge to protect, restore, and make some room.

http://www.calvin.edu/go/no-more-room

From us, to you.

Gabrielle Eisma

Leah Knoor

Hannah Riffell

203

No More Room

Up in the sky, their wings unfurled,
The dark and sharp-eyed eagles whirled.
But there is no more room on Earth
for the eagles in the world.

So soft and white
in every way,
The polar bears just
loved to play!
But there is
no more room
on Earth for the
polar bears
today.

Though slow, the elephant
was strong,
And had a special
trunk long.
But there is
no more room
on Earth
where the
elephants
belong.

With flippers but no foot or hand,
Sea turtles laid their eggs in sand.
But there is no more room on
Earth for turtles now to land.

Quite big enough
to cause
a scare,
The rhinoceros did not
have hair!
But there is
no more room on Earth
for the rhino
anywhere.

Inside a hive hung
from a tree,
The yellow bees
made sweet honey,
But there is
no more room on
Earth for the
buzzing honeybee.

And so to you who've had since birth
An idea of another's worth,
Will you make room for beasts on earth?

ADDITIONAL
RESOURCES

Appendix 1

DISCUSSION QUESTIONS

Preface

1. Have you ever taken the time to consciously consider how much energy and other resources you use on a daily basis? Does it disturb you that our daily activities produce so much pollution?
2. Why do you think the Christian church isn't leading the way in promoting and practicing environmental sustainability?
3. Do you have any preliminary responses to the perennial question "How shall we live?" What are you seeking from this book to help you answer that question? Are you receptive to learning new themes and principles for understanding the relationship between humans and the nonhuman creation?

Introduction

1. Do you often encounter people who are cynical or uncaring in the face of creation's degradation? How do you respond to such cynicism? How do you think Christians should respond?
2. Have you heard about stewardship in church? What did the word mean? Have you heard other meanings of stewardship in other contexts? What is your personal understanding of the term *stewardship* at this point?
3. Have you noticed or considered the limitations of the Christian Environmental Stewardship (CES) paradigm? What do you think about the weaknesses and blind spots identified by the editors? Do you agree or disagree that CES is problematic? Why?

4. Where in our world today do you see the creation being valued primarily instrumentally? What are some practical problems with instrumental valuation?

Chapter 1: Smashing Prototypes

1. Have you ever felt a deep sadness (lament) for a part of God's creation? When and where? What was your response to this lament—despair, cynicism, action?
2. Have you ever grown closer to someone through grief or lament? How can you use lament about the state of the nonhuman creation to cultivate your relationship with God?
3. When and where have you observed creation's lament? Does this lament spur you to action, as the author suggests it should?

Chapter 2: Words Matter, but Audience Matters More

1. How do you understand and view the concept of stewardship? What has led you to this understanding? How about climate change or global warming?
2. Why might a population or group dislike or misuse the term *stewardship*? The author cites stewardship's financial connotations in a political context as one example. In what other situations or for what other groups might *stewardship* be an inappropriate or unhelpful term to use?
3. Can you think of some words or phrases (other than stewardship) that better describe Christian responsibility to the nonhuman creation?
4. How would you go about discussing creation care with an elderly member of your church? A college student? A coworker? What words would you use for each audience? What aspects of creation care would you emphasize? Which would you avoid?

Chapter 3: From Foreign to Family: Kinship as Pathway toward Radical Care for the Earth

1. Have you encountered a theology of stewardship that emphasized using the earth's resources for human benefit above all else, such as

was articulated by the mountain-town pastor? Where and when? How did you respond to it? Affirmation? Rejection? Somewhere in between?

2. When have you felt kinship with the nonhuman creation? With a family pet, perhaps, or while walking in the woods? In the middle of a city? Describe the experience.

3. The author defines kinship as "commonality in difference." List some of the commonalities and differences between humans and the nonhuman creation mentioned by the author. Can you think of any important commonalities or differences that the author didn't mention?

4. How might you implement kinship practices in your church? Your school? Your workplace?

Chapter 4: The Responsibility of Earthlings for the Earth: Graciousness, Lament, and the Call of Justice

1. In which inanimate things (like a nail) do you already see intrinsic value? How does this view change your behavior toward them?

2. Explore the story of the bent nails that need straightening, the grandfather and grandson, etc. How does this story enliven your understanding of God's care for us and how we should care for God's creation?

3. How do you generally view yourself in relation to the nonhuman creation? Does the concept of humans as earthlings challenge, affirm, or deepen your understanding?

4. The author refers to our debt of gratitude to the earth for sustaining us. Do you feel this debt of gratitude? Why or why not? Does it impact how you act toward the earth?

5. Brainstorm some ways Christians can carry out their ethical responsibility to protect the creation.

Chapter 5: Symbiotic Stewardship

1. How would you articulate the drama of salvation in one hundred words? How could you include the importance of the creation in that description?

2. Are you surprised by the deep integration of humans and microbes? How easily (or not easily) does this idea sit with you? What is your reaction to the term *holobiont*?

3. When you think of the Fall, do you think of it in terms of humans acting *lower* than they were made to be (behaving more like animals), or do you think of it in terms of humans attempting to be *higher* than they were made to be (attempting to be God)? How might the way you view the Fall impact your view of the nonhuman creation and your relationship to it?

4. Do you perceive tension between the acknowledgment of human creatureliness and the traditional Christian ideas of the image of God? What are some ways we can hold these concepts in tandem? Are they antagonistic? Neutral? Synergistic?

5. How do you see matter stewarding you? Contributing to your redemption?

6. In the Scriptures, what other nonhuman creatures (besides the Jordan River) did God choose to include in the economy of salvation?

Chapter 6: From Stewardship to Earthkeeping: Why We Should Move beyond Stewardship

1. Have you had a moment of awakening similar to what Mitch experienced? What led to the change? How did it impact your life?

2. Do you agree with the five shortcomings of stewardship the author lists? Why or why not? Compare/contrast these "shortcomings" with the "weaknesses" given in the introduction.

3. Do you agree that it is time to retire the notion of stewardship? If so, why? If not, why not?

4. What do you see as the key difference(s) between stewardship and earthkeeping? What can you do in your life to move from being a mere steward of the creation to being an earthkeeper?

Chapter 7: Stewardship and the Kingdom of God

1. How have you seen the effects of human finitude on human efforts to care for the nonhuman creation? Where and when have you seen

successes in spite of our finitude? What factors do you think contributed to those successes?

2. What are some steps you can take to be a more informed, ecologically sensitive consumer?

3. Think of some examples of systemic sin in your culture. How does it impact the nonhuman creation? Humans? Can you think of any ways to work toward redemption in that fallen system?

4. Brainstorm some practical ways to start living out the Kingdom of God in your care of the nonhuman creation.

Chapter 8: What's That? Naming, Knowing, Delighting, Caring, Suffering

1. What are some creatures or features of the natural world, perhaps in the region where you live, that you would like to know more about? How might you start to learn?

2. Are you a subject matter expert with knowledge that others might find delightful and useful as they become better earthkeepers? How can you share that knowledge?

3. What are some features of your home region that you already care about? Have you felt some grief or lament over the abuse, destruction, loss, or potential loss of those features? What have you done in response? What could you do?

Chapter 9: Reimagining Our Kinship with Animals

1. Reflect on a recent time when you felt defensive; this could be in response to a disagreement with a friend or family member, a discussion in a class or at work, etc. What underlying value, attitude, or belief led you to feel defensive in that circumstance? If you had allowed this defensiveness to give way to curiosity, how might the encounter have gone differently?

2. Reflect on a time when you felt engaged and curious. What piqued your curiosity in the first place? How did you act in response to your curiosity? What did this curiosity enable you to learn or experience?

3. Reflect on an experience that shifted your vision of the world in some way. This experience could have occurred in a class or as a result of

watching a documentary, listening to a presentation, or traveling to a new culture. What was the cause of the shift, and what was the result of the shift? Did your behavior change in any noticeable way? Did the change last?

4. If you are persuaded by this chapter that we ought to imagine our relationship with animals differently, what might this reimagination mean in your daily life? Could you imagine shifting your diet a little or a lot? What would that shift look like? How would your family and friends respond? Do you expect such a shift would be difficult or easy for you?

5. If you are unpersuaded by this chapter or maybe still on the fence, what questions remain for you and why?

Chapter 10: A New Worldview

1. Where do you see the "human ingenuity can solve anything" mentality in your culture? To what degree do you think that humans can invent or develop our way out of environmental problems (for example, by developing alternative energy sources)? What are technology's limitations for overcoming creation care challenges?

2. What are some examples of human technology interfering with natural systems? Can you brainstorm ways that humans could work with natural systems instead of destroying them?

3. How can you educate yourself more about the natural systems that surround you?

4. How can you cultivate humility in your approach to our understanding of the earth? Can you think of ways to let the earth teach us rather than assuming that humans know best?

Chapter 11: Making Visible the Invisible: Environmental Racism

1. Have you observed examples of or suffered under environmental racism? If you have suffered under environmental racism, what were the circumstances and how did you react? If you have been an observer of environmental racism, are you now more likely to empathize with marginalized people?

2. What are some policies that might have prevented the environmental racism in the first place? How could you work toward environmental justice in that situation, either as the observer or the sufferer?
3. How can you increase your awareness of upstream-downstream connections? How can you take moral action to help prevent injustices?
4. Can you think of ways to cultivate recognition, empathy, lament, and restorative action in your church or community?

Chapter 12: Who Can Be a Steward?

1. In what ways do you have agency to care for the creation? In what areas might you lack agency?
2. Who has a voice on environmental decisions in your community (neighborhood, school, church)? Your country?
3. What are some examples of connecting disempowered people to the nonhuman creation in your community/nation?
4. Is there an environmental protection group that you work with or support? Who is underrepresented within the group? What could you do to involve them in the group's work?

Chapter 13: From Stewardship to Place-Making and Place-Keeping

1. Is there a place that you deeply love? Briefly describe it. Why do you feel so connected to it?
2. How have you previously engaged in place-making and place-keeping (moving into a new house, cleaning up the church landscaping, getting involved in local politics or planning, etc.)? Share a few examples.
3. How have you tended to view cities and urban areas? If you have viewed them as "unnatural" in comparison to rural settings, how can you work to change those perceptions?
4. What are the most pressing social, economic, and environmental issues in your place? How can you more actively engage in making and keeping your current place?

Chapter 14: Walking through a World of Gifts

1. Have you ever received a gift that you valued more highly than a comparable store-bought item? What made you value it more?

2. This chapter states that "to receive a gift is inspiration to give a gift." When have you experienced this dynamic? How (from this chapter or your own ideas) do you think you could start giving back to the nonhuman creation?

3. Contemplate the nonhuman creation as a gift from God to you. Have you accepted this gift with reciprocal, restrained gratitude, or have you grasped it as a possession, to use as you please? How might cultivating gratitude for this gift improve your relationship with God?

4. Contemplate the nonhuman creation as a gift from God to current and future others. Does this recognition influence the way you think about interacting with the gift?

5. What hope have you gleaned from this book? Can you envision ways to heal the nonhuman creation and our relationship with it rather than contributing to its thoughtless destruction? What are some ways you can start to "live into that better, reconciled future"?

Appendix 2

FURTHER READING

Chapter 1: Smashing Prototypes

Calvin College. "Senior Design Projects." Accessed March 18, 2019. https://calvin
.edu/academics/departments-programs/engineering/student-experience
/senior-design-projects/.

Lee, Nancy C. *Lyrics of Lament: From Tragedy to Transformation.* Minneapolis, MN:
Fortress Press, 2010.

Simon, Paul. "Born at the Right Time." *Rhythm of the Saints.* Warner Bros., 1990,
compact disc. Originally released October 16, 1990.

Chapter 2: Words Matter, but Audience Matters More

George Mason Center of Climate Change Communication. Accessed March 18,
2019. http://www.climatechangecommunication.org/.

Larson, Brendon. *Metaphors for Environmental Sustainability: Redefining Our Relationship with Nature.* New Haven, CT: Yale University Press, 2011.

Peterson, Tarla Rai. *Sharing the Earth: The Rhetoric of Sustainable Development.*
Columbia, SC: University of South Carolina Press, 1997.

Chapter 3: From Foreign to Family: Kinship as Pathway to Radical Care for the Earth

Davis, Ellen F. *Scripture, Culture, and Agriculture: An Agrarian Reading of the Bible.*
New York: Cambridge University Press, 2009.

Oliver, Mary. *New and Selected Poems.* 2 vols. Boston: Beacon Press, 1992.

Quinn, Daniel. *Ishmael: An Adventure of Mind and Spirit.* 5th ann. ed. New York:
Bantam/Turner Book, 1992.

Woodley, Randy. *Shalom and the Community of Creation: An Indigenous Vision.*
Grand Rapids, MI: Eerdmans, 2012.

Chapter 4: The Responsibility of Earthlings for the Earth: Graciousness, Lament, and the Call of Justice

Foltz, Bruce V. *The Noetics of Nature: Environmental Philosophy and the Holy Beauty of the Visible*. New York: Fordham University Press, 2014.

Joldersma, Clarence W. "Earth Ethics for Education." Oxford Research Encyclopedia of Education. Last modified December 19, 2017. http://oxfordre.com/education/view/10.1093/acrefore/9780190264093.001.0001/acrefore-9780190264093-e-54.

———. "Earth Juts into World: An Earth Ethics for Ecologizing Philosophy of Education." *Educational Theory* 67, no. 4 (August 2017): 399–415.

———. "Earth's Lament: A Friendly Supplement to Zuidervaart's Societal Principles in an Era of Climate Change." In *Seeking Stillness or The Sound of Wings: Works on Art, Truth, and Society in Honor of Lambert Zuidervaart* (forthcoming), edited by Peter Enneson, Michael DeMoor, andMatthew J. Klassen Eugene, OR: Wipf & Stock, 2019.

Llewelyn, John. *Seeing through God: A Geophenomenology*. Bloomington: Indiana University Press, 2004.

Chapter 5: Symbiotic Stewardship

Bonhoeffer, Dietrich. *Creation and Fall: A Theological Exposition of Genesis 1–3*. Minneapolis, MN: Fortress Press, 1997.

Deane-Drummond, Celia, and David Clough, eds. *Creaturely Theology: On God, Humans, and Other Animals*. London: SCM Press, 2009.

Moore, Stephen D., ed. *Divinanimality: Animal Theory, Creaturely Theology*. New York: Fordham University Press, 2014.

Muers, Rachel. "The Holy Spirit, the Voices of Nature and Environmental Prophecy." *Scottish Journal of Theology* 67, no. 3 (2014): 323–39.

Chapter 6: From Stewardship to Earthkeeping: Why We Should Move beyond Stewardship

Berry, Wendell. *Home Economics*. San Francisco: North Point Press, 1987.

Bouma-Prediger, Steven. *Earthkeeping and Character: Exploring a Christian Ecological Virtue Ethic*. Grand Rapids, MI: Baker Academic, 2019.

Brown, William P. *Sacred Sense: Discovering the Wonder of God's Word and World*. Grand Rapids, MI: Eerdmans, 2015.

Moo, Douglas J., and Jonathan A. Moo. *Creation Care: A Biblical Theology of the Natural World*. Grand Rapids, MI: Zondervan, 2018.

Wirzba, Norman. *From Nature to Creation: A Christian Vision for Understanding and Loving Our World*. Grand Rapids, MI: Baker Academic, 2015.

Chapter 7: Stewardship and the Kingdom of God

Berry, Wendell. *The Unsettling of America: Culture and Agriculture*. San Francisco: Sierra Club Books, 1977.

Wright, N. T. *New Heavens, New Earth: The Biblical Picture of Christian Hope*. Grove Biblical Series. Cambridge: Grove Books Limited, 1999.

Yordy, Laura Ruth. *Green Witness: Ecology, Ethics, and the Kingdom of God*. Eugene, OR: Cascade Books, 2008.

Chapter 8: What's That? Naming, Knowing, Delighting, Caring, Suffering

Belkin, Douglas. "Rhododendron? Hydrangea? American Doesn't Know Anymore." *Wall Street Journal*, August 14, 2018. https://www.wsj.com/articles/rhododendron-hydrangea-america-doesnt-know-anymore-1534259849.

Hiebert, Theodore. *The Yahwist's Landscape: Nature and Religion in Early Israel*. New York: Oxford University Press, 1996.

Lopez, Barry, and Debra Gwartney, eds. *Home Ground: A Guide to the American Landscape*. San Antonio, TX: Trinity University Press, 2013.

Powers, Richard. *The Overstory: A Novel*. New York: W. W. Norton, 2018.

Chapter 9: Reimagining Our Kinship with Animals

Alexis, Nekeisha Alayna. "Doesn't the Bible Say that Humans Are More Important Than Animals?" In *A Faith Embracing All Creatures: Addressing Commonly Asked Questions about Christian Care for Animals*, edited by Tripp York and Andy Alexis-Baker, 39–52. Eugene, OR: Cascade Books, 2012.

Clough, David. *On Animals, Volume I: Systematic Theology*. New York: Bloomsbury T&T Clark, 2012.

———. *On Animals, Volume II: Theological Ethics*. New York: Bloomsbury T&T Clark, 2018.

Halteman, Matthew C. *Compassionate Eating as Care of Creation*. Washington, DC: Humane Society of the United States, 2010.

King, Sarah Withrow. *Animals Are Not Ours (No Really, They're Not): An Evangelical Animal Liberation Theology*. Eugene, OR: Cascade Books, 2016.

———. *Vegangelical: How Caring for Animals Can Shape Your Faith*. Grand Rapids, MI: Zondervan, 2016.

Wirzba, Norman. *Food and Faith: A Theology of Eating*. New York: Cambridge University Press, 2011.

Chapter 10: A New Worldview

Anderson, M. Kat. *Tending the Wild: Native American Knowledge and the Management of California's Natural Resources*. Berkeley: University of California Press, 2005.

Diamond, Jared. *Collapse: How Societies Choose to Fail or Succeed*. Rev. ed. New York: Penguin, 2011.

Moore, Steven A. *Alternative Routes to the Sustainable City: Austin, Curitiba, and Frankfurt*. Lanham, MD: Lexington Books, 2007.

Ross, John F. *The Promise of the Grand Canyon: John Wesley Powell's Perilous Journey and His Vision for the American West*. New York: Viking, 2018.

Chapter 11: Making Visible the Invisible: Environmental Racism

Bonilla-Silva, Eduardo. "Rethinking Racism: Toward a Structural Interpretation." *American Sociological Review* 62 (1996): 465–80.

Bryant, Bunyan. *Environmental Justice: Issues, Policies, and Solutions*. Washington, DC: Island Press, 1995.

Bullard, Robert D. *Confronting Environmental Racism: Voices from the Grassroots*. Boston: South End Press, 1993.

———. "Solid Waste Sites and the Black Houston Community." *Sociological Inquiry* 53 (1983): 273–99.

Taylor, Dorceta E. *The Environment and the People in American Cities: Disorder, Inequality, and Social Change*. Durham, NC: Duke University Press, 2009.

Chapter 12: Who Can Be a Steward?

Hunjan, Raji, and Soumountha Keophilavong. *Power and Making Change Happen*. Fife, Scotland: Carnegie United Kingdom Trust, 2010.

McKibben, Bill. *Hope, Human and Wild: True Stories of Living Lightly on the Earth*. Minneapolis, MN: Milkweed Editions, 2007.

Ostrom, Elinor. *Governing the Commons: The Evolution of Institutions for Collective Action*. New York: Cambridge University Press, 1990.

Robbins, Paul. *Political Ecology: A Critical Introduction*. Hoboken, NJ: Blackwell Publishing, 2004.

Wondolleck, Julia M., and Steven Lewis Yaffee. *Making Collaboration Work: Lessons from Innovation in Natural Resources Management*. Washington, DC: Island Press, 2000.

Chapter 13: From Stewardship to Place-Making and Place-Keeping

Bartholomew, Craig G. *Where Mortals Dwell: A Christian View of Place for Today.* Grand Rapids, MI: Baker Academic, 2011.

Cresswell, Tim. *Place: An Introduction.* 2nd ed. Hoboken, NJ: Wiley-Blackwell, 2014.

Cronon, William, ed. *Uncommon Ground: Rethinking the Human Place in Nature.* New York: W. W. Norton, 1996.

Sack, Robert David. *Homo Geographicus: A Framework for Action, Awareness, and Moral Concern.* Baltimore, MD: Johns Hopkins University Press, 1997.

Chapter 14: Walking through a World of Gifts

Kimmerer, Robin Wall. *Braiding Sweetgrass: Indigenous Wisdom, Scientific Knowledge, and the Teaching of Plants.* Minneapolis, MN: Milkweed Editions, 2013.

Kramer, Kyle T. *A Time to Plant: Life Lessons in Work, Prayer, and Dirt.* Notre Dame, IN: Sorin Books, 2010.

Maathai, Wangari. *Replenishing the Earth: Spiritual Values for Healing Ourselves and the World.* New York: Doubleday, 2010.

Maté, Ferenc. *A Reasonable Life: Toward a Simpler, Secure, More Humane Existence.* Vancouver, Canada: Albatross, 1997.

Moore, Kathleen Dean. *Wild Comfort: The Solace of Nature.* Boston: Trumpeter Books, 2010.

Van Wieren, Gretel. *Restored to Earth: Christianity, Environmental Ethics, and Ecological Restoration.* Washington, DC: Georgetown University Press, 2013.

Woodley, Randy S. *Shalom and the Community of Creation: An Indigenous Vision.* Grand Rapids, MI: Eerdmans, 2012.

LIST OF CONTRIBUTORS

Mark D. Bjelland's first career as an environmental engineer exposed him to scores of forlorn, polluted, and poverty-stricken places. His engineering training prepared him for the technical problems he encountered but not the social and ethical questions they raised. He returned to graduate school, studying environmental ethics and theology with Loren Wilkinson at Regent College and earning a Ph.D. in urban geography from the University of Minnesota. His research explores the interface of urbanization, justice, and the environment. He taught geography and environmental studies at Gustavus Adolphus College for fifteen years prior to coming to Calvin College in 2013. He is co-author of *Human Geography: Landscape of Human Activities* and has published articles in *The Geographical Review*, *Urban Geography*, *The Professional Geographer*, and the *Research Journal of the Water Pollution Control Federation*.

Dietrich Bouma is a doctoral student in city and regional planning at Cornell University, where he studies land security, environmental governance, and conservation and development in developing countries. He has a B.S. in biology from Calvin College and a M.S./M.P.P. in environmental policy from the University of Michigan. He has worked with the Huron River Watershed Council, United Nations Food and Agriculture Organization, Au Sable Institute of Environmental Studies, World Resources Institute, and the University of Michigan Graham Sustainability Institute.

Steven Bouma-Prediger is the Leonard and Marjorie Maas Professor of Reformed Theology at Hope College in Holland, Michigan. A graduate of Hope College, his Ph.D. is in religious studies from The University of Chicago. He has won numerous teaching awards, including being selected by the Hope class of 1999 as the recipient of the Hope Outstanding

Professor-Educator Award. His most recent book is_Earthkeeping and Character: Exploring a Christian Ecological Virtue Ethic. Other books include For the Beauty of the Earth: A Christian Vision for Creation Care, revised second edition, and Beyond Homelessness: Christian Faith in a Culture of Displacement, co-authored with Brian Walsh.

Aminah Al-Attas Bradford, doctoral candidate at Duke University's Divinity School, writes at the intersection of Christian theology and ecology. She is a fellow at the Forum for Theological Exploration and ordained in the Christian Reformed Church in North America (CRCNA). She is the author of a recent article entitled "Living in the Company of Beasts: Karl Barth, the Microbiome, and the Unwitting Microbial Witness of the Divine Bearing of All Things."

Calvin B. DeWitt is professor emeritus, Nelson Institute, University of Wisconsin-Madison. His research is on integrative knowledge of earth's biosphere and application of science, ethics, and praxis in its care and keeping as our common home. Among his many articles are the titles "Earth Stewardship and Laudato Si'" and "Carbon, Climate, and Earth Stewardship." His books include Earthkeeping: Christian Stewardship of Natural Resources, Missionary Earthkeeping, Earth-Wise: A Guide to Hopeful Creation Care, Caring for Creation, and Song of a Scientist.

Eugene Dykema is retired from George Fox University where he was the founding director of the Graduate Program in Business and taught economics and business classes. He taught economics at Calvin College for 18 years. He has a background in chemical engineering and management consulting. He has published articles in various journals and been a contributing author to several volumes including Earthkeeping and Responsible Technology. He is currently writing on topics related to Christian economic choice.

Gabrielle Eisma is a first-year student at Calvin College, with a major in writing and studio art and a concentration in illustration. She plans to work as an illustrator for young adult and children's literature.

Kathi Groenendyk is professor of strategic communication at Calvin College, teaching classes in persuasion, visual rhetoric, and communication and conflict resolution. She earned her doctorate from the Pennsylvania State University and her master's degree at Texas A&M University. Her research has focused on environmental communication and has included the study of environmental attitudes in faith communities. Her varied interests have led to articles with titles "Reconfiguring Borders: Health-Care Providers and Practical Environmentalism in Cameron County, Texas" and "The Populist and Faith Appeals in William Jennings Bryan's 'The Menace of Darwinism.'"

Matthew C. Halteman is professor of philosophy at Calvin College and fellow in the Oxford Centre for Animal Ethics, UK. He teaches and writes on twentieth-century European philosophy (especially hermeneutics and philosophy as a way of life) and applied ethics (especially food and animal ethics) and is the author of *Compassionate Eating as Care of Creation* and co-editor (with Andrew Chignell and Terence Cuneo) of *Philosophy Comes to Dinner: Arguments about the Ethics of Eating*.

Becky Roselius Haney is associate professor of economics at Calvin College and earned her PhD in economics from the University of Chicago. Her research interests include the economics of sustainability, resource depletion, and energy transitions. She works on the forefront of economic research methodology by applying agent-based computer simulation models to these macroeconomic phenomena. She also has a Master's of Divinity from Duke University and is interested in the interaction of faith and sustainable economic activity. Becky is an author of *Beyond GDP: National Accounting in the Age of Resource Depletion*.

Gail Gunst Heffner is a member of the faculty at Calvin College, currently serving as the director of community engagement in the Office of the Provost. Her PhD is in Urban Studies and Resource Development from Michigan State University. Gail is one of the founders of Plaster Creek Stewards and is serving as the principal administrator for several large grants designated for watershed restoration in the Plaster Creek watershed. She is an editor of *Commitment and Connection: Service-Learning and Christian Higher Education*. Gail has also published articles on community-based research, engaged scholarship, social capital, community development, environmental service-learning, and reconciliation ecology.

Matthew Kuperus Heun is professor of engineering at Calvin College. He earned an MS and PhD from the University of Illinois at Urbana-Champaign and later worked at NASA's Jet Propulsion Laboratory and at Global Aerospace Corporation. He has been a visiting scholar at the Centre for Renewable and Sustainable Energy Studies at the University of Stellenbosch, South Africa. His long-term research question is "What is the relationship between energy and the economy when viewed through the lens of sustainability?" In addition to scores of articles, he is lead author of *Beyond GDP: National Accounting in the Age of Resource Depletion*.

Clarence W. Joldersma is professor of education at Calvin College where he teaches philosophy of education. He has a broad range of research interests, including Levinas, phenomenology, embodied cognition, neuroscience, social justice, and the environment. Recent books include *A Levinasian Ethics for Education's Commonplaces: Between Calling and Inspiration* and *Neuroscience and Education: A Philosophical Appraisal*. He has co-edited, with Sean Blenkinsop a themed issue of *Educational Theory* on environment and philosophy and published essays on environmental ethics.

Leah Knoor is a first-year student at Calvin College, with majors in Biology and Biochemistry. She plans to pursue a career in microbiological research after graduation.

Bill McKibben is the Schumann Distinguished Scholar in Environmental Studies at Middlebury College and a fellow of the American Academy of Arts and Sciences. He was the 2013 winner of the Gandhi Prize and the Thomas Merton Prize and holds honorary degrees from 18 colleges and universities. In 2014 Bill was awarded the Right Livelihood Prize, sometimes called the "alternative Nobel." His 1989 book *The End of Nature* is regarded as the first book for a general audience about climate change and has been translated into 24 languages. He has written more than a dozen additional books, most recently *Falter: Has the Human Game Begun to Play Itself Out?* He is a founder of 350.org, a planet-wide, grassroots climate change movement.

Kyle Meyaard-Schaap serves as the National Organizer and Spokesperson for Young Evangelicals for Climate Action, a national network of young Christians taking action to address the climate crisis as an expression of their Christian witness and discipleship. Kyle holds an undergraduate degree in religious studies from Calvin College, a Master of Divinity degree from Western Theological Seminary, and is ordained in the Christian Reformed Church in North America (CRCNA). His work on climate change education and advocacy has been featured in national and international news outlets such as PBS, NPR, NBC News, Reuters, and US News and World Report. Recent articles from Kyle include "Stopping Climate Change is a Part of Following Jesus" and "Renewing Evangelical Engagement on Climate Change: The Birth and Growth of 'Young Evangelicals For Climate Action.'"

Debra Rienstra is professor of English at Calvin College, where she teaches early modern British literature and creative writing. She earned her undergraduate degree from the University of Michigan and her PhD in English literature from Rutgers. She is the author of three books of nonfiction as well as many essays, writing regularly for *The Reformed Journal's* blog, "The Twelve," on topics including spirituality, worship, arts and literature, higher education, and pop culture. Her current writing projects focus on spirituality and place, particularly in connection with the dunes ecosystems of the West Michigan shoreline.

Hannah Riffell is a first-year student at Calvin College, with a major in English Writing. She plans to pursue a career in writing after graduation.

James R. Skillen is associate professor of environmental studies at Calvin College. He writes about both federal lands in the American West and the relationship between Christian faith and creation care. His favorite class to teach, a May field course in Yosemite National Park, combines both interests. He has published *Federal Ecosystem Management: Its Rise, Fall, and Afterlife* (2015) and has a forthcoming book, *This Land is My Land* from Oxford University Press.

David Paul Warners is professor of biology at Calvin College, teaching classes in botany, biological research, evolution, and restoration ecology. He received an MS from the University of Wisconsin and a PhD from the University of Michigan. With colleague Gail Gunst Heffner, he initiated a campus-based group called Plaster Creek Stewards that works with the broader community to restore health and beauty to the local watershed. Among his recent articles are "Assessing a reconciliation Ecology Approach to Suburban Landscaping: Biodiversity on a College Campus" and "Reconciliation Ecology: A New Paradigm for Advancing Creation Care."

Loren Wilkinson is Professor Emeritus of Interdisciplinary Studies and Philosophy at Regent College. His teaching interests include Christianity and the arts, philosophy, literature, and earthkeeping. He has written many scholarly and popular articles developing a Christian environmental ethic and exploring the human relationship to the natural world in its environmental, aesthetic, scientific, and religious dimensions. He edited *Earthkeeping: Christian Stewardship of Natural Resources* and co-authored *Caring for Creation in Your Own Backyard* with Mary Ruth Wilkinson. He is currently working on a book entitled *Circles and the Cross: Cosmos, Consciousness, Christ, and the Human Place in Creation* and has recently completed two works related to that project: *Imago Mundi*, a book of poems, and *Making Peace with Creation*, a documentary film directed by Iwan Russell-Jones.

Megan Halteman Zwart is Associate Professor of Philosophy at Saint Mary's College (Notre Dame, IN). Megan received her bachelor's degree from Calvin College (Grand Rapids, MI) and her PhD from the University of Notre Dame. She teaches classes in the history of philosophy and applied ethics, including food ethics and medical ethics. Megan has published articles in the areas of engaged pedagogy, the ethics of eating, and philosophy as a way of life. Her current research examines how to reduce polarization in classroom environments, enabling students to engage in dialogue across difference.

INDEX